'Extraordinary conversations with
and most inspiring figures of our
and presented with enormous liter
they form a snap-shot of where the peoples of the Black diaspora
stand, today in the early twenty-first century, and how much has
been overcome to get here.'   —David Olusoga

'Sarah Ladipo Manyika brings an intimate, eclectic and
delightfully startling freshness in this remarkably curated
celebration of the African diaspora. Her curiosity and ranging
insights sharpen the genius, and the humanity, of her (already
familiar) subjects and our appreciation of them, and what an
absolute joy to savor *Between Starshine and Clay*.'
                                        —NoViolet Bulawayo

'Sarah brings us an important book full of inspiring voices and
leaders engaged in the most important issues of the day. It is an
amazing collection that will inspire readers young and old.'
                                        —Dame Vivian Hunt

'Even though Sarah Ladipo Manyika's medium is language, to
read her *Between Starshine and Clay* is like seeing an animator
at work. Little by little, we see her subjects taking shape, and
then, with a sudden blink, we are being invited to participate
in choices made, joys, regrets and lives fully lived. A lesson in
magic from Manyika's writing.'   —Ato Quayson

'What draws me to this work is what inspired it: a desire to
bring Black voices from the African diaspora to the foreground.
And Sarah Ladipo Manyika has assembled her subjects very
carefully; each person in this book indeed conveys the power,
strength and sheer diversity of the African diaspora. This is a
one-of-a-kind book, a necessary and important one.'
                                        —Delroy Lindo

'Sometimes, I feel discriminated against, but it does not make me angry. It merely astonishes me. How can any deny themselves the pleasure of my company? It's beyond me.'

– Zora Neale Hurston, *How it Feels to be Colored Me*

BETWEEN STARSHINE AND CLAY

Conversations from the African Diaspora

Also by Sarah Ladipo Manyika

Novels
In Dependence
Like a Mule Bringing Ice Cream to the Sun

As editor
The Weaverbird Collection: New Fiction from Nigeria 2008
(with Akin Adeṣọkan, Ike Anya and Ike Oguine)

Sarah Ladipo
Manyika

Between
Starshine
and Clay

Conversations
from the
African Diaspora

Foreword by
BERNARDINE EVARISTO

First published in 2022 by
Footnote Press
www.footnotepress.com

Footnote Press Limited
4th Floor, Victoria House, Bloomsbury Square, London WC1B 4DA
Distributed by Bonnier Books UK
Owned by Bonnier Books
Sveavägen 56, Stockholm, Sweden

First printing
1 3 5 7 9 10 8 6 4 2

Zora Neale Hurston quote taken from *How it Feels to be Colored Me*,
with permission from the Zora Neale Hurston Trust; 'Between Starshine
and Clay' is taken from Lucille Clifton's poem 'won't you celebrate with
me' first collected in *The Book of Light*, Copper Canyon Press, 1993; 'Toni
Morrison: In Conversation', 'Michelle Obama: On Meeting' and 'Margaret
Busby: On Meeting' first published on *Granta*, 2017, 2019, 2020; 'Toni
Morrison: On Meeting' first published in *Transition 124*, 2017; 'Willard
Harris: On Meeting' is an extended and updated version of 'Mondays
with Mrs. Harris' first published on *Medium*, 2017; 'Evan Mawarire:
On Meeting' first published on *Africa Is a Country*, 2019.

A CIP catalogue record for this book is available
from the British Library and the Library of Congress.

ISBN (hardback): 978-1-804-44008-7
ISBN (trade paperback): 978-1-804-44019-3
ISBN (ebook): 978-1-804-44009-4
Cover design by Anna Morrison
Book designed and typeset by Victoria Heath Silk
Printed and bound in Great Britain by
Clays Ltd, Elcograf S.p.A.

MIX
Paper from
responsible sources
FSC
www.fsc.org   FSC® C018072

For Julian

TABLE OF CONTENTS

FOREWORD

by Bernardine Evaristo

Reading this book felt like entering a large house with twelve successful Black people sitting in their own rooms inside of it, and then being guided by Sarah Ladipo Manyika from one room to the next, in order to sit down with each person and hear about their careers, ideas and lives. I was enthralled and felt emotionally and intellectually nourished by their stories, each one impressive, all of them so different. Between Starshine and Clay is quite unlike anything I've ever read before, playing as it does with form and structure, but also in terms of its transcontinental and trans-cultural expansiveness, which thereby opens up a world of riches to the reader.

Most of the people featured in its pages are known to me because they have, or had, global reputations as leading intellectuals, activists and creatives. I have been a fan of many of them and it was fascinating to read more about them and to gain valuable insights behind their public personas. However, the only one profiled whom I actually know in person is the pioneering British publisher Margaret Busby. The essay about her life fills in the gaps of my knowledge about one of our literary trailblazers who broke two records: as Britain's youngest and first Black woman publisher. Here, as elsewhere, Ladipo

Manyika's writing is so beautifully written and descriptive the reader is immersed in Busby's backstory: her extraordinary family ancestors who were also pioneers, the childhood in Ghana, education in Britain, setting up what would become an important publishing house in the Sixties when she was just a twenty-year-old university student, the world-renowned friends and associates, the seminal Daughters of Africa and New Daughters of Africa anthologies.

As I read on, I realized that this book reveals, through various life stories, what it has taken for these people to succeed; what it takes to have a vision and work toward it; what it takes to be an original thinker who forges your own path, and what it takes to become a leader, whether it's in the arts, academia, politics or public service. But this isn't a dry manual for success, far from it, it's a series of interviews and profiles that engage and illuminate its subjects, while revealing something of their personalities and personal narratives.

It's worth noting that profiles and interviews with successful people only tend to appear in print and other media to promote a new creative venture or to celebrate a landmark event. So it's highly unusual to read pieces that exist to honor and celebrate people without a marketing motive behind them. It provides the opportunity for a more open and unexpected exploration.

Ladipo Manyika is genuinely interested in everyone she writes about, some of whom she knows well, and all of whom are from her wider communities. Her style is affirming and empathetic without appearing hagiographic. She recognizes the talents and achievements of these exceptional individuals with a tacit awareness that, especially in societies where we are minoritized, we ourselves can and indeed should set the terms of appreciation and acknowledgment of each other, without hanging around waiting for others to anoint us. There is nothing anthropological or sociological about her perspectives or perceptions. She is a politicized, thoughtful, observant writer who has an instinct for what is interesting and illuminating, what is fun and enjoyable, and this book is a powerful testament to who we are and who we can be in the world – beyond reductionism and homogeneity, and beyond the annoyingly toxic tropes that dominate and misrepresent. While the more familiar narratives of discrimination and marginalization exist, these individuals have not been crushed by society's inequalities, especially in the case of Evan Mawarire, the pro-democracy activist and pastor in Zimbabwe, who has been imprisoned as a political prisoner and continues to fearlessly battle oppressive forces.

In a racialized world where Black achievement is often overlooked, this book is a welcome addition, one I would press into the hands of anyone interested in expanding their understanding of how we can shape the world according to our values, philosophies and interests – proactively and positively – rather than adhere meekly to structures that have long attempted to control, restrict and impose definitions on us. While the subjects in this book are widely divergent, which is to be welcomed, common denominators among them include self-determination, ambition, commitment to social and cultural change and achievement against the odds. Whether they like or accept the term or not, these people are role models, not just for younger generations, but for those who need guidance finding their way in the world.

Sarah Ladipo Manyika herself has led an atypical life, living in parts of Africa, Europe and North America, which she recounts in her introduction – the outline of her own life story as the daughter of a Nigerian man and English mother. The author of two celebrated novels, her story is as engrossing as the people she writes about. She has now lived for decades in the United States, but her gaze and experience, family ties and cultural interests extend far beyond its national borders. It's not surprising that someone with her background has conceived of a book that brings people's stories together from different parts of the world. It's not surprising that in this book Willard Harris, who is not a public figure, would be seated at the table with Michelle Obama, Toni Morrison and Henry Louis Gates, Jr. While Between Starshine and Clay is inspirational to the nth degree, the person who most surprised me is Willard Harris, a San Francisco resident, a former director of nursing and friend of the author. Born over a century ago, in 1919, she is still living a full and independent life: Harris goes for weekly walks and, wait for it, still works part-time. It's fitting that Ladipo Manyika thought to have included her alongside some very starry names because she encapsulates the enviable spirit of survival, resilience and triumph – still here, still active at her phenomenal age, still learning, still communicating, still enjoying life. Like the other people so carefully explored in this fascinating book, we have a lot to learn from her.

NOTES OF
A NATIVE DAUGHTER

Introduction

Not far from where I live in San Francisco is an outdoor athletic
stadium where I walk, usually on the upper track watching the
athletes down below. People of all ages and walks of life come here
to exercise or just to enjoy the outdoors – school children, hospital
workers, personal trainers and their clients. In recent years, I've
come to recognize the regulars, including a man with a suitcase
and other belongings neatly tucked away in one of the alcoves.
When I see him, he's either sitting close to his bags or nearby in
the bleachers, eating a sandwich or reading. Occasionally, he's
joined by a friend and sometimes he plays music from a boombox.
He's Black, heavyset and wears suspenders and a dark trench
coat. We've never spoken, but we nod 'hello' to each other. I
wonder what his story is, where he grew up, who his people are,
what's in his suitcase, where he sleeps at night.

Wondering about other people's life stories is what I do. I
have lived on three continents and find that my eye is constantly
drawn to stories of people in Africa and in its diaspora, whether
recent or hundreds of years removed. Take the middle-aged
woman dressed in iro and buba whom I see in Berlin, sitting on

a park bench with an arm around a white child. She reminds me of the woman in Njideka Akunyili Crosby's painting *Mama, Mummy and Mamma* and I wonder . . . what is this woman's story? Is she related to the child or does she work for the child's family? Or take the young woman with a spectacular afro whom I see in San Francisco's Chinatown bargaining with a fruit seller. Who is this Angela Davis lookalike speaking fluent Mandarin? Where does she come from, what is her story? Or what about the Uber driver named Toussaint who tells me his Haitian mother named him after someone in history, but he doesn't know the details. Once at the White House I found myself wondering about the Black staff who served President Obama and his family. What were their stories and how might their stories compare to those who worked there during President Lincoln's time? These are the sorts of stories that fascinate me. How many are still waiting to be recorded, heard and understood?

Stories are always shaped, or at least buffeted, by history and circumstance, and recent years have felt particularly turbulent. Seen through my eyes, as a Black woman, the combination of everything – from the pandemic, to police brutality, to the rise of virulent nationalism and repressive regimes – seems to have fallen disproportionately hard on Black people around the world. I have found myself wondering how our experiences and stories compare to those of previous turbulent periods and to what degree I and others have changed in the process. In these precarious times I've been searching for answers, perspective – and hope.

My search has led me back to 'Oyinbo', an essay I wrote twenty years ago, in which I explore my experiences with blackness in countries where I've lived. Reading it now, much of what I wrote then still resonates, but at the same time the world has moved on and changed, as have I. This introductory essay is titled 'Notes of a Native Daughter' in a reverent nod to James Baldwin, whose *Notes of a Native Son*, with its personal exploration of race, histories and countries lived in, is as resonant today as it was in 1955 when first published. I begin by revisiting 'Oyinbo' and retitling it 'Autobiographical Notes'. Later, in 'Notes on Encounters', I turn to the twelve people who are the focus of this book and who have been a source of inspiration to me in my search for perspective and hope. This book is a celebration of personal and collective stories, of histories, of people making a way where there seems to be no way, making a difference, making history. It's a celebration of the joy that comes despite the hurdles and barriers meant to discourage, dishearten or destroy.

I. AUTOBIOGRAPHICAL NOTES

OYINBO IN NIGERIA

I grew up in Jos, a city in northern Nigeria, in the 1970s and early 1980s. At that time, Jos was a desirable, idyllic hill town with a broad ethnic and religious mix of Nigerians, some Europeans, Americans, Indians and Lebanese. My father was an Anglican vicar from a Muslim family in the south-west of Nigeria, and my mother was a physiotherapist from a white, nonreligious home in the north of England. Our family friends came from a cross-section of nationalities, religions and ethnicities, and my brother and I attended a missionary school for children of missionaries and others. As a child, my identity reflected my family – Christian, half Nigerian (Yoruba, to be ethnically precise), and half English. The word 'syncretism' was one I used with pride to describe the mixed and harmonious ethnic, national and religious milieu in which I was raised.

There were many mixed-race couples among our Jos friends, so my mixed-race status was not unusual. That said, as a child I was frequently called 'oyinbo' which was a reference to my fair skin. Literally translated, 'oyinbo' means 'peeled skin' or 'pale skin', but in the Nigerian context the term had less to do with race than with distinguishing foreigners (or 'expatriates') from

3

locals. While I didn't like being singled out as different, 'oyinbo' was not rooted in a social construct of race. Nigeria, unlike other countries in Africa, has no history of pervasive settler colonialism of the sort in southern Africa, and no legislated social hierarchies categorized along racial lines. Nigeria was certainly exposed to the racial implications of colonialism during the colonial period, but there were few reminders of these explicit racial constructs as I was growing up.

One of my most vivid memories of childhood is of listening to adults, mainly men, talking politics. My father and his friends would debate for hours the state of the nation and which political party was thought best suited to lead the country. As Nigeria lurched from one military coup to another, I remember American-style democracy being admired, especially for its orderly transition of power. Even as corruption rose and the nation's infrastructure continued to crumble, hope persisted and I parroted the grownups around me saying that at least Nigeria, in contrast to other nations, could take pride in its freedom of expression. But by the time my family left Nigeria in the mid 1980s, electricity cuts and power shortages had become the norm, armed burglaries were on the rise and the military was back in power. It wasn't long before any illusions I had about freedom of expression were shattered: in 1986, a parcel bomb killed Dele Giwa – a journalist known for his fearless investigative exposés of government corruption – and in 1995 beloved writer and outspoken environmental activist Ken Saro-Wiwa was executed by the military government.

As I grew older, I found myself wanting to better understand how Nigeria went from the hopes of independence to its shattered dreams. I also began to realize how expatriate and America-centric my early missionary education had been. I hadn't been taught Nigerian history, literature or languages. It was only later through reading books, such as Wole Soyinka's childhood memoir *Aké*, that I found windows into Nigeria's past. His prison memoir, *The Man Died*, gave me the first real glimpse into the events of the Biafran War, Nigeria's Civil War. Later still, Chris Abani's novella-in-verse, *Daphne's Lot*, and Chimamanda Ngozi Adichie's novel *Half of a Yellow Sun* would convey to me a greater sense of the events and conditions of this war. Chinua Achebe's *A Man of the People* and *Anthills of the Savannah* were the first books that I read capturing the era of rampant corruption and 'big-men' politics. Out of a desire to read different sorts of stories from Nigeria, I wrote my first novel, *In Dependence* – a transcontinental love story spanning the final four decades of the twentieth century.

In the early 2000s, my once tranquil hometown of Jos was the site of deadly religious and ethnic strife. This became one of my first personal lessons in understanding that peace and progress can never be taken for granted, and that when simmering societal issues go unresolved for too long they will at some point come to a boil.

AFRICAN IN ENGLAND

I moved with my family to north London in 1984. Just as skin color was a marker of foreignness in Nigeria, it (as well as accent and class) was a marker of hierarchy and otherness in England. As in Nigeria, my difference triggered curiosity but not hostility. What was unfamiliar to me, however, were the encounters with those whose parents came from other countries, but who themselves claimed to be British. I also encountered Black people who hadn't grown up on the African continent but said they were African. I felt insulted by their seemingly rudimentary understanding of Africa. Why appropriate elements of *my* cultural heritage and label it as yours? At the time, I didn't fully understand the history and circumstances of West Indians coming to England, or the ideological or political histories that resulted in such identifications with Africa. It was only later, especially when reading Andrea Levy's *Small Island*, that I acquired a more vivid sense of the experiences of the Windrush generation who came from the Caribbean to Britain after World War Two to help rebuild the country and address its labor shortage. Similarly, Zadie Smith's *White Teeth* was the first novel I read depicting a modern-day culturally diverse London.

While my knowledge of history was lacking, I did know something about racial discrimination from my maternal grandparents who'd disowned my mother for marrying my father, a Black man. I understood my grandparents' racism to be born out of ignorance and a lack of education and as something of the past. As a teenager, I didn't give racism in England much thought; I continued to identify primarily with Africa, and with Nigeria more specifically. Eager to learn more about my home continent, I opted for a degree in African Studies and French at the University of Birmingham. After graduating, I applied for jobs at the BBC as well as the civil service, where I hoped to join the diplomatic service. When I wasn't successful with either, I blamed the economic recession. I did notice, however, that some graduates – frequently those with lower qualifications than mine – seemed to have an easier time obtaining the jobs I'd been rejected for. I speculated that this had to do with class – their double-barreled names, or having studied at Oxford or Cambridge. I noticed they were all white, too, but at the time didn't consider the role institutional racism might have played.

The job I did eventually find was as a secretary at Penguin Books. It wasn't what I'd hoped for, but at least I was surrounded by books, albeit few by or about people that looked like me. What Black authors were present were African American – writers such as Alice Walker, Maya Angelou and Toni Morrison.

At the time, I didn't realize that where I lived in south London was a place of historical significance for many Black creatives and activists, some of whom might have lived there when I did. My commute to work took me from Herne Hill to Brixton, along the Railton Road, where, activist-writer Darcus Howe, photographer Rotimi Fani-Kayode and writer

C. L. R. James once lived. James was brought out of obscurity by the legendary Margaret Busby and her pioneering publishing house Allison & Busby, founded in 1967. Back then, I hadn't heard of Busby and many of the authors she'd published over the years. I wish I had. But in 1993 I discovered her landmark anthology, *Daughters of Africa*, and it changed the way I thought about our stories – so many of them, and over centuries and continents. How little I knew about Black British writers was made clear to me years later through a keynote address given by writer and scholar Bernardine Evaristo at the 2015 African Literature Association conference in Bayreuth, Germany. It was the first time I'd heard anyone give a historical overview of Black British writing and with an emphasis on women writers.

While at Penguin I wrote a short essay, entitled 'Brown Friendly', advocating for the right to hold to both my whiteness and my blackness – my 'brownness', as I called it. I was proud of this essay, which won a writing award. I was twenty-three and thought I knew a lot about race. I was, after all, the child of Black and white parents and had found a way to balance my whiteness and my blackness. Looking back on the piece now, I wince at my naiveté but even more so at how hard my younger self tried to forge her own path to circumvent society's discrimination and pigeon-holing of Black people.

ARAB IN FRANCE

In 1989, I spent my third year of study at the University of Bordeaux. I'd never lived on my own in a foreign country and I didn't find it easy. At first, I struggled with the language and the French bureaucracy and worried about the high incidence of sexual assault against women on campus.

Those who quickly befriended me were fellow international students. Chantal became my closest friend and helped me navigate my way. She also explained the system of French '*départements*', of which her island, Guadeloupe, was one. Chantal wrote poetry and was the first to introduce me to Black francophone writers, including the novelist Maryse Condé. At the University of Bordeaux, I studied *Lettres modernes* (Modern Literature) which did not include Black French writers or any women writers that I can recall. I would discover writers such as Frantz Fanon and Aimé Césaire who were addressing France's colonial history only much later.

I didn't arrive in France thinking of it in terms of race, but soon came to see that the land of *liberté, égalité, fraternité* was not as united as it sounded. I remember the TV room in the student dormitories where we gathered each evening to watch *Antenne 2* news. Arab students sat in one corner, Africans in another, and those from the Caribbean in another, while the occasional white student filled the gaps in between. None of us liked Jean-Marie Le Pen, the then leader of the French National Front, and most of us supported Harlem Désir, the leader of SOS Racisme, an organization devoted to fighting racial discrimination. These shared views at least gave some unity to our divided room.

My time in Bordeaux coincided with the highly publicized controversy over whether Muslim girls should be allowed to wear veils to school. I followed the debate with interest along with many students in my hall of residence. I was saddened by the tensions between whites and Arabs but didn't feel directly affected by it, until one afternoon when I was attacked by a group of skinheads. I was waiting to catch a bus from town back to campus. Though I'd become fluent in French, I shouted in English for them to leave me alone. They laughed and told me to stop pretending not to be Arab. For the first time, I experienced the true arbitrariness of ethno-racial attacks. It didn't matter where I was from or who I was – in their eyes I was an Arab and that was all that mattered. Nobody came to my aid, but when a bus finally arrived they let me go.

I often wonder what I would have made of Baldwin's essays about France in his collection *Notes of a Native Son* had I read them while I lived there. In 'Equal in Paris' he notes the scorn with which those in power treated the poor, many of whom were Arab, and in 'Princes and Powers' he writes with insight of the gulf between Black Americans and Africans in France. I wonder how Baldwin might have reflected on the 2005 uprisings that took place in the *banlieues* of Paris, born of discontent and alienation amongst young Muslims and North African immigrants. What would Baldwin make of France today?

I stayed in touch with Chantal and over the years she's shared her struggles with racism in France, particularly in the work setting. She, like me, is alarmed that Le Pen's daughter Marine Le Pen has become a serious political contender, in a way her father never was, winning nearly forty-two per cent of the vote in the recent 2022 presidential elections in an era where rightwing nationalism has become increasingly mainstream.

COLORED IN ZIMBABWE

Many years before I visited Zimbabwe, my father described it as one of the most beautiful countries in Africa. He spoke of its stunning jacaranda season, of the beauty of the lush Eastern Highlands, and of how smoothly everything ran.

On my first visit in 1992, with my then boyfriend, now husband, I saw what my father meant. Zimbabwe's capital, Harare, was beautiful and blessed with well-functioning infrastructure, but what struck me most were the number of white people. I'd never before seen so many white people in an African country who were African. I also encountered a new racial category into which I was slotted – 'colored'. Not colored in the British or American sense (that old-fashioned, now widely considered offensive term for 'Black') but colored as defined under apartheid, when the country had been Rhodesia, a category in between Black and white and of mixed heritage, and the distinction was important. In Zimbabwe's relatively recent history as Rhodesia, coloreds were placed by whites below themselves but in a category above Blacks and therefore treated slightly better than Blacks. I came to know more about Zimbabwe's colonial, then white minority rule from Tsitsi Dangarembga's 1988 debut novel *Nervous Conditions*, depicting pre and postcolonial 'nervous conditions'; from Dambudzo Marechera's semi-autobiographical work, *The House of Hunger*, about growing up Black under Rhodesia's oppressive white rule; from Alexandra Fuller's childhood memoir, *Don't Let's Go to the Dogs Tonight*, about growing up as the child of white farmers living close to where the war of liberation raged.

Not long after my first trip to Zimbabwe and before we were married, my fiancé asked if I identified as 'Black'. The question rattled me. I thought it obvious that I identified as Black even though I was, 'technically' half black and half white. But in holding to my bi-racial space in a way that could be seen as detracting from a collective and wider Black cause, was, perhaps, where some of my fiancé's concerns lay. He had grown up under white minority rule which employed a divide-and-conquer approach based on racial categories. He'd also grown up in Mbare, a segregated township of Salisbury (now Harare) where he experienced segregation and racism very much as African Americans would have experienced it in 1960s America, with whites-only schools, shops, toilets and pools.

I've returned to Zimbabwe many times since and watched as the rule of Robert Mugabe – a leader of the liberation struggle who became Zimbabwe's first Prime Minister – stretched from one decade to another, moving from independence in 1980 through the thriving early 1990s to the 2000s when the country was clearly in political then economic decline. In 2005, after a summer visit, I wrote a short story entitled 'Zvakwana', meaning 'enough is enough' – the word I saw scrawled in graffiti at bus stops and on durawalls everywhere in Harare. This was in the wake of Operation Murambatsvina ('clean up'), the politically motivated forcible demolition of slum dwellings that displaced up to 700,000 people. At the time, Zimbabwe's unemployment rate was estimated at eighty per cent, and with its increasingly crumbling infrastructure, power cuts and water shortages, it reminded me of Nigeria in the 1980s. The opposition bravely led by Morgan Tsvangirai was constantly being beaten up and imprisoned. I kept wondering when Mugabe might be toppled in a military coup d'état, as per the pattern of regime change I'd experienced in Nigeria.

Meanwhile, I read many of Zimbabwe's novelists who were shining a light on the complex truths of the nation through stories. Writers such as Petina Gappah and Tendai Huchu documented the ills and hypocrisies that had come to plague Zimbabwean society: hyperinflation, misogyny, corruption and the unchecked AIDS epidemic. Brian Chikwava and others captured the 'lost decade' and displacement, as well as the dark underbelly of Gukurahundi, the hidden genocide that took place in the 1980s. Then in 2017 the unthinkable happened – a coup, and long-time ruler Robert Mugabe was deposed after thirty-seven years. The #ThisFlag citizens' movement led by Pastor Evan Mawarire played no small part in helping mobilize people to press for change. With regime change came hope, but hope that was short-lived. NoViolet Bulawayo's 2022 novel, *Glory*, is a scathing political satire of Zimbabwe's last few years. *Glory* is also eerily similar, in its depiction of the breadth and depth of corruption, to *Chronicles From the Land of the Happiest People On Earth*, the most recent novel from Nigerian Nobel Laureate Wole Soyinka.

BLACK IN AMERICA

I moved to the US in 1994, excited to live in a country that had loomed large in my cultural imagination thanks to the music, films and books I'd enjoyed growing up. Moreover, I was going to San Francisco, with its reputation for beauty and liberal attitudes, not unlike my childhood city of Jos. What I didn't know when I first moved was the extent to which my glowing picture of San Francisco would be marred by the reality of race in America, and how race would become the thing I could never shake from my thinking and work.

Initially, I learned about America from observing social interactions across racial lines. I observed easy mingling at work but not in most social contexts, including, most depressingly, the churches – the persistence of what Martin Luther King, Jr, had once called the 'most segregated hour' in America. Frequently, my husband and I would bump into people whom we knew from work but who didn't notice us outside the workplace: the 'out-of-context' phenomenon, as we came to label it. I also learned from the news. I'd seen the shocking events of the Rodney King beating prior to arriving in America and would continue to be shocked by news of other racially motivated attacks. Returning now to my original 'Oyinbo' essay of twenty years ago, it's harrowing to rediscover the 1997 Abner Louima police torture case, the 1998 murder of James Byrd, Jr, who was chained by the ankles to the back of a pickup truck and dragged to his death, and the 1999 Amadou Diallo police shooting – names and incidents I'd almost forgotten in the deluge of new names that have since replaced them. From Rodney King to Trayvon Martin to Andre Hill, Ahmaud Arbery, Breonna Taylor, George Floyd, Tony McDade, Casey Goodson, Jr, Patrick Warren Sr, Ma'Khia Bryant, and on and on . . .

Living in America, I came to feel closer to racial violence than I'd ever felt. I was fearful for my husband who, as a Black man, was most at risk from these 'random' acts of racial violence, and then with the birth of my son my fears increased. I would go on to encounter race in America in the context of my Ph.D. research on the comparative experiences of African students in America and Britain. My work presented me with an uncomfortable tension. By talking about race and studying its effects on my subjects, it felt as though I was perpetuating and legitimizing race and giving it the fixed status that it should never have. But *not* to talk about race or to try ignoring it was not only impractical but irresponsible. So I tried heeding what James Baldwin advocated, which was to remain committed to struggles against injustices while keeping my heart free of hatred and despair. With Barack Obama running for President this seemed doable.

In the run-up to the 2008 presidential election my wardrobe consisted mainly of Obama T-shirts, many of them emblazoned with: *HOPE. CHANGE. YES WE CAN.* I will never forget the euphoria of the night he won. The election of Barack Obama gave me hope for America, for the world, and for my son. It felt like there was a collective Black exhale that ricocheted around the globe. At the presidential inaugural ball Beyoncé sang Etta James's 'At Last' and Black people everywhere seemed to walk with a little more swagger. America looked more golden than ever.

But.

Racial discrimination, in all its nasty, nefarious forms, didn't stop with the election of Obama. Nor did the shooting of unarmed Black people – by those supposed to protect them, and those who thought they had a right to shoot.

In December 2014, when a grand jury in New York decided not to indict the white officer in the choking death of Eric Garner (captured on video for all the world to see), my son had just turned fourteen. I remember his utter disbelief and anguish. I also remember talking to fellow Black mothers about the ease with which others seemed able to go about the business of the holidays, without giving much thought to the pain and fear that gripped us. Trying to protect our young ones, we told them not to play with toy guns, not to wear hoodies and not to walk too close to white women. Not that this was new. Black parents have been telling their sons this for generations. We also did our best to alert everyone else to their presence in the hope that our children would not be harmed or mistaken as 'trouble'. We presented them all smart and smiley to the local police and to our neighbors – 'Look at my son, please recognize him, don't be afraid of him' – knowing all the while that nothing we did, absolutely nothing, would guarantee their safety. But we couldn't stop trying. As Elizabeth Alexander puts it so poignantly in her book, *The Trayvon Generation*, we parents of Black children are constantly exhausted and must 'sleep with one eye open'. In an attempt to explain the anguish and fears of any Black parent raising a child in America I wrote, in 2015, what would become my most widely read and shared essay, *Coming of Age in the Time of the Hoodie*. Usually, a writer longs for works to be perennially timely and relevant. My piece is. I wish it were not.

Then came the election of Donald J. Trump. Having grown up in Nigeria and spent two years in Kenya in the mid 1980s, I was well aware of how quickly democracies can unravel. I'd seen the appeal of a 'big man' promising to make a country great, and I'd seen how these men stay in power by muzzling the press, intimidating the opposition and rigging elections (with or without foreign help). But the fact that I'd anticipated America's election result, albeit hoping I was wrong, didn't reduce the shock or horror of it nor of the attempted coup four years later when Trump lost the 2020 election. What's more, at the time that Obama had been elected, I had forgotten about the rollback and violent backlash that followed the Reconstruction period more than a century earlier and so wasn't prepared for history to repeat itself with an ominously similar rollback in the post-Obama years. It was only with the publication of Henry Louis Gates, Jr,'s *Stony the Road: Reconstruction, White Supremacy, and the Rise of Jim Crow,* in its exploration of America's Reconstruction period and the violent backlash against it, that I would be reminded of this and come to understand the true fragility of America's progress.

In the wake of the Trump years with the virulent rise of white nationalism that is now out in the open and embraced by many, it's hard, very hard, to keep my heart free of anger and despair. My son became a man in the Trump years, and I continue to worry not only about his physical safety, but also about the cost to his emotional and mental well-being while being Black in America.

II. NOTES ON ENCOUNTERS WITH THE AFRICAN DIASPORA

Beyond my own story lie many more life stories of us. When I think of stories from Africa and its diaspora, especially in these last few turbulent years, it's Lucille Clifton's poem 'won't you celebrate with me' with its titular invocation that stays with me. The poem speaks of survival through adversity and combines a blunt acknowledgement of how hard it is to survive, to forge one's own path and yet to pull through and have something to celebrate. It is from her lines 'here on this bridge between / starshine and clay' that this book takes its title. Clifton's poem points to the aching distance between the clay of human potential and the starshine of our desires and aspiration.

This book highlights twelve people who illustrate, for me, the essence of Clifton's poem. Each of them has charted a new path, often in the face of danger and fierce opposition. They've told stories past and present through fiction, autobiography, film and theater; they've uncovered, collected and curated old histories. And they've continued, each in their own way, to push for change and progress. This book is also a meeting of people and perspectives about Africa and its diaspora, with chapters that speak to each other, almost in call and response – sometimes in agreement, sometimes not – highlighting the diversity of views and experiences.

From such a vast continent and its diaspora, there are many inspiring voices that could be included in a book like this, including those mentioned throughout my 'Notes', but these twelve are among those whose work I've engaged with deeply and whose voices I find particularly resonant in these times. They are also people whom I've spent time with over the past few years. Several were a part of my series *Conversations Across the Diaspora* created and hosted for the Museum of the African Diaspora (MoAD) in San Francisco from 2020 to 2021. Some I've come to know quite intimately through multiple interactions and conversations. We've met on different continents, in cities and towns, from Peckham to Boston, Harare to Johannesburg, Lagos to Oak Bluffs on Martha's Vineyard and beyond, sometimes in each other's homes and with each other's families. We've laughed, joked, shared meals, danced and cried together.

THE CREATORS

When I'm asked who inspires me as a writer, it's **Toni Morrison** that I mention first. To me, she's in a category of her own in capturing the stories of peoples forgotten or ignored, and she writes like no other. Whether in the rich history of *A Mercy*, set in the 1680s when slavery was still in its infancy, or in the deep pain of *Beloved* where the action takes place at the time of the Emancipation Proclamation, or in *God Help the Child* set in present day, Morrison's work enriches American literature and history in a singular way. The afternoon I spent with her in her home is one I will never forget. Towards the end of our conversation, I asked her how she thought of old age and what excited her. Her immediate response has stayed with me. Writing, she said, was what excited her most: 'Everything is either connected to it, or not.'

Another writer who speaks of us, particularly in the past few years, is the poet **Claudia Rankine** with the ever-timeliness of her work. In *Citizen* she depicts the many 'daily diminishments' faced by Black people whose rights to full citizenship are perpetually being undermined. I especially appreciate the examples she includes that take us beyond America to France and England thereby providing a broader perspective of the Black experience. Her latest book, *Just Us*, invites all of us to have conversations across racial divides, and does so in a form that fiercely insists on historical facts in an age of fake news. When I consider Claudia's work, I'm reminded of the great sisterhood of poets, those 'unacknowledged legislators of the world' spanning generations from Gwendolyn Brooks to Warsan Shire and to Amanda Gorman.

Then there is **Xoliswa Sithole**. One evening, as she and I sat curled up on my living-room sofa, I asked her: what's your favorite word? 'Beautiful,' she answered immediately, which struck me as a poignant choice for a filmmaker whose work draws attention to human suffering and the uglier side of life. Many of Xoliswa's films focus on the suffering of women and children in the context of pandemics, war and poverty. These are heavy topics that make for heart-wrenching documentary films. And yet, because Xoliswa's work is driven by a fundamental belief in the beauty of humankind, we are left to believe that not only can we do better, but we must. Xoliswa's work reminds me of other great filmmakers, including Ousmane Sembène, Spike Lee, Isaac Julien, Abderrahmane Sissako, Steve McQueen, Ava DuVernay and many others telling difficult, necessary and under-told stories.

In 1986, **Wole Soyinka** rose to global prominence as the first Black Nobel Prize winner in Literature. As with his fellow Nobel Laureate Toni Morrison, I'm always struck by the elegance of his voice and the majesty of his presence underscored by his magnificent halo-fro of white hair. Whenever I meet him, no matter where in the world, from Lagos to Bayreuth, he's always followed by an excited crowd, yet his celebrity doesn't distract him from his lifelong focus on basic human dignity for all, wherever we might live – be it the townships of South Africa or between checkpoints in Palestine. Another iconic writer I associate with standing up for human dignity, both for the oppressed and for the dignity of African languages, is Ngũgĩ wa Thiong'o whom I've come to know and who would have been in this collection had time and schedules permitted.

THE CURATORS

The idea of 'curation' is very important to me as I consider the need to find and gather our stories and histories, record them and make them accessible. In this respect, the scope of **Henry Louis Gates, Jr** (aka 'Skip')'s life work and the rich tapestry of scholars and students he has championed or mentored over the years is breathtaking. At Harvard University he has created one of the largest centers for African and African American research in the world. In addition, he's author, editor and filmmaker of what amounts to hundreds of works on art, literature and history. Skip is also a gifted storyteller, as seen here when he's recounting his tale of hitch-hiking across the equator from Dar es Salaam to Accra. I'm also convinced that Skip, in another life, must have been a griot or a stand-up comedian, or both. Whenever we meet, be it in our homes – his being like a museum filled with art and photographs of the 'who's who' from across the African diaspora – or via email, deep conversations often end in fits of laughter as we play our version of the dozens.

Like Skip, **Margaret Busby** has been an exceptional champion and curator of writers. As a pioneering publisher and editor for over half a century, her work includes the two landmark anthologies *Daughters of Africa* and *New Daughters of Africa*. Her curatorial work also quietly extends to Wikipedia, where she's constantly making entries for people, literally making us and our stories visible. As with Skip, each time I speak with Margaret I discover more about her friendships from across the decades and continents – from Nina Simone to Stevie Wonder to Hugh Masekela. Margaret's friends and their corresponding stories read like a compendium of the world's Black greats. Through her work she has inspired many more. I think especially of publisher and founder of Cassava Republic Press, Bibi Bakare-Yusuf, a pioneer in her own right, whose approach to African literature has had a seismic effect on publishers world-wide as she strives to broaden Africa's stories and stable of authors with an 'African archive of the future'.

I've chosen to place actor and playwright **Anna Deavere Smith** with these curators because her one-woman plays are a vital archive of our oral histories. Each of her plays chronicles the effects of inequality and discord in American society, from *Twilight: Los Angeles 1992* in the wake of the Rodney King beating to *Notes From the Field* on America's school-to-prison pipeline. Several years ago, I had the privilege of teaching with Anna and observing how gifted she is as an educator. I'll always remember one of her students wrestling with how to perform a role she was assigned to play. The role was of a Rwandan refugee and the student didn't feel she had the cultural or lived experience to play the part. Anna's response was a response to all of us: what makes you think you cannot play that role? Art is about being able to put oneself in other people's shoes. Art demands this of us.

At the age of 102 'and a half', as she reminds me, **Willard Harris** is a living archive of us, and her life is the very essence of Clifton's poem – from picking cotton as a young woman to becoming the first Black head of nurses at a major Californian hospital, and to running my local polling station at the age of 100. Born in 1919, the year women won the right to vote in America, she has lived through an extraordinary century, from the Harlem Renaissance to World War Two, from the civil rights era to the feminist movement and *Roe v. Wade*, from America's first Black president to the subsequent era of rollbacks to civil, voting and reproductive rights. She has lived through all the turbulence and upheaval and yet continues to be full of joy and hope.

THE CHANGEMAKERS

As I've reflected over the last several years, the question of progress is always on my mind. On the one hand I see where we have made progress, and some of the people in this book symbolize progress that is certainly worth celebrating. Yet even as our countries make progress, that progress doesn't always carry everyone along or work well for all. We've also seen how even progress attained can't be taken for granted. I've come to appreciate that progress requires leaders or movements to continually fight for it and inspire us. This book includes four leaders that have either launched movements for change or have used their platforms to drive change.

I had managed to convince myself that I would never be in awe of famous people, until the day I met **Michelle Obama**. I was gobsmacked by her radiance and cool. And then she talked to me so ordinarily as writer to writer, mother to mother. I've been inspired by how confidently she has stepped into her public roles and blossomed in spite of the intense racism and negativity directed at her. Becoming the first Black American First Lady was monumental and symbolic for all of us and shows what is possible. In this way I think of other 'first' women, from Graça Machel to Vice President Kamala Harris and to Supreme Court Justice Ketanji Brown Jackson.

The unevenness of economic opportunities and of criminal justice systems are issues that affect the lives of many in Africa and its diaspora. People such as Angela Davis, Bishop Desmond Tutu and Bryan Stevenson have worked relentlessly, often for decades, on these issues. **Michael Hastings**, who began his career as a teacher, has also spent a lifetime focused on the plight of the poor and the disadvantaged, as well as those in prison. From his work as an educator, to government service, to his current seat in the House of Lords, he has dedicated his time to building racial equity and to supporting and mentoring young leaders around the world. I find it telling that Michael, like others in this book, embraces the maxim of planting trees in whose shade another generation will sit.

Once in a while, a leader comes out of nowhere, from the bottom, with nothing more than their passion, which galvanizes a national movement for change. Pastor **Evan Mawarire** is one such leader. He was the first person to harness the power of social media to mobilize the masses in Zimbabwe and take on a powerful President who'd been in power for thirty-seven years. Evan ignited a social-media-fueled citizen movement using the weight of the nation's flag to speak truth to power. What Evan did through the movement that formed around him was, in the famous words of late US Senator John Lewis, 'good trouble, necessary trouble'. In thinking of good trouble and bottoms-up leadership, I'm reminded of other movements from the student-led protests of America's civil rights era all the way to the Black Lives Matter movement, which also took on monumental and institutionalized challenges.

I first met **Cory Booker** when he was a student at Oxford. At the time, I didn't know that he would become a tireless warrior for social justice issues, ranging from helping tenants take on slumlords to fixing America's broken criminal justice system and ending mass incarceration. And what stands out for me now, just as much as what Cory does to push for equality and justice, is the depth of his commitment to those he represents and his desire to understand their lived experiences. Cory still lives in Newark's Central Ward. What also stands out to me is that Cory never misses a chance to speak of love, hope and joy. Who can ever forget the power and emotion of his words in Ketanji Brown Jackson's nomination hearings for Supreme Court Justice: 'Nobody's stealing my joy! Nobody's going to make me angry.'

—

There is much to learn from those featured in this book, the stories told and also the joy shared. We feel this joy in the laughter that comes across in between the lines of conversations, and we see it in the delight of memories and in the sharing of friendships. For me, one of the most magical moments comes at the end of Wole Soyinka's chapter, when he's in a playful conversation with his friend Skip Gates. It's a moment of levity and joy that shows the interconnectedness of great Black lives that we so rarely have occasion to observe or to celebrate. Soyinka and Gates teasing each other and riffing on their late friend Toni Morrison is priceless. There is power and delight in the joy of being alive, of having survived and come through all that was meant to break us. 'Won't you celebrate with me' is repeated in Clifton's poem. I invite you to do just that.

Sarah Ladipo Manyika

CREATORS

What I'm going to say is going to sound so pompous, but I think an artist, whether it's a painter or a writer, it's almost holy. There's something about the vision, the wisdom.

– Toni Morrison

1.

TONI MORRISON

On Meeting

I.

'Here is the house'
– Toni Morrison, *The Bluest Eye*

The house commands a view. Square and solid, it sits on an embankment rising from the Hudson river. Meticulously maintained, its clapboard sidings and balcony railings are painted in shades of tan and river gray, with an ivory picket fence around the perimeter. The entrance is on the side of the house, hidden from public view. The door opens and a woman who says she is Nadine lets us in. I've come with Mario Kaiser, friend and writer, who has arranged this interview with *Süddeutsche Zeitung Magazin*. Nadine leads the way downstairs to the study and announces us.

Ms Morrison is dressed in black – trousers, kaftan, woolen cap – and seated opposite a woman whose back is towards us. This other woman is a journalist and asks us if we can give her more time. We look to Ms Morrison, who seems to sense our concern. 'I'll give you all the time you need,' she says. 'Just make yourself at home.'

Back upstairs, Nadine is frying onions and peppers, sending out a comforting smell of any number of cuisines that I love. The aroma from the kitchen has me thinking of food in Ms Morrison's novels and how she often uses food to hint at what simmers beneath the surface. There's the smoke curling from the soft white insides of biscuits in *Beloved* (1987), the terrible crash of Mrs Breedlove's berry cobbler in *The Bluest Eye* (1970), the hastily abandoned vegetable chopping in *Paradise* (1997). In *God Help the Child* (2015), her most recent novel, Queen prepares a 'united nations' soup that tastes like 'manna'. I imagine the soup smelling like Nadine's cooking. 'Something healthy for Mrs Morrison,' says Nadine, who is from Jamaica.

Ms Morrison has said make yourself at home. I glance at Mario, whose look of concentration is befitting of the award-winning writer that he is. Meticulously, he writes in a reporter's notepad, while my gaze darts from kitchen to living room to the deck jutting out over the Hudson. A flock of seagulls transports me to the opening pages of *Jazz* (1992), then to Ms Morrison's Nobel Prize lecture and her parable of an old blind woman. In this parable, several children have come to visit the blind woman, thinking they can test the limits of her wisdom. One asks, 'Old woman, I hold in my hand a bird. Tell me whether it is living or dead.' The woman is silent for a long time before she finally speaks:

'I don't know,' she says. 'I don't know whether the bird you are holding is dead or alive, but what I do know is that it is in your hands.'

The bird becomes a metaphor for language, and the story a profound meditation on the complex truths surrounding narrative – its dangers and its power. Have we thought hard enough, deeply enough, about the questions we are about to ask this eighty-six-year-old writer? Will we be able to go beyond the limits of questions and answers and gain wisdom?

As we wait for Ms Morrison to receive us, and I'm trying to take in what surrounds me, I reach for a photograph album. Such albums were ubiquitous in my Lagos-Jos-Nairobi childhood, so I smile at the familiarity of posed family shots, flicking through wedding photographs of Ms Morrison's eldest son, Ford. Later, I will wish that I had breathed more deeply, more slowly, had taken in more details of the home, the books on tables and the memories in the pictures.

What I do remember is that the ceiling, walls and carpet of the living room are all subtle variations of the dove-gray Hudson river they overlook; that light pours through the windows on all sides – not a bright light, but enough to give the room an airy feel. The warmth comes from the kitchen. Someone has thought carefully about the home's furnishings – understated, modern and contemplative, with accents from Africa. A Dogon figure, an Akuaba fertility doll and a small Shona sculpture are all on display. And on the wall above the Shaker-inspired stairs leading to the top floor hangs a prayer board, reminding me of one of Victor Ekpuk's decorative pieces which are fast becoming collectors' items. I smile, feeling at home; this is simultaneously Kingston, Accra, Lagos, Harare and New York. I wonder if Ms Morrison has ever visited the African continent. Nan in *Beloved* arrived in America 'from the sea', speaking a language that was not English. Would Ms Morrison ever write a story set in Africa? And, if so, what century would she set her story in? What would she say about slavery on the motherland?

Ms Morrison's other interview has finished; I hurry to use the guest bathroom. Even though I know I must be quick, I linger in the bathroom adorned with photographs of Ms Morrison and other writers who I've long admired – Soyinka, Márquez, Baldwin. In the spot above the sink, where I'd hoped for a mirror, hangs the letter from the Nobel Prize Committee announcing its decision to award Professor Toni Morrison its highest honor. On the opposite wall hangs a 'Publication Denial Notification' outlining why Ms Morrison's novel *Paradise* was banned from

Texas correctional facilities for fears of 'inmate disruption such as strikes or riots'. I smile at where the letter hangs, just above the toilet, thinking I might do the same with the copy of a recent school letter that has deemed my first novel 'morally distasteful' and called for it to be banned from Nigeria's school syllabus. Ms Morrison's letter is placed above the toilet's April Fresh air freshener, under a photograph of Muhammad Ali. Ali famously boasted of wrestling with alligators, handcuffing lightning and throwing thunder in jail. Ms Morrison was once his editor; I hear she wrestled him to the page.

Of the downstairs area where we return to talk to Ms Morrison and where she tells us she writes, I remember almost nothing except that on the table between us, next to our water glasses, lay a copy of Mohsin Hamid's *Exit West* (2017), which she had yet to read and I had just read. At first, I was conscious of the house noises that interrupted the flow of our interview, especially the shrill pinging sound each time the front door was opened. There was also the intermittent clatter of Nadine's pots and pans and her footsteps overhead, but in the presence of Ms Morrison, these noises soon fade. For the two hours that she generously grants us, my attention is fixed on her, the softness in her gaze, the light freckles on her hand, but, above all, on the sound of her voice. That voice.

II.

'Once upon a time there was an old woman . . .
Her reputation for wisdom is without peer and without question'
– Toni Morrison, Nobel Prize lecture

For weeks, I had been wondering what she would be like. It was one thing to have encountered Toni Morrison through her writing and to have watched her lectures and interviews, but another to meet her in person. Having just written a book about a seventy-four-year-old woman, I am curious to see what Ms Morrison reveals about her experience of older age. I had heard that she is wheelchair-bound and often in pain. I hope she won't be in too much pain (any pain) on this day.

The first thing that strikes me when I meet her is that she looks like one of my friends. You know that feeling when you see someone and think, 'Wow, this person is just like so-and-so!' Ms Morrison has the same light complexion, wide-set eyes and thick hair as my friend, the documentary filmmaker Xoliswa Sithole. All but one of Ms Morrison's silver-gray locks are hidden beneath her beret. The lone lock pokes out, resting on the nape of her neck. But it's her presence, more than the physical resemblances, that most reminds me of my friend, making her feel familiar. She exudes confidence from an erect and still posture, from her large stature. She is regal even when, as she occasionally does, dabbing at a watering eye.

I begin by asking how should we address her. Does she prefer Professor, Doctor, Mrs, or Ms?

'I like Toni,' she says, smiling.

Her smile portends a playfulness and openness that will remain one of my lasting memories of our conversation. Twice during the interview, we are interrupted by friends or family, and on each occasion she introduces us as 'friends'.

I've known of Toni's sense of humor both from her books and from watching interviews, but I'm surprised by how much she will make us laugh. She frequently jokes about herself and sometimes about others. Occasionally, she does both simultaneously, such as when a friend drops by with Easter flowers and has to squeeze past us to give her a hug. 'You're too fat, you're like me!' she exclaims. This ability to joke with others and laugh at herself not only reminds me of people I'm most fond of, but it's a trait that I most associate with Nigerians. Toni is also prone to laughing at moments that are sometimes the opposite of funny, and this too feels familiar, as a mechanism for enduring what is otherwise traumatic. I claim Toni as an honorary Nigerian, and she may well be, originally – Igbo, Yoruba or any of the many ethnicities that make up Nigeria. Like a true Nigerian, she is also fond of exaggerations. She talks of publishers who 'beat you up' over titles and boasts of a great-grandmother, Millicent, who, she says, is probably 'still alive'. Toni is not bitter in her old age, which was something I'd wondered about while reading *God Help the Child* and sensing cynicism or, like the old woman in her parable, just keeping her distance from younger generations. On this day, at least, she's not bitter.

Toni's humor and playfulness are magnified by her love of theater. As an undergraduate at Howard University, she belonged to a traveling theater group. She speaks fondly of this time, telling us that if she could, she'd like to return to those days. As she talks, she becomes like an actor on stage. She uses silence, shouts, songs, cursing, recitation and fake-crying, all to great dramatic effect. At one point, she takes a long pause before launching into the retelling of a ghost story told to her as a child. Half cooing, half singing, she begins: 'Gonna whop, gonna chop my wife's head off! . . . Tam-tam, tam-tam, tam-tam. Gonna cut my wife's HEAD OFF!' Toni is such a thespian that I find myself ineluctably drawn in with 'umhs' and 'ahhs', as if in call and response, as if in church, as if I'm in Nigeria where respect and appreciation for an elder is vocalized in variations of 'ehe-ehe', 'oo', and 'yes, ma'. Her theatricality also causes me, without realizing it at times, to mimic the cadence of her voice and her accents.

When I ask what President Obama whispered to her after presenting her with the Presidential Medal of Freedom, I play the role of co-conspirator, adopting her American accent in anticipation of what she'll say next, only to be surprised when she says she doesn't remember. 'I knew then!' she explains, 'But soon as I left, I thought: What did he say? I was so embarrassed!' Trying to make her feel better, I joke that she can make it up. Little do I know that the story is only just beginning. Masterfully, she weaves a longer story, revealing only at the end that her son later asked Obama if he remembered what he whispered to his mother. Obama said, 'Yeah, sure I remember. I said, "I love you."' Toni knew all along.

As a writer, I'm particularly drawn to Toni's choice of words. She is fond of interjections, exclamations, repetition and made-up words. Toni-isms, I shall call them. 'Pank,' she says mimicking the sound and action of switching off the TV whenever President Trump appears (a man she never calls by name but as 'this so-called "president"') and 'Google-shot' when referring to the use of Google Earth to view a location. Sometimes she speaks in a childlike voice, sometimes in a stern voice, sometimes she trails off at the end of a sentence on the cusp or middle of a thought, poised before diving into deeper thought. What is especially fascinating for me is recognizing in her speech many of the same rhythms and phrases that she uses in her writing. She sounds like Frank Money in *Home* (2012) when she says: 'I want you to know,' 'You have no idea,' 'Think about it,' and in that voice.

I've read that writing and being a mother are the two things that matter the most to Toni. As a mother of a son, I'm curious to know about her experience of motherhood and how she balances the two things. A large, glass-framed photograph of her youngest son, Slade, hangs by the front door. This is the son who died of cancer, and when we ask if there are things she would like to bring back from her past, it is Slade she mentions first. I feel pain for her. How does any parent cope with the death of a child? I wonder how it has affected Toni's relationship with her remaining son, Ford, whom we are lucky to meet. The interaction between mother and son is warm and playful. Toni takes great pride in Ford, and he in her. 'Whadya bring me,' she asks as soon as he arrives, 'a sam-wich?' – to which he responds that he's brought her books. She is especially excited by a book about Richard Nixon that he's brought for her new writing project. Ford is polite and kind and takes no umbrage when his mum bosses him around. 'Take that book from here!' she play-shouts, instructing him not to clutter the area where we're sitting. Our laughter, like in *Tar Baby* (1981) is 'sprawling like a quilt over the command'.

This is Toni. Mother. Nobel Laureate.

III.

'Berries that tasted like church'
– Toni Morrison, *Beloved*

Toni Morrison begins her first novel, *The Bluest Eye*, with several paragraphs' worth of lines written in the style of the best-selling *Dick and Jane* children's books:

> *Here is the house. It is green and white. It has a red door. It is very pretty. Here is the family. Mother, Father, Dick, and Jane live in the green-and-white house. They are very happy.*

In Nigeria, where I learned to read, the equivalent primers (courtesy of Nigeria's former colonial masters) were the 'Peter and Jane' Ladybird books with the same stock white characters and no Black characters. Both Janes were blond. So, even before reading Toni Morrison's work, or knowing about the society she was writing about, I understood what it meant not to find reflections of oneself in literature. When Toni says at the beginning of our interview that she is 'writing to, about and for other Black people', and that she writes about Black people because she finds us 'interesting', I cannot help but respond with a resounding 'Yes!' F.U.B.U. as Solange sings – For us, by us. This is why I often quote Toni Morrison who has said that if there's a book you want to read but cannot find, then you must write it. This is what compels me to write.

The first Toni Morrison book that I bought was *Jazz*. At the time, I knew little about the author or her standing in the literary canon, but I was drawn to the book's title. It sounded 'real cool' to me in my 'Jazz June' days, as Gwendolyn Brooks puts it. I was twenty-something, with little exposure to literary fiction and only superficial knowledge of the history of Black people in America. I knew about the history of West Africa and had some textbook knowledge of the Atlantic slave trade, but no deep understanding of the scale or lived horror of slavery, and knew virtually nothing of the legacy of racism in America. The images I saw of America on TV were ones that made America look happy and prosperous. African Americans, I assumed, led lives like the Huxtables from *The Cosby Show*. Reading Toni Morrison was the beginning of my education on America then and now, Black and white.

As soon as I started to read *Jazz*, I knew that the sound of Toni Morrison's stories mattered. Professor Henry Louis Gates, Jr, renowned literary critic and historian, refers to her novels as 'talking books' and, just a few days before our interview, he encouraged me to ask her about this. I love the phrase 'talking books', harkening back to the talking drums of my childhood. And even before we ask her about the oral tradition in her work, Toni tells us: 'I like the act of reading my works because I measure their value in terms of how they sound.' I'm elated to hear this, as the sound of stories has always been very important to me as both reader and writer. I also prefer listening to Toni narrate her own audio books before I read them. Never before have I heard a writer state the importance of a book's sound so explicitly, and certainly never a Nobel Laureate. It makes me question why the literary establishment continues to privilege text on the page over the orality of read-aloud prose.

As Toni expands upon America's legacy of racism and skin privileges, I am struck, as I was when looking around her home, by the interconnectedness of history. There are many similarities between America's civil rights era and apartheid Southern Africa. When she mentions Hecht's, the only department store in Washington DC where colored girls of her generation were allowed to use the restroom, I remember my husband's stories of not being able to try on clothes in Rhodesia's department stores, not being able to use white-only restrooms, not even being able to use the main elevators. Black people either took the stairs or, for the tallest buildings, used the service elevator in then-apartheid Rhodesia.

Toni's discussion of the importance of names and naming in her work also resonates. Names and nicknames matter within the African American community just as they continue to matter within the African continent. I have recently been reminded of this through exchanges with students in Nigeria who study my novel *In Dependence* (2008) for the university entrance exam – students with names such as Favour, Happiness, Precious, Marvelous and Godswill. Toni has these wonderful names too, each of which signifies, often ironically, something essential about the character. In her family, nicknames, she tells us, were 'usually about your weakness. Whatever your weakness is, that's what they call you. So you can get that out of the way right away.' In *God Help the Child*, she names her characters Bride, Brooklyn, Queen, Booker and Sweetness. Bride is no Bride and Sweetness is not sweet. Toni tells us about a 'horrible slave owner' called 'Goodmaster' in her forthcoming book, *Justice*, who insists that his slaves take his name as theirs. I wonder if she has read NoViolet Bulawayo's novel *We Need New Names* (2013), which celebrates names with characters such as Darling, Bastard and Godknows. Morayo, the adventure-loving protagonist of my most recent novel, means 'I see joy' in Yoruba. In each case, the naming captures something essential about the character, sometimes opening the door to irony, but always making them memorable.

Then we get to sex. 'Can we talk about sex?' I ask. 'Yeah,' she smiles, 'I'm in a good position to talk about it, since it's been like a thousand years. What do you want to know?' Writing about sex is notoriously difficult. There's even a well-known prize – the Bad Sex in Fiction Award – that ridicules how badly it can be done. How then does Toni do it so well? She tells us that it's not the clinical descriptions that make for good writing about sex (or indeed sex itself); rather, it's how to associate sex with something else, something surprising that makes the writing about sex more interesting and more compelling.

A linguistic agility with metaphor is a hallmark of Toni's language. One of my favorite lines comes from *Beloved*, from the scene in which the ferryman, Stamp Paid, having helped Sethe cross to freedom, goes to the river's edge in search of blackberries. These berries, we are told, 'tasted so good and happy that to eat them was like being in church. Just one of the berries and you felt anointed.' Much is conveyed in the startling juxtaposition of berries with church – much that speaks not only to the storyline but to the history of slavery, to America's history, to salvation, exaltation and ecstasy.

The history of slavery and its legacy is so horrific that I wonder how Toni manages to write about slavery and persistent racism without the heavy weight of this history collapsing her stories. How does she remain sane when writing about horrors that have not ended? How is she able to write about racism in America while, as James Baldwin put it, keeping her heart 'free of hatred and despair'? How does she hold on to hope? I ask her how she strikes the delicate balance in her writing between memory and forgetting – forgetting in the sense of needing to heal, which is a sentiment frequently voiced by characters in her novels. Toni's response to my question, as with many of her responses, goes beyond what is asked, to what, like the children in the parable, I've dared not ask. What's required, she replies, 'in order to get to a happy place – what I call happy, even though people are dropping dead all over my books – is the acquisition of knowledge. And if you know something at the end, or toward the end, that you didn't know before, it's almost wisdom. And if I can hit that chord, then everything else was worth it. Knowing something you didn't know before [. . .] It's not the battles,' she adds. 'A lot of books are about winning something.

I'm not interested in that so much as the way the intellectual life and the emotional life should be.' Hearing this is one of the many moments when I feel grateful that we are recording our conversation so that I can return to it to re-listen and learn something new each time I listen. For now, it's this, that what matters both in life and in stories is wisdom. The emphasis, thoughtfully illustrated in her Nobel lecture in her parable of the old woman, is on how hard we must try and how hard language must work. 'Language can never "pin down" slavery, genocide, war. Nor should it yearn for the arrogance to be able to do so. Its force, its felicity, is in its reach toward the ineffable.'

Before we leave, I ask Toni if she will sign my son's copy of *The Bluest Eye*. It's his favorite book, and he's asked me to ask how she finds the language in which she writes. 'Tell him I'm a genius,' she replies, smiling. And we laugh and laugh.

In Conversation

April 15, 2017

SARAH LADIPO MANYIKA: Do you prefer being called Professor, Doctor, Mrs or Ms?

TONI MORRISON: I like Toni.

LADIPO MANYIKA: Toni?

MORRISON: Yes, I answer to that.

LADIPO MANYIKA: Toni, thank you for giving us this opportunity to talk to you.

MORRISON: I'm glad.

LADIPO MANYIKA: I come from Nigeria so, a minute ago, I was convening with Wole Soyinka in your bathroom. [Among the photographs on the walls of Morrison's guest bathroom is one that shows her with the Nigerian Nobel Laureate.]

MORRISON: Ah! Yeah, we used to go to Paris and have meetings and talk – elegant talk – and solve world problems. And Soyinka always knew how to solve everything.

LADIPO MANYIKA / MORRISON: He still does.

MORRISON: Yes, yes. In that voice he has!

MARIO KAISER: Sarah and I became friends because of a book of yours. We were at a writers' residency, and when I told Sarah that I was working on a story about my grandfathers, who were soldiers and didn't come back from the Second World War, she gave me *Home* – the book and the audio book.

MORRISON: Oh, that's right, because I read them. I like the act of reading my works because I measure their value in terms of how they sound. That's not the only thing, but it's an important thing to me. I remember, when I first started publishing, the publisher would give a book of mine to somebody to read – to sell in disc form. And they were excellent actresses, but I never listened to them. But one day I turned on one, and I said, 'That's not right!' It was *Beloved*, I think. I said, 'It goes, "Dat-da-da-da-dat-dat-boom-dat-dat-dat-dat-dat. 124 was spiteful. Full of a baby's venom." And she was reading it straight. So, I started reading them all. Now I have learned – to my great horror – that I have to read them all again, because they said that the ones I did were abridged. I want you to know: that's one of the worst experiences of my life – sitting in that little room, with the people outside doing the recording. You have no idea how many mistakes you make when you read into a microphone.

KAISER: Your latest book, *God Help the Child*, begins with a striking sentence: 'It's not my fault.'

MORRISON: That's right.

KAISER: A mother looks at her newborn daughter.

MORRISON: And was scared.

KAISER: She realizes that the child's skin is much darker than her own, and she fears for the child's future.

MORRISON: And her own.

KAISER: Unlike your previous books, this story is set in the present. Why can skin color still make or break people in this country?

MORRISON: We got started that way. The country got started with a labor of Africans – to do work for free and reproduce themselves as more workers. When I did *A Mercy*, that book was supposed to be just before racism became the letter and the characteristic of the land. It's just before the Salem witch trials, when they were running around killing people for religious reasons. Religious people got upset about all that, but not about color. But following that, it became this. The 'healing' – it was the way in which people got together: white become white. Think about it: if you come to this country from Germany, or Russia, or anywhere, you get off the boat, get on the land. But in order to become an American, you have to be white. That's the quality that brings the country, its people, together: having a non-white population. Some things along those lines may be happening in Europe now. My concept is that if you were from Sweden, you were Swedish. You didn't have to say, 'I'm a white Swede.' You know what I'm saying?

KAISER: I do. I am German, and until I came to live in the US I never felt white.

MORRISON: That's such an important part. When somebody like Frederick Douglass wrote a book, he was writing to white people – legitimately – because he wanted them to behave, set him free. That was the audience. Not for me. Tolstoy was not writing for little girls from Ohio. He was writing for Russians, right? I'm writing to, about and for other Black people. And if it's good enough, it will be read by and appreciated by people who are not African Americans. That's the simple way to put it. But the point is, I just thought we were interesting.

LADIPO MANYIKA: Yes!

MORRISON: See, the funny thing is: what people outside this country, particularly in Europe, think about this country, what they like about it is generally something that comes out of Black culture. It's jazz. It's even language. Think about what this country would be like without us. I wouldn't even visit! I came with my first book trying to say, 'Look, racism really and truly hurts. If you really want to be white and you're not, and you're young and vulnerable, it can kill you.' That was when I first began to write, and finally, after all these years of reading books, editing books, working in libraries, I thought, 'Wait a minute, there's no book in there about me!' So, if I wanted to read it, I would probably have to write it.

KAISER: In *God Help the Child*, like in other books of yours, children suffer. You brought two children of your own into this world, in the 1960s, during the struggle for civil rights. Did that give you hope that America would hold a brighter future for your children?

MORRISON: No. No. No, I've been here a long time. Look, they've only just started putting lynched people, murdered Black boys in the newspaper. Nobody talked about that. That wasn't newsworthy. Now someone like Trayvon Martin or that other little boy they shot, they get a lot of press. I was telling my son, 'Do you realize that I was in the world fifty, sixty years before anybody ever thought that was worthy of an article? Or that you should feel bad about it?' It just wasn't there. There have been some changes, although now I think we may be taking a step back with this so-called 'president'. That's so dangerous and so awful that I don't even want to think about it. I try not to. That man can make me really sick.

LADIPO MANYIKA: 'Make America Great Again.'

MORRISON: 'Make America Great Again' means 'Make America White Again'. So now you have this other explosion of people who want to feel above something, better than something. And who is that? That's me.

LADIPO MANYIKA: Listening to you reading your stories underscores the orality and musicality of your storytelling. Do you intend your writing to be read out loud?

MORRISON: I intend the reader to hear it. I come from a house in which they did that all the time. I remember the story about my grandfather, about whom it was always said – with pride – that he had read the Bible from cover to cover. Five times. I knew at some point that it was illegal for Black people to read. And it was illegal for white people to teach them to read. You could go to jail or be fined.

My grandfather didn't go to school. He went one day, and that was to tell the teacher he wouldn't be back. He would rely on his sister to teach him to read. They called him Big Papa. And I was thinking, much later, What else could he read? There were no books, no libraries. There was just the Bible. But, at the same time, it was an act of taking power back.

In my house, there were books everywhere. My mother joined the Book of the Month Club. That was like resistance. Along with that thing about reading was telling stories, which they did all the time. Sang stories. There were about ten, and they were all insane.

LADIPO MANYIKA: Were the stories changed along the way?

MORRISON: You could change them, because they made us tell them. They would say, 'Tell that story about such-and-such!' And they would get up, little kids, and you could edit them a little bit. But they were just mad. I liked them because they were like . . . [She pauses, then starts to sing – first in a low voice, then louder.] . . . 'Gonna whop, gonna chop my wife's head off!' It was a loud song. 'Tam-tam, tam-tam, tam-tam. Gonna cut my wife's HEAD OFF!' And then the wife comes back with her head in her arm and says, 'It's cooold out here. It's cooold out here.' That was our entertainment. That and singing.

My mother sang all the time – day, night, whatever. She had the most beautiful voice I have ever heard. She's hanging up clothes, she sings. She's washing dishes, she sings. That sound for me was part of the effort, even though I didn't write until I was thirty-nine, or something. But when I did, it was very important that the language had that sound. A lot depended on the sound of a tale – the meaning often would lie in the sound of it. They were all dumb, scary stories. Do you remember reading stories when you were kids? Hänsel and Gretel? That's horrible! All those stories of people dying, throwing their kids out. And then a witch throws you in the oven. Oh, God!

LADIPO MANYIKA: One of the refrains in your books is the tension between memory and forgetting – forgetting as a way of overcoming. It's in *Beloved*, with this repeated line: 'It was not a story to pass on.' It's in *God Help the Child*, where you write that 'memory is the worst thing about healing.' How do you deal with this tension?

MORRISON: In order to get to a happy place – what I call happy, even though people are dropping dead all over my books – is the acquisition of knowledge. If you know something at the end that you didn't know before, it's almost wisdom. And if I can hit that chord, then everything else was worth it. Knowing something you didn't know before. Becoming something. There are certain patterns in the books and in life that look like they're going one way. And then something happens and people learn. *God Help the Child*, which I thought was a horrible title . . .

KAISER: What title would you have given the book?

MORRISON: I think I gave it one. I don't remember what it was. It was beautiful!

LADIPO MANYIKA: Why did you not get your own way?

MORRISON: Because they beat you up.

LADIPO MANYIKA: Isn't that one of the privileges of winning the Nobel Prize – that you can tell people what to do?

MORRISON: No! [She imagines an argument with her publisher.] 'Go fuck yourself, this is my title!' – 'No, you don't get to get that!' They think they're doing you a favor by publishing it, even though they're making tons of money – and will forever. After I die, after my children die, my grandchildren, they'll still be making money. I worked in that industry for a long time. I'm unimpressed. So, what were we talking about?

LADIPO MANYIKA: The tension between memory and forgetting.

MORRISON: Oh, yes, yes, yes, yes, yes. It's not the battles. A lot of books are about winning something. I'm not interested in that so much as the way the intellectual life and the emotional life should be. You move along a trail and you come to some place. You don't want to come to the place where you were at the beginning. In the book where the girl . . . Where is that book? What's that book?

LADIPO MANYIKA: *God Help the Child.*

MORRISON: That's the one! They're all beginning to merge into one. This girl is very, very black and very, very beautiful. Her lover is a smartass. Both of them are very self-involved, and then they come to a place where they have to take care of somebody else, not themselves. And that experience takes them out of their little shell of 'me, me, me', so that they are able at the end to have some respect, and even affection, for each other.

KAISER: You write in the book about what you call 'skin privileges' – how the shade of your color affects your status, even within the Black community. Could Barack Obama have become President if his skin were darker?

MORRISON: He looks dark to me!

KAISER: But not what you call 'Sudanese black'.

MORRISON: No, not Sudanese black. That's a nice black. Ethiopia black. All Ethiopians are beautiful! There are no ugly Ethiopians. The color thing. I come from a little steel town.

KAISER: Lorain, Ohio.

MORRISON: Lots of immigrants, one high school. I go away to college – first one in my family – and then I discover, at Howard University, this thing you're talking about: skin privileges. And Washington at that time was full of middle-class Black people. They worked in the census bureau, and there were organizations, sororities that were one color and another color. I didn't know what they were talking about. They just seemed sort of unintellectual to me – because I couldn't make friends based on that.

When I went back there to teach, one of my students was Stokely Carmichael. I said, 'What are you gonna do, Stokely, when you graduate?' He said, 'I've been accepted at Union

Theological Seminary. But first I'm going down South.' It had gotten very political, so that color was not the important thing. It was about civil rights.

But when I was a student there, it was very much that. In Washington, there was one department store where we – colored girls – could go to the bathroom. Hecht's it was called. They wouldn't let you go to the bathroom in any other place. And they had these little signs in the buses: *White Only*. I stole one and sent one to my mother. It was a visually segregated town. Water fountains. I always thought that they couldn't be serious. Why were they paying for two fountains? It didn't make sense that they would spend all this money so that they could feel better than somebody.

KAISER: When Donald Trump asked African Americans to vote for him, he said, 'What do you have to lose?' What is your response?

MORRISON: I just thought it was a stupid question. What I would have to lose would be everything. What I'm losing now is you're throwing bombs around. But it was so nasty and so superior. This con man who has seventy-seven words in his vocabulary. We have counted them. Philip Roth counted them. Seventy . . . seven . . . words.

LADIPO MANYIKA: Let's leave Trump for Obama. What was it like to receive the Presidential Medal of Freedom from him? And what did he whisper in your ear?

MORRISON: Were you there?

LADIPO MANYIKA / KAISER: No, we saw the video.

MORRISON: He did whisper in my ear. And I'll tell you, this is important: I didn't know what he said.

KAISER: You seemed very pleased.

MORRISON: I knew then! But soon as I left, I thought: What did he say? I was so embarrassed! I went to Paris, and the guy who was the ambassador to France, I told him that story. I said, 'He whispered in my ear, and I don't know what it is. Something's wrong!' And he said, 'Listen, I had a forty-five-minute conversation with him, and I don't remember a word.'

LADIPO MANYIKA: You were awestruck.

MORRISON: I think that's it. But when I went to the party, my son was my date. He said to Obama, 'You said something to my mother, and she doesn't remember. Do you remember what you said?' And Obama said, 'Yeah, sure I remember, I said, "I love you."' [She covers her face with her hands and pretends to be sobbing.] I can see why I forgot that! I forgot it in the way that you can have a conversation with somebody that you really like or who is really impressive. And it's so impressive that you just blank.

LADIPO MANYIKA: Let's stick to love and talk about your friend James Baldwin.

MORRISON: Oh, yes!

LADIPO MANYIKA: Baldwin once said, 'The role of the artist is exactly the same as the role of the lover. If I love you, I have to make you conscious of the things you don't see.' How do you see the role of the artist?

MORRISON: Oh, it's funny that he says that. Jimmy. What I'm going to say is going to sound so pompous, but I think an artist, whether it's a painter or a writer, it's almost holy. There's something about the vision, the wisdom. You can be a nobody,

46

but seeing that way, it's holy, it's godlike. It's above the normal life and perception of all of us, normally. You step up. And as long as you're up there, even if you're a terrible person – especially if you're a terrible person – you see things that come together, and shake you, or move you, or clarify something for you that outside of your art you would not have known. It really is a vision above, or beyond.

It's hard to think of paintings, particularly, any other way. I can't imagine how they do that. I mean, what's the connection between the thing you're doing and your mind? That's why criticism is so awful. Not all of it, but much of it. Because the language of the criticism can't quite reach the plane where the artist is.

LADIPO MANYIKA: Do you name your characters, or do they name themselves?

MORRISON: They name themselves. I have sometimes written characters with names that were wrong, and they never came alive. I have to ask them, 'What's your name?' You just wait and something clicks – or not. And, if not, the writing feels clunky, or they don't talk. Sometimes it's just the opposite. When I wrote *Song of Solomon*, there was this woman in there named Pilate. And once I envisioned her, she never shut up. She really took that book over, and I just had to stop her. So, I said, 'You have to shut up, this is not your book!' She has one scene where she's mourning her granddaughter and she says, 'And she was loved.' That's all the space she got. Although she's influential, she doesn't talk.

KAISER: You were baptized a Catholic when you were twelve years old, and you took the name Anthony, which later became Toni. Saint Anthony was a towering figure in the scripture.

MORRISON: Saint Anthony of Padua!

KAISER: He was known for his forceful preaching, and he's the patron saint of lost things. What are the lost things you would like to bring back?

MORRISON: Two things. One is my son. And there are certain periods in my life I'd like to live over.

KAISER: Is there one period in particular?

MORRISON: Yeah, undergraduate school. There were some very good things with that place, and I learned a lot. I was in this little theater group, and we used to travel in the summer. It was the first time I'd been in the South – the real South, not the Washington DC type. I remember when we got to a hotel and the faculty figured out that it was a whorehouse or something like that. So one of them went to the phone booth. Remember they used to have phone booths? He looked in the back of the phone book to find a Black preacher, which you could because it would say AME, African American Zion, or something. He found one and called them up and said that he was there with some students from Howard, and that they needed a place to stay, because there's no places for Black people. The preacher said, 'Call me back in fifteen minutes.' And he did, and he had gotten some of his parishioners to accept us. I went with a girl, stayed in this woman's house. It was fabulous! God, she had dried her sheets on bushes that had that odor. Oh, it was heaven! And they fixed us fabulous food. We tried to give them money, but they wouldn't take it. So, we put it in the pillowslip.

KAISER: The story is reminiscent of Frank Money, the protagonist of *Home*, when he's looking for a place to stay.

MORRISON: Oh, yeah. There's that Green Book he uses, which I have a copy of, which was where Black people could stay. You know, I didn't identify him as a Black man until my editor said,

'Nobody knows if he's Black or white.' And I said, 'So?' And he said, 'Toni, I really think it's important.' So, I gave in. But I was interested in writing the way I did in *Paradise*, in which I announce color: 'They shot the white girl first.' But you don't know who that white girl is. And that was very liberating for me because sometimes you can say 'black' and it don't mean nothing. I mean, unless you make it mean something. That was a learning thing because of the other side of town, where blackness was purity – and legitimacy. See, my great-grandmother lived in Michigan, and she was like the wise woman of the family. She knew everything. She was a midwife. Every now and then, she would visit. This was a tall woman. I mean, she looked tall. She had a cane that she obviously didn't need. And she came in the house and looked at me and my sister and said, 'Those children have been tampered with.' I thought that was a good thing. But she was pitch black, and she was looking at us as soiled, mixed. Not pure. She was pure – pure black, pure African – and we were kind of messed up a little bit. I thought that was interesting, because I had been 'othered' since I was a kid – but from the other side.

LADIPO MANYIKA: Can we talk about sex?

MORRISON: Yeah! I'm in a good position to talk about it, since it's been like a thousand years. What do you want to know?

LADIPO MANYIKA: You are known for writing great sex scenes.

MORRISON: I do! I think I write sex better than most people.

LADIPO MANYIKA: How do you do it?

MORRISON: The worst thing about sex scenes is that they're all clinical. They say 'breasts', or 'penis' or what. I mean, who cares? The goody part about sex and writing about it and having it is not that. It's something else. In *The Bluest Eye*, when she goes all the way, she claws away the skin to get to the ivory – you know, she's going down. Deep! But if you can associate sex with some other behavior that is interesting, then the sex becomes interesting.

LADIPO MANYIKA: In *Beloved*, it's the cornfield, but it's also the eating of the corn, the suggestiveness.

MORRISON: The corn tops are waving. The guys are looking.

LADIPO MANYIKA: 'It had been hard, hard, hard sitting there erect like dogs, watching corn stalks dance at noon.'

MORRISON: Somebody told me that Denzel Washington was asked to be in the movie of *Beloved*. And he said, 'I'm not gonna be in a movie where Black men have oral sex with white jailors.'

There was a scene where these men are in jail digging, you know, but they're all chained. He acted like that was bizarre. And then you read about Choate, this school where everybody was raping all the students from the sixties on. I don't know why he was so hostile to it. But that's OK, Denzel! I'm interested in how to make it really beautiful, really intimate, and distributed. It has to be something that everybody can relate to – not just the sex act, but what I'm saying about it. I read other people's sex scenes and I think, 'Yeah, so?'

KAISER: What will your next book be about?

MORRISON: Oh, it's so good! It's called *Justice*, although it's not about justice. There's a family in there, and their slave owner. His name was Goodmaster, and he made all the slaves call themselves Goodmaster. They hated it because he was horrible, but they kept the name because they could keep in touch with each other generations later. There's a guy in there who has three children, two girls and a boy. Their names are Courage, Freedom and Justice, but that's not good when they go to school. So, instead of Courage, they write Carrie. And Freedom, they say Frida. And the boy, whose name is Justice, they call Juice. Names matter. The naming is vital because we didn't have any names. They just gave us stupid names. I tried to remember my father's friends. They had nicknames. Cool Breeze, and one was called Jim the Devil. All kinds of names. Some are lovely, some are horrible. Whatever your weakness is, that's what they call you. So you can get that out of the way.

KAISER: You have said that you don't want to be remembered as an African American writer, but as an American writer.

MORRISON: Did I?

KAISER: Yes.

MORRISON: America? I couldn't relate to the country. It's too big. It's like saying, 'How would you think about Europe?' I mean, what? But I was somewhere with Doctorow, the writer, at an event. He was introducing me, and he said, 'I don't think of Toni as a Black writer. I don't think of her as a female writer. I think of her as . . .' And I said, 'White male writer.' And everybody laughed. That's what I remember. He was trying to move me out of the little sections. But what was there besides woman, Black? There was only white men. He probably meant to say just a plain writer, you know, a writer writer.

2.

CLAUDIA RANKINE

In Conversation

Claudia Rankine is the author of five books of poetry, including Citizen: An American Lyric *and* Don't Let Me Be Lonely; *four plays, including* Help, *which premiered in March 2022 (The Shed, NYC) and* The White Card, *which premiered in February 2018 (ArtsEmerson / American Repertory Theater) and was published by Graywolf Press in 2019; as well as numerous video collaborations. Her recent collection of essays,* Just Us: An American Conversation, *was published by Graywolf Press in 2020. She is the co-editor of several anthologies, including* The Racial Imaginary: Writers on Race in the Life of the Mind *(2015). In 2017, Rankine co-founded The Racial Imaginary Institute (TRII). Among her numerous awards and honors, Rankine is the recipient of the Bobbitt National Prize for Poetry, the Poets & Writers' Jackson Poetry Prize, and fellowships from the Guggenheim Foundation, the Lannan Foundation, the MacArthur Foundation, United States Artists and the National Endowment for the Arts. She teaches at NYU in the Creative Writing Program.*

November 16, 2020

SARAH LADIPO MANYIKA: Claudia, you have won many awards. Do you have a favorite or one that really surprised you?

CLAUDIA RANKINE: What an interesting question. Favorite award – I think they were all surprises, so I have a lot of surprise awards! But no, it's just always a delight that people are actually engaging with the work. As a writer you spend a lot of time creating different pathways and following lines of inquiry, trying to actualize a thing. Then the work goes out in the world and finds its people. I try not to be too invested in either the awards or the rejections, because I feel, once it's out, it's its own thing.

LADIPO MANYIKA: It is interesting that you bring up the word rejection. 'Rejection?' Have you had any rejections? Has *anyone* said no to your work?

RANKINE: Many, many, many people!

LADIPO MANYIKA: Can you tell us about your connection to the African diaspora?

RANKINE: The connection is unavoidable. As a Jamaican immigrant to the United States who comes from a country colonized by the British, it's impossible not to understand the relevance of the slave routes and the Middle Passage. In terms of my writing, I would say that some of the most influential writers on my own work are the poet Aimé Césaire and the psychoanalyst Frantz Fanon; with Fanon, for me, being maybe the most crucial in the way his work addresses the psychological ramifications of anti-Blackness within a society.

LADIPO MANYIKA: Your book *Don't Let Me Be Lonely* begins with a quote from Césaire, to paraphrase, 'Life is not a spectacle,' which is just really powerful.

RANKINE: Exactly. The quote: 'And most of all beware, even in thought, of assuming the sterile attitude of the spectator, for life is not a spectacle, a sea of grief is not a proscenium, a man who wails is not a dancing bear . . .' imprinted itself on my consciousness the very first time I read it in *Notebook of a Return to the Native Land.*

LADIPO MANYIKA: You grew up in Jamaica for the first few years of your life. Talk about your childhood and what kindled your love for literature and the arts.

RANKINE: Well, my mother tells a story; I'm going to believe her. She said I was one of those kids who was reading even before I could read. I was always holding books. So obviously I must have been around readers, people who had books. My mother was always reciting poets like Countee Cullen and Emily Dickinson. Once I came to the United States, when I was around seven, I spent a lot of time in the library. I was one of those kids where the library was my closest friend. I would go there with tote bags and come home with them full of books all by the same author. I just read alphabetically in the library and, when I finished all the books by one author, I went on to the next.

The thing that I remember most clearly was I read all of those books that are called *Best American Plays,* and equally the *Best American Short Stories* . . . So whenever I watched a movie, I always knew the plot. Someone in my family was always asking, 'How do you know what's going to happen?' And I would answer '*Best American Plays!*'

LADIPO MANYIKA: It's interesting what your mother said about you starting to read before you could read. That seems to be a metaphor for the ways in which you read situations, the ways in which you read conversations. Maybe we'll explore that a bit more when we talk about your latest book. But for now, let's discuss *Citizen*, which is the middle book of your trilogy. One of the fundamental rights of a citizen is the right to vote. Given where we are in America at this point in time, what reflections would you make on what it means to be an American citizen?

RANKINE: I think you're absolutely correct that the right to vote is at the center of our power as citizens. We know this because of how active voter suppression attempts are in this country. Right now, the unwillingness to concede has to do with an attempt to delegitimize one vote, one person. The pushback in Georgia against a recount in January is also an example of this. I'm going to pause here just to give a shout-out to Stacey Abrams, who I think is the superhero of this whole election. I really feel that it's criminal, the ways in which elected representatives in this country are trying to delegitimize our democracy by 1) suppressing the vote, 2) preventing counts, and now 3) endorsing legal challenges against a legitimate election. It's very sad and I'm frightened by the fragility of our democracy. We are apparently on the brink of being citizens of a fascist state and therefore must continue to fight to keep some semblance of a democracy.

LADIPO MANYIKA: Your latest book, *Just Us: An American Conversation*, is, at its core, about the necessary conversations we must have about whiteness, and it's about the fictions that we tell ourselves. But before we actually dive into it, tell us a little bit about the title, taken from the punchline of a Richard Pryor skit.

RANKINE: Why don't I play it for you?

[VIDEO CLIP BEGINS – Pryor makes a joke about the injustices of the American criminal justice system with the punchline**]**

RICHARD PRYOR: *'You go down there looking for justice, that's what you find, just us.'*

[VIDEO CLIP ENDS]

RANKINE: It was actually the reverse: the title was always JUST US, but its resonance with Richard Pryor's joke came later. Given the premise of the book, *An American Conversation*, appropriately I was in conversation with Alexandra Bell. I love her work, the series *Counternarratives* that she does and the way in which she has brought back an examination of the media. Bell asked if the title of my book was a reference to Richard Pryor's joke. At the time, I wasn't familiar with it. She pointed me to it and, when I heard his routine, I was fascinated because obviously the 'just us', when used by Pryor, means Black people.

I also love the fact that when you think about justice, it could also mean that justice is only for white people. There is a kind of slipperiness in the collision of 'just us' with 'justice'. Pryor's quip seemed like the right portal to enter this book, because he suggests you cannot talk about anti-Black racism without talking about white people or institutions of whiteness.

LADIPO MANYIKA: It's a brilliant title for me in that it can also be read as a question: just us? I read it that way. Also, justice reminded me of a conversation I had with Toni Morrison a few years ago. She was working on a novel at that time, and its working title was *Justice*. So there are many resonances to your particular title.

I also want to talk about humor – the power of humor, and how you draw on humor at different points in the book and in previous works. Humor can often say things that are just hard to say straight up. That is the power of humor. That said, there's not a ton of humor in your new book. A lot of it is very, very serious, and needs to be serious.

RANKINE: I think it's funny at times, but OK.

LADIPO MANYIKA: More not-funny.

RANKINE: I know, by virtue of reality, it's sometimes not funny. But depending on the day, you can either be attuned to the dark or the humor in the 'dark humor'.

LADIPO MANYIKA: I'm going to read just a little bit toward the beginning when you talk about what you've set out to do with this book. This is on page nineteen.

> *The running comment in our current political climate is that we all need to converse with people we don't normally speak to, and though my husband is white, I found myself falling into easy banter with all kinds of strangers except white men. They rarely sought me out to shoot the breeze, and I did not seek them out. Maybe it was time to engage, even if my fantasies of these encounters seemed outlandish. I wanted to try.*

Tell us about these conversations, some of the things that you learned, maybe some of the things that surprised you.

RANKINE: I gave my students an assignment to interview people about the role of whiteness in their lives. They interviewed strangers, their family members and friends, their suitemates and roommates. I thought, Maybe I should do that myself. I'm one of those people who is constantly trying to figure out how I can multitask. It occurred to me that, when I'm in airport terminals waiting for the plane, it's dead time where I'm usually surrounded by white people, many of them white men traveling in either first class or business class. I realized I could use that time to try and talk to them about their privilege, about their understanding of whiteness.

What I learned is that that phrase, white privilege – and it's interesting to me that the phrase was developed by a white woman, Peggy McIntosh, who later disavowed it – is a term that makes white men think that I want to talk about their economic privilege. I hadn't gone into those conversations thinking I was always going to get a bootstrap narrative about how hard they worked. Every once in a while there would be a guy who was like, 'I have a lot of money and I've always had a lot of money and it's good to be me.' But most of the time it was people who worked hard, and I could see that they worked hard. They were falling asleep on these long flights and they were surrounded by computers and papers and phone calls and all of that stuff that we spend our day doing.

So I began to stop using that term, white privilege, and started asking them about their white living. 'What does it feel like to be a white man moving around in space?' Because I got tired of having to say, 'I'm not talking about money. I'm not talking about economic privilege. I just want you to tell me how it feels not to be policed, not to be racially profiled, to have freedom of movement where you're not constantly questioned. Where a door opens and people assume you're going to walk through it.' I cannot tell you how many times I've watched my husband mindlessly enter rooms where he's not even invited, but he's welcomed as if he's expected. But before I can follow him, they step in front of me to ask: 'What are you doing here? Can we help you? Who are you?' That kind of mobility is a thing to watch in the world.

LADIPO MANYIKA: What you just said about the different responses to you and your husband reminds me of something I've heard you say about a moment when you had left your house and the alarm went off. Perhaps you can tell that story.

RANKINE: Well, this happened not long ago, actually. I think I was distracted and I left the house to walk the dog. The way our alarm is set up, it goes off when you exit as well as when you enter. So I left the house unaware that I had engaged the alarm, which alerts the police. So I just locked the door behind me and took the dog and, when I came back, there were all these policemen in our yard. An officer approaches me, and I sheepishly admit, 'Oh, my God. I accidentally did this, let me go inside and turn it off.' We have a code to get in the house. Then you have to put in another code to turn the alarm off. All these things are happening.

When I go back outside, we joke about this and that. Meanwhile, my husband has received a notification on his phone, saying the alarm is on. He drives home, jumps out of the car, comes bounding up the steps, and the policeman turns to him and says, 'She said she lives here.' Even before asking him, 'Who are you?' or, 'Can we help you?' or saying to me, 'Do you know this man?' he just says, 'She said she lives here.' It was like someone had been caught fraternizing with the enemy.

Those are the kinds of moments that are always, to me, revealing of how anti-Blackness lives just below the surface of civility in white people. If you're listening, it shows itself.

LADIPO MANYIKA: *Just Us* is a very brave and courageous book, and it's a book that is worth reading quite slowly. One of the things that really spoke to me was just how many times you shine a light on the fictions that we weave and what we want to believe: things that don't actually compute with reality. Also, speaking of being brave and courageous . . . There's a chapter entitled 'Social Contract', the unwritten code being that one doesn't talk about race. But you go right there and you use the term white and white privilege. Terms and encounters that make people feel uncomfortable. Sometimes in society there's a desire to feel like we've moved beyond this when we haven't at all.

And I want to highlight another conversation. There was a cross burning back when you were at college some years ago and you spoke to a friend who actually saw it. Perhaps you can talk about it.

RANKINE: I wondered who would remember that event among my friend group. After all, it was nearly forty years ago. It occurred outside a Black Student Union party. I contacted a good white friend from college and was surprised to learn that it was actually her who saw it and called the campus police. They brought her into a basement and she had to go through pictures of suspects. When I asked her to write down what she remembered about the event, she wrote, 'I wonder if the people, the possible students who did this, are looking back and regret that they had behaved in such a way.' It just reminded me of how quickly white people want to believe in the benevolence of white people.

Look at the 2020 election, for example, how disappointed people were that it wasn't a landslide election, that, in fact, it was so close. Her inability to believe they are what they performed still baffles me. I asked, 'Why would you think that they're any different today than they were then?' Another thing she said to me recently, because we talk pretty often, was, 'The thing I only recently thought about is why did they show me those students? That must mean that they had done other things to be people of interest at that moment.'

I requested the police files and when they arrived I noticed they named two white male students. When I looked them up, to my horror, I found that they were both working in the justice system now. One was an attorney general and one was a judge. Hopefully they had a big transformation or something, but given the way the justice system has worked out, as Richard Pryor told us, I wouldn't be surprised if they hold the same beliefs today that they held when we were eighteen, nineteen, twenty.

LADIPO MANYIKA: This business of wanting to believe in the benevolence of people – I mean, it's not just white people, but as a Black person, I always want to believe. We always want to believe in the best, but sometimes we just have to look at facts, especially in this era when facts are always questioned. One thing that really struck me was a little graph toward the end of your book which shows the percentages of people that voted for President Obama the first time around and the second time around. One thing I frequently hear is, 'Well, how can we be where we are when everyone was behind President Obama?' The most President Obama got was forty-three per cent of the white vote and then, the second time around, it was thirty-nine per cent. There are some things that we either conveniently forget, or we don't want to look at for what they are.

Claudia, there's great hybridity in your work. You draw on images, you draw on video, film. In this book, you have a narrative on the right-hand side and then on the verso you have photographs, evidence, be it anecdotal or factual. What went into the form of this book?

RANKINE: Well, part of my practice is that the content and form have to be married for me to be satisfied in the process of making a book. These two elements really have to be working in tandem. For this book, I was interested in the ways in which fake news, anti-science, anti-facts have become *de facto* during and since the Trump administration. I wanted the book to reinsert factual information into quotidian conversations. The idea was for the page to reenact our constant negotiation of images, facts and news, everything that makes up the day. I was more committed to the process of this active management than the facts themselves. It's ideally an archive of the act of processing.

The question was, how do I then organize it so that it's not in the back of the book, as often happens. I came up with a system where the essays would run on the recto side of the page and the facts and images would be on the verso side of the page.

The question then became how to get a reader to move fluidly between the recto and verso pages. We came up with a red dot to indicate a moment where the sentence was dependent on outside information. So that if a sentence butterflied out into other referential material that might destabilize or confirm its veracity, those facts, those images ended up on the verso side of the page. I wanted the text to be as open as possible, so if a reader didn't want to read the citations and factual information, they didn't have to. If they wanted to read it and think about it relationally, then they could. It inserted an autonomy into the act of reading and, more importantly, gave a blueprint regarding the process of thought that foregrounded my own conversations. In many ways I was more committed to offering a blueprint of the process of thought than to the fact of the content.

LADIPO MANYIKA: Let's spend a minute or two talking about some of the blind spots that you found, in particular a chapter entitled 'José Marti'. In addition, there's an audience question that I'll insert here which is: 'Wouldn't interviewing white men in airports eliminate white men who earn much less and might feel differently about their own well-being?' Such a question touches on privilege and also perhaps your own privilege as someone who is able to, first of all fly, at least pre-Covid, business class. What have you learned about your own blind spots?

RANKINE: Well, I wouldn't consider that a blind spot in the sense that it was intentional. I intended to document *my* world. I wasn't going to pretend to have a neutral position when I didn't. I wanted to show the positionality from which I was speaking, and the fact that precarities that I experience are not ones that are necessarily based on financial privilege. Not that those are not important. Normally, I don't show up in my books in a way that's fully me. But I wanted this book to do that.

I did hear from other white men in different economic positions when the piece ran in the *New York Times*. I received over 200 letters and emails. Those were from everybody, both very wealthy people and also very poor people. Some of them felt I wasn't taking them into account. That's true. But ultimately, their assumptions about and treatment of Black people were more or less consistent. Because what we are really talking about is unconscious bias, and that doesn't have a dollar sign attached to it. If anything, less-advantaged white Americans take solace in the fact that they aren't Black, or at least that's what I take from Lyndon B. Johnson's statement, 'If you can convince the lowest white man he's better than the best colored man, he won't notice you're picking his pocket. Hell, give him somebody to look down on, and he'll empty his pockets for you.' Class does not eliminate racism.

The blind spots I did have existed more along the lines of being too focused on the world of anti-Blackness without taking into account the experiences of, say, Asian or Latinx people living under the umbrella of 'People of Color'. I was grateful to be challenged on my knowledge of the history of the multiple positions of Latinx identity. In the past, I was guilty of using shorthand to suggest any community can be talked about as a monolith, capable of being reduced to a single experience.

LADIPO MANYIKA: You used the word 'precarity' in the book and I hear you use it a lot as you're speaking. And also the word 'swerve'. 'Swerve' is a word that I associate with Michelle Obama. She uses it a lot in *Becoming*, how she swerves to do something that maybe she ordinarily wouldn't do, and it's a confidence thing. Tell me about 'swerve' and your use of it in this book.

RANKINE: Well, I think one of the things that I have run into over the years – and I don't know if it's an age thing, or I'm not understanding something – is that I've always felt that part of being human is to adjust to the person in front of you. I've had the experience most recently with my play *The White Card*, in which a Black woman artist is attempting to broker a deal with white collectors whose racism is on full display. When we were trying to cast the Black female artist, we brought in some very well-known, but younger, Black actresses. And they kept saying, 'I don't understand why this character would stay in the room with a white person who is racist.' And I say, 'Well, don't you swerve in your own life? Don't you adjust because you want to stay in that room, because you want to do the thing you want to do?'

And they kept saying to me, 'I would just leave,' and I responded, 'You would walk out?' I have never seen anybody walk, just get up. I mean, on occasion in fits of anger, but mostly in business meetings you see people adjusting, you see people attempting to manage the environment. The swerve to me is an active negotiation of real life. I will say, though, upon second thought, I have seen people think about something and then walk away, but not in real time.

LADIPO MANYIKA: Is that possibility of the swerve what gives you hope?

RANKINE: Well, I think it's an accommodation in the sense of one wanting to be able to negotiate a life. What gives me hope is that it will become less necessary to swerve in order to get the things that you should just have, to live the same quality of life that white people get to live. I don't think racism will ever disappear, but I think we now have a public that is much more literate and educated around some of these issues. I don't feel like I am necessarily the one who has to bring certain things up when they're occurring, other people are speaking to those moments. I don't have to get out of the way of a weaponized insult, other people are jumping in to say no to that. Then the swerve is less necessary because somehow the environment is addressing those moments. But we also have this very new and weird dynamic where people are being very racist in their attempts to be anti-racist.

LADIPO MANYIKA: Say more.

RANKINE: Well, students and other people are telling me that they're getting calls, for example, saying, 'We had the perfect job for you and it would've been yours, except that we are being forced to hire a Black person.' That language is now becoming more and more acceptable. Nobody says, 'We have realized that our institution is all white and therefore can only represent one perspective.' Instead, they're 'being forced' to do anti-racist work and, 'Sorry, you white person, you would be here, but we're going to have to . . .' In a way, it's what Amy Klobuchar did. Remember she said, I am going to step aside for consideration as VP, so that Biden can get a woman of color, get a Black woman in there. And, in fact, she was stepping aside because of what was going on in Minneapolis, in Minnesota, her state, where policing was out of control. But there's this new way of acting like they're doing a favor to Black people.

LADIPO MANYIKA: It's another sort of fiction making. Should we look at a clip of your collaborative piece with John Lucas, *Situation 11*?

RANKINE: Sure. I was often asked, 'What's a conversation that would've been in *Just Us* had the publishing date been later?' And it's this interaction that happened between Christian Cooper (a Black man) and Amy Cooper (a white woman, no relation) in Central Park regarding her refusal to leash her dog in a protected area of the park. After the Amy Cooper conversation and what happened, a lot of white friends said, 'Oh, my God. That Amy Cooper is racist, but should she have lost her job? Isn't that going a little too far? Isn't that too much?' Every time those moments happen, I'm like, 'What? *Et tu, Brute?*'

[VIDEO CLIP BEGINS]

AMY COOPER: *There is an African American man, I'm in Central Park, he's recording me, threatening myself and my dog.*

RANKINE: *Amy Cooper calls the police on a Black man bird-watching. Hers was a quotidian reminder. Reminder of the normalcy of, how can I put it, having not been meant to survive? Christian Cooper, no apparent relation, asked Amy Cooper to put her dog on a leash. It was a simple ask in accordance with the rules of Central Park's Ramble. I am enthralled with Cooper's affect, her plaintive 911 call of distress.*

AMY COOPER: *I'm in trouble and there's an African American man threatening my life.*

RANKINE: *Intensified with each repetition of the phrase, 'I am being threatened.'*

AMY COOPER: *And there's a man, African American . . .*

RANKINE: *'I am being threatened.'*

AMY COOPER: *He's recording me, and threatening . . .*

RANKINE: *By the third repetition, her voice quivers.*

AMY COOPER: *African American man, I'm in Central Park.*

RANKINE: *But she's able to multitask and re-attach the leash to the dog as she speaks. Like an actor, heightening her fear in her performance of a line, she pushes on.*

AMY COOPER: *I am being threatened!*

RANKINE: *Cooper and I both recognize she can bet on racism, racial profiling and possible unwarranted murder of a Black person to be supported systemically by random policemen, prosecutors, judges and the carceral system at large. Our mutual socialization into repeated patterns of discrimination* *allows her to do what she does and prepares me to understand what she is doing in the daylight of what I am seeing.*

Where we part company, where we part, where I am no longer a part, is in her expectation that I will agree that she is afraid. Do fantasies create real emotions? Is Christian Cooper's possible death an acceptable loss? History says yes. Yesterday said, yes. If fantasies are relevant to the moment, are they not also relevant to the consequences of the moment? Can I categorize Amy Cooper's behavior as an American story that plays fast and loose with notions of imagined fear? To imagine herself as a rescue, to imagine herself into a rescue narrative is to activate a covert white female power trigger that can easily call in the violence of white men.

One white friend puts it this way: 'Amy Cooper assumed her role as a piece of high value white property in jeopardy. Tapping into what she knows to be a salient catalyst for swift and deadly intervention.' Given this, is her performance more incredulous rage than fear? The rules, the rules don't apply to her. Am I to understand her as thinking, or is it feeling, the fullness of 'don't you see who I am?' Is that white living right below, just below, a level of civility? Unspoken, but believed, rage tied to white identities, assumed sense of ownership of all property. Her park, her city, her apartment building, her, her, her president, her business. Cooper's exact words were, 'I'm going to tell them there's an African American man threatening my life.'

Hers is the language of good manners, weaponizing the narratives of white racism. 'Excuse me,' she says to Christian Cooper as she dials the police. There are so many Amy Coopers, women like Sarah Page, the white woman who served as justification for the Tulsa massacre. The white woman behind the Rosewood massacre, the two white women behind the imprisonment of the Scottsboro Boys. Carolyn Bryant Donham, who finally admitted to lying, but whose admittance could not bring back to life Emmett Till. Or Linda Fairstein,

who prosecuted the Central Park jogger case, and willfully
sent five Black and Latinx teenagers to prison for years. For
years on false and suppressed evidence. Do I need to go on?
The various modes of behavior that white women weaponize
in service of Black death are there to be metabolized. It's an old
script supported by this one.

VIDEO: *A crowd scene, people chanting, 'Hands up, please
don't shoot me.'*

[VIDEO CLIP ENDS]

LADIPO MANYIKA: It's an old script and these are things we
have to look at and have conversations about, as uncomfortable
as they are. I want to reiterate just how brave and courageous
you have been in giving us all of your works and in really
looking at what the facts are and not swerving away. Claudia,
this is not easy work and these are not easy times. What grounds
you in these times?

RANKINE: I have a daughter and it sounds corny, but it's true:
you want to leave the world a better place than you found it. For
me, the only way I know how to do that is by writing and doing
the kind of hybrid work that I do.

I just watched Dave Chappelle the other day and he said
that he was not as optimistic as Donald Trump because Trump
says, 'There are good people on all sides.' Chappelle thinks there
are bad people on all sides, and I agree with him. People, by
their very nature, are conflicted and complex. But the tragedy
is that white violence, racism is supported by the apparatus of
our supposedly democratic structure that was built on white
supremacy. So, one form of being human is criminalized, and the
other form is governing.

This culture of whiteness has caused so much damage and
we have managed to somehow divorce white people from the

equation. We have managed to go 400 years where people talk about what's happening without talking about actual American history and the role ordinary white people have played in that. The only person I know who really did that work was James Baldwin, and to some extent bell hooks. Baldwin insisted that we've got to understand that racism is not about Black people as much as it is about white people and their fantasies and their psyche. In fact, Toni Morrison said it bluntly in her interview with Charlie Rose:

> *If I take your race away, and there you are, all strung out. And all you got is your little self, and what is that? What are you without racism? Are you any good? Are you still strong? Are you still smart? Do you still like yourself? I mean, these are the questions. Part of it is, 'yes, the victim. How terrible it's been for Black people.' I'm not a victim. I refuse to be one . . . if you can only be tall because somebody is on their knees, then you have a serious problem. And my feeling is that white people have a very, very serious problem and they should start thinking about what they can do about it. Take me out of it.*

LADIPO MANYIKA: Claudia, if you could change anything about the way that people think of the African diaspora, what would it be?

RANKINE: I think that often our discussion of the diaspora and colonization feeds into a disproportionate centralization of the power of whiteness and the ways in which white people can show up to help Black people when, in fact, they're showing up to cause the problems again and again. Countries that are devastated, are devastated because their resources were taken. They're not devastated because they're devastated. We are also a part of everything that is vibrant and contributing.

LADIPO MANYIKA: To that point, in terms of celebrating all that is amazing, and I know this is an impossible question, who is your favorite artist from the African diaspora?

RANKINE: John Akomfrah is somebody whose work I adore and often return to in my own. His work *Vertigo Sea*, which touches on history, migration and the Middle Passage. The way that he juxtaposes images to create multiple narratives has profoundly influenced my view of hybridity. I also am really interested right now in Arthur Jafa's work. In some ways Jafa and Akomfrah are in conversation in the way they are bringing the history up against the ordinary, the high meets the low, all of it into one genre, into one art form of excellence.

I just read and loved Natasha Brown's *Assembly*. The series *Small Axe* by director Steve McQueen on London's Black immigrant communities. Teju Cole's writing and art. The poet Hafizah Geter who has a new memoir out. Zadie Smith. Roxane Gay. There are too many to list, these writers and artists I am fed and inspired by.

3.

XOLISWA SITHOLE

In Conversation

Xoliswa Sithole is an award-winning producer and director whose films focus on women and children, justice, human rights and poverty. Her many films include Shouting Silent *(2002),* A Ribbon in the Sky *(2002),* Projek Mandela *(2009) and* Orphans of Nkandla *(2005), for which she won her first BAFTA and an International Emmy nomination. Her documentary* Zimbabwe's Forgotten Children *(2010) was shot entirely undercover and won Peabody and BAFTA awards. Sithole is also the producer and director of* Child of the Revolution *(2016) and* Standing on Their Shoulders *(2018), a feminist documentary on the 1956 Women's March in South Africa and its domino effect on Black women's activism till present day. She is the director of Nayanaya Pictures.*

February 12, 2021

SARAH LADIPO MANYIKA: When you were very young, you came from apartheid South Africa as a refugee, with your mum and your sister, to what was then Rhodesia, now Zimbabwe. You have written a lovely piece about your childhood in the book *Township Girls: The Cross-Over Generation,* in which you write:

> *I would walk to Chitsere Primary School, where I also fought my own wars of being very light skinned. The kids used to call me mukaradhi, meaning colored. And I did stick out, and my Bantu bottom stuck out as well. I was teased quite a lot, but what may have saved me was that I was quite smart, and I always fought for the underdog.*

Talk about your childhood and how this has shaped you.

XOLISWA SITHOLE: My mother left South Africa with my sister and myself, and first went to Zambia. A lot of South Africans were going to Zambia because the ANC was stationed there. Then we ended up in Rhodesia, at that time. My mother was a nurse and she subsequently got a job and waited for my dad, and he didn't come. My mother met Joshua Sithole and married him – she was madly in love with him. But what was interesting is that I was then raised by, or plunged into, a highly political family in Zimbabwe. My uncle, Ndabaningi Sithole, was a founding member of ZANU (Zimbabwe African National Union). All these politicians would always come to our house and discuss politics.

Someone else who was very, very important to us was Edson Sithole. Dr Edson Sithole was my cousin and lived in my parents' house. He was the first Doctor of Laws in Southern Africa, and he was a political activist. He disappeared in 1976 under Ian Smith's regime, never to be found again. Edson Sithole was really, I think, my first love. As an older cousin/

brother he used to take me everywhere. He was a lawyer and he taught me a sense of justice. He would be imprisoned a few times. I didn't know what this meant when I was young. When he disappeared, and then my father died, who had raised us as Sitholes, it broke my mother because we were refugees in what eventually became Zimbabwe. Edson Sithole had a huge impact on my need to fight for justice.

LADIPO MANYIKA: I was struck, in your piece, by how you say you were 'quite' smart, which is the understatement of the year. You were *very* smart. And there are lots of things that you could have done. You were a great dancer, you could have been a great academic, but instead you went into acting and filmmaking. How did that happen?

SITHOLE: I always wanted to be an actress. I had this flamboyant mother. My mother, God bless her, she was married and divorced four times. I grew up in conservative Rhodesia, which became Zimbabwe. It was totally scandalous in that environment. And I had a desire for just being creative. When I was very young, my mother bought me this swimming costume for two dollars and I would wear it and hold a broomstick and start singing songs. I remember when Lena Zavaroni came to Rhodesia. It was Rhodesia then, and we were not allowed to go to movie theaters with white people. Black people had to sit right at the back of the theater in the Black section. And I cried for a ticket. It was three dollars. It was a lot of money for my mum, but I wanted to go and see Lena Zavaroni. It was the biggest thing for us!

The only Black people we saw on television were the Jackson Five and Diana Ross. I would say to my mother, 'I'm going to be on TV one day.' My mother would say to me, 'My child, if you want to be Diana Ross, you can be Diana Ross.' So, I just grew up with this thing in Rhodesia, went to a Black school. And I just imagined that I was going to be someone in front of the screen.

LADIPO MANYIKA: So, you were Diana Ross and more! You are Xoliswa Sithole. It's making me smile as you're describing how you were as a child. In this essay you also write about living in England for a short while when you were working in care homes. You did some acting then, as well. Tell us about that.

SITHOLE: Went to England – no plan – with my friend Ruramai. Worked in old people's homes. And I would act for these old people – go behind those curtains and Ruramai would be holding the curtain. 'Ladies and gentlemen—' we would line up the elderly people who were like eighty and ninety with cataracts '—clap your hands for Miss Xoliswa Sithole!' I would come out and I would sing 'It's a long way to Tipperary, it's a long way to go . . . ' Or I'd just act something. And then they would clap their hands and say, 'Very nice.' But, of course, half of them, or most of them were half blind. But I was just this performer for these people in those old people's homes. It's just about making lemonade when you've been given lemons. It's just making the most of whatever situation you're in.

LADIPO MANYIKA: I love this. There is the performer in you but then you are also so understated about your accomplishments and what you can do. I would like to run a clip from your award-winning film *Shouting Silent*, and then we'll talk about it.

[VIDEO CLIP BEGINS]

SITHOLE: *My name is Xoliswa. It means 'I give you my peace'. Although, I do not think that my mother thought that I gave her peace. We had a very cantankerous relationship.*

I live in Johannesburg, and I am a filmmaker. I am starting a new project, and, like every new venture in my life, I always visit my mother's grave in the Transkei. I ask her for wisdom and guidance. I am making a film about young women who have lost their mothers to AIDS, women like me. My mother passed on in 1996. The girl child is so vulnerable, and so many of these girls are just slipping through the cracks of society. I want to know how they are really coping without their mothers. I feel blessed to have had my mother until adulthood.

[VIDEO CLIP ENDS]

LADIPO MANYIKA: That's just the beginning of what is an extremely powerful film. In that film, in addition to talking a little bit about your own story, you are interviewing and speaking with other people who are losing (or who have lost) their parents to HIV/AIDS. Xoliswa, for as long as I've known you, women's stories, young girls' stories, have been at the core of what you do. Why is that?

SITHOLE: I just think that there is no agency in society – especially a society which is actually very misogynist and globally patriarchal – there is no agency to actually make stories about women that have resonance. Being a documentary filmmaker, you are bearing witness. You are recording and bearing witness. It makes sense for me, as a woman filmmaker, to make films around such topics. And, of course, I'm a filmmaker. But I need to say something. When I had the idea to make this film, I had just finished working for CNN where I had met Charlayne Hunter-Gault, who was my mentor, really. Toni Morrison talks about how all a child wants is for a person's eyes to light up when the child walks into the room, and Charlayne's eyes used to light up for me.

When I told her I wanted to make this film, Charlayne is the person who got me the money for it. Charlayne was very pivotal, and I'm going to get emotional here. Pivotal in pushing, in pushing constantly, being generous, advising. She has continued to be like that. This film was very difficult emotionally because I felt very exposed. But she was such a big support. She just said, 'I will get you the money. This is important.' South Africa was dealing with its own issues of AIDS denialism. So, it was a very difficult film to make. Even when the film came out, I was persecuted. And Charlayne was very supportive at that time. I think that it's important for us to tell women's stories and I think we just need to be brave and unapologetic about that.

LADIPO MANYIKA: You are in many of your films and you are a documentarian, so you're sharing stories. Yet, at the same time, there are scenes where the people you're talking with cry with you – you're a shoulder for them to lean on. I wonder, what is it like, this tug, for you as someone telling a story. You're bearing witness, and yet you cannot help but be part of the story as well. Often, as I'm watching your work, I think of Bryan Stevenson's work when he talks about being broken. You cannot help but be broken yourself when in the midst of these kinds of things – these heavy and difficult subjects and hard experiences that people are going through.

SITHOLE: Oh, it's very hard. I mean, making that film was very hard for me. We went throughout the country, people asking, 'What is this thing?' People didn't have a full grasp of what HIV/AIDS was at that time. I would come home. I would cry. I felt defeated. And at moments you feel like, 'You know what? I think I must just throw the towel in.' But something tells you to just keep on. It makes you vulnerable, because there's a thin line where you could be very exploitative in terms of what you are doing. And then you also need to be compassionate. It's a very difficult line.

Fortunately, I did have people around me who felt it was a very important story to tell. And also the fact that my own mother had passed on. And I know that the film traveled globally to other places. Even here, when we showed it to people, you would have grown women saying, 'Thank you. You've given me the strength to tell my story. I've been positive for five years, but I've never had the guts to tell anybody.' Some of it was a catharsis for a lot of people, and some of it wasn't. It's just what it is. And you do it. It's difficult. It's very difficult.

LADIPO MANYIKA: Many of your films have been impact films. Maybe you can describe this term. These films have raised a lot of money for various causes. For HIV orphans, for ending poverty and so forth. With this particular film, *Shouting Silent*, could you say more?

SITHOLE: Yes, the impact. I was slaughtered by the media with this film and I was so upset and so jaded. Actually, for the whole year I couldn't work after that because I was so . . . I don't know. It was my first time being so exposed and feeling vulnerable. Soon after that, the BBC and True Vision TV wanted to make a film in South Africa, but I refused. I said, 'No, I'm not going to make any more films about orphans and everything.' But they kept coming back to me. So, I worked with them on this ninety-minute film called *Orphans of Nkandla.* That was in 2005. But, when that film came out, Richard Curtis, who started Make Poverty History (he's also one of the founders of Red Nose Day, which raises money for global charities), used a clip of that film to raise money for Make Poverty History.

The film was also shown on Red Nose Day, and a clip was also used by Sir Elton John. He has his AIDS charity, and he does a ball every year. Two years in a row he showed that clip, and he raised £7m over two years. That money was actually meant to come to South Africa, but Thabo Mbeki wasn't interested. So, the money went to Kenya for some trials that they were doing about the spread of HIV from mother to child.

The reality is that there are sad stories, and, at that particular time, that was the reality we were dealing with. We were dealing with the reality of people not being able to access HIV medicines, mothers and children dying because Nevirapine wasn't made available, and people had to fight the government for it to be available. So, you are bearing witness and documenting because this was a war that we were fighting.

LADIPO MANYIKA: In a way, we've come full circle. The film you're working on now is looking at the history of fighting to get those drugs for AIDS, and now we're wondering whether people will be able to have access to the Covid-19 vaccine. But, before we get there, you mentioned Sir Elton John. In the course of your work, you've also been able to meet some incredibly famous people. Elton John, Bill Clinton, Oprah Winfrey. What was it like meeting Elton John?

SITHOLE: Actually, we were filming for Red Nose Day and Sir Elton John came to *Nkandla*. Then he came to me and said, 'Darling, would you like to come to the Elton John Ball?' And, see, I don't like being starstruck because I guess I think, deep down, I'm a bit of a diva myself. I just said to him, 'Yeah. OK, thank you.' Casually, I got out of the hut (we were filming in a hut) went around the corner, pinched myself and jumped up and down. I went to the Elton John Ball. Danced the night away with all the superstars. Diana Ross was there. There were about five Black people, and I was one of them. And they were all wondering who is she. Who is she? Who is she? And I just loved it.

Elton John was playing music two meters away from me. Each time he got up to take a break, he would come past my table. 'Hello, darling, are you having a nice time?' I think they just thought that I was probably some African princess or something, and I just loved it. I loved it. Charlayne, culprit. She was having a dinner for President Bill Clinton at her house. And, she said to me, 'Xoliswa, I want you to be available on this day to cook.' Because I can cook. She didn't tell me anything. Day before, she said, 'You are cooking for Bill Clinton, sixty people.' I cooked.

The one thing that I loved about President Bill Clinton: he was the sort of person who would go to the kitchen, speak to all the people who were working in the kitchen. Not just, hello, hello. Spend time talking. And Mandela was also like that. Just really, really engaged. Yes, my life has been serendipitous, if I may say so. Oprah Winfrey. I was asked to be the South African producer for the Oprah Winfrey Leadership Academy for Girls documentary.

I was six months pregnant with my daughter. I did that. And, she was lovely. But, I really, really don't get starstruck. I'm sorry to say that. Because, I think, like Rudyard Kipling's poem . . . if you can treat people, kings and queens, and have the same reverence for the common man, then you are a man, my son – something like that. I've always wanted to keep that. You know what I'm trying to say? To not have excessive reverence for powerful people. Also, being a documentary filmmaker, it does keep you grounded.

LADIPO MANYIKA: Well, you can stay grounded while we all remain starstruck by you. I'd like to go back to women and girls and note that in addition to documenting people's stories through your films, you also have done some spectacular films on history, one of them being about the history of women's activism in South Africa. Let's play a little clip from this film, *Standing on Their Shoulders.*

[**VIDEO CLIP BEGINS** – Shireen Hassim speaking in reference to the 1965 Women's March in Pretoria protesting the pass laws]

SHIREEN HASSIM: *To some extent, the men in the ANC, in particular, weren't sure that the march was a good idea. They were worried about what would happen if women got arrested. And the women said, 'Well, we're not carrying passes and we're prepared to go to jail.' And the men said, 'Well, if you go to jail, who will look after the children?' So, the very idea that women could leave their children was considered to be radical.*

LADIPO MANYIKA: I always smile when I hear her say that. Who will look after the children? I hope everyone will see it in full and appreciate the various themes dealing with the erasure of women's stories – the erasure and the invisibility of the history behind women's movements. And even the way the world still sees people such as Winnie Mandela or Albertina Sisulu and refers to them as 'wives of' activists when they themselves have such bigger stories. I wonder if you could say a few more words about that.

SITHOLE: Yes, we are supposed to actually contest the erasure of women out of history. We're supposed to fight that. When I thought of making this film, it was to celebrate the 1956 Women's March in Pretoria. Because, as you know, men were already carrying passes and the law was now wanting to force women to carry passes. And women organized. 20,000 women marched to Union Buildings and they said, 'No, we are not.' And they never carried passes.

But, in making this film, the most disappointing thing for me was that there's nothing on women in terms of archives, in terms of recorded stories. It was just really, really difficult to get that information. Also what was interesting for me was to research how the 1956 Women's March created a domino effect where Black women in this country ended up continuously fighting, right up until the 2015 #FeesMustFall movement, which had a lot of women in the forefront.

Because, women, we are really in danger of actually being Tippexed out of history. As a result, when I finish these other two films I'm working on, I actually just want to do women's films. Because it's frightening. Even if you do get the archive, it's hideously expensive. It was a very challenging film to make. Also what was fascinating for me is that you have women who brought some of these famous men into politics, and they are never referenced. Epainette Mbeki was a Communist long before Govan Mbeki was. Mamphela Ramphele was one of the founding members of the Black Consciousness Movement. But all people have to say is that she slept with Steve Biko. I mean, Mamphela Ramphele did so much, even during that time. And so, what? For a woman, it's different when you sleep with your comrade, but for a guy, it's OK.

Albertina Sisulu, when she died, the obituaries, they were saying *wife of* Walter Sisulu. You know what I mean? I think we need to seriously work at contesting erasure, contesting all of these stereotypes, and just fighting. Fighting for more and better funding for women's stories. Because it's easy to get more money for some guy. But it's difficult to even get a lot of money to make a film on Winnie Mandela, let alone anyone else who is female. I think there's a lot of work to be done there.

LADIPO MANYIKA: You mentioned being 'slaughtered', using your words, for *Shouting Silent*. Why was that?

SITHOLE: South Africa at that time was seriously dealing with denialism around HIV. It was a mixed bag. There are also issues around pharmaceutical companies probably thinking that they were going to make a lot of money. And the budget alone: for South Africa to provide drugs through pharmaceutical companies, that would've wiped out the health budget. And then there was Thabo Mbeki's thinking and the way he was doing things that created problems. When I did the film, I think people were just honestly shocked at the images they were seeing. And so, the media accused me of paying people to act in the film.

The same thing with *Zimbabwe's Forgotten Children*. When you've got about ninety kids being kicked out of school for not having two dollars, one or two friends of mine said, 'But, Xoliswa, did you stage that?' I just think that it's the denialism, especially of Black middle-class people who don't want to see those images, and who don't want to know that, actually, this is happening in your backyard. So, yes, I was slaughtered. It was ugly. I didn't work for a year. I was in a lot of pain. But also that was the price you paid for going in and exposing the real situation. Because the country was tiptoeing around the issue. That's the price you pay.

LADIPO MANYIKA: Speaking about difficult receptions, but also difficulty in making films, parts of *Child of the Revolution* were filmed in secret. That was very dangerous work. We'll show clips from *Child of the Revolution*, but, before we do that, tell us about your character, Colin.

SITHOLE: Basically, doing a documentary, you do research. People had suffered during the clean-up operation. I wanted to go to a squatter camp where people had been put, as in forced to move there, after the clean-up operation.

LADIPO MANYIKA: And, the clean-up operation?

SITHOLE: Murambatsvina was the clean-up when Mugabe said that the towns were getting crowded. The idea behind it, really, was to dismantle dissent that was happening within the urban areas. I went to this place and, lo and behold, I came across a character called Colin Mbawa. And, while I was talking to Colin Mbawa, I discovered that he and I had gone to the same school. I went to a mission school in Zimbabwe from the age of nine to eleven, in the rural area of Wedza, and I left when the school was closed due to the war, the liberation war. And he mentioned a teacher, teacher Kunonga, and I remembered him as my grade six teacher. And he said, 'Oh, he also taught me.' It was just one of those fortuitous moments that happen when you are making these films. Also, when I work, it's a very spiritual process. I honestly actually go to my parents' graves. I burn some herbs. I speak to my ancestors. I always find these fortuitous situations. So, that's the Colin Mbawa story.

[VIDEO CLIP BEGINS]

SITHOLE: *The clean-up operation has dumped these people into a life of hopelessness. I had never thought that a Zimbabwean would not be able to educate his children. Meeting Colin left me feeling defeated and powerless. The fact that Colin had had a similar start in life to me, all I could think was, 'There, but for the grace of God, go I.'*

[VIDEO CLIP ENDS]

LADIPO MANYIKA: I think in many ways, what you said at the end summarizes this idea of growing up in Zimbabwe, a country that gave you so much, and then going back and seeing how things had not worked out.

SITHOLE: The whole idea of doing *Child of the Revolution* was that I was raised in a very political family. When the Chimurenga War (War of Liberation) was being fought, which I also experienced in Wedza, we were raised to believe that we were the future custodians of the country, that we were going to one day be leading the country. And so, I go back to Zimbabwe thirty-five years after independence to ask what happened to the revolution. It's an interrogation of that.

At the same time, it's a holistic approach on the importance of fighting for the land. The importance of the autonomy of Black people ruling and having ownership of their resources. That's important. At the same time, we also need to be critical of ourselves as Black people, especially the middle-class, because they are the ones who are in charge of all this mess that we are dealing with at the expense of the working poor.

It was really that. But also to pay homage to a country that raised me, that made me who I am. I'm very much a Zimbabwean, as I am a South African. And also to really, really pay homage to Dr Edson Sithole, who was pivotal in my upbringing.

In Matabeleland, I met one of the top political leaders – someone whose brother had disappeared. And this guy they believed was thrown into a mine shaft. Edson Sithole, it was believed also that he was thrown in a mine shaft. There was a commission, the Catholic Commission, that discovered mass graves of people.

Filming was very dangerous. I had a very brave camera woman. She kept on going inside and wanting to take this angle. And I kept saying, 'Please, let's go, let's go, let's go. They're going to catch us.' Because the tentacles are that much and we would've been meat! The moment we finished, I put the footage somewhere where you don't want to know where I put it, and we just drove to Harare from Bulawayo.

It was very, very, very scary filming in Matabeleland. The film took nine years. It's never been distributed because I don't have money to pay for the footage, for the archive. Because it's archived wall to wall. I'll get the money one day and it'll be released because I think we are bearing witness. I was bearing witness for a certain time in history.

LADIPO MANYIKA: It's interesting as you were talking about what happened to the revolution, and looking back in time. I'm in America right now and thinking back to the civil rights era. Why are we *still* talking about these [same] issues? I think a lot of what you're saying resonates with different parts of the world, at this time.

Let's circle back to Nelson Mandela. You have produced one film about Nelson Mandela and you're working on another. It's not easy making films about Nelson Mandela as a Black woman filmmaker. Tell us about this.

SITHOLE: OK. The film on Nelson Mandela I have been working on for about five years. Basically, Nelson Mandela is just a very expensive person to make a film about. Part of it is that he's been culturally appropriated. But also, at the same time, you don't have Black women making films about Nelson Mandela. It's really white men who've got access to a lot of money. Charlayne has made films on Nelson Mandela. But, Charlayne is Charlayne.

I'm doing a film that looks at Mandela's global peace efforts; how Mandela brought peace to countries like East Timor. East Timor was under Indonesian occupation and Mandela went to speak to Indonesia for them to release Xanana Gusmão, and they refused. Second time he went and then they released Gusmão who became the first democratically elected president there.

Mandela brought peace to Burundi. He brokered peace between Libya and the Lockerbie bombing. Mandela tried to broker peace between Palestine and Israel. Peace within Ireland. I don't think that people actually are aware of these global peace efforts or missions that he was on. But I'm not really focusing on that now because I'm really focusing on *We Shall Not Die Quietly*, which is a very important film.

I was very fortunate to be headhunted to be the director. The producer, Achal Prabhala, a brilliant, brilliant young man from India, and the executive producer, brilliant, brilliant producer, David France. His film, I hope, is going to win this year's Oscar. It's called *Welcome to Chechnya*. And, basically, we are looking at how Brazil, South Africa and India fought for people to get cheaper HIV/AIDS drugs. South Africa really was very pivotal in creating the language and activism.

But, while we were doing the sizzle to raise money, Covid happened. The film is also looking at how this global activism created a domino effect in the West, where you now have people like Bernie Sanders and Elizabeth Warren whereby one of the things they were campaigning about was access to cheaper medicines. How Big Pharma is really exploiting people and how, in the UK, people are also fighting that as well. But that activism was created by the Global South. Now we are seeing that domino effect going into the Western world, and with Covid we are saying, because people are dying, lift the moratorium on patent laws for us to create cheaper Covid medicines for the rest of the world. Lift it for a short space of time. And, of course, pharmaceutical companies are not going to do that. But we managed to fight them in South Africa and other parts of the world: Brazil, India. It's possible. This film is really taking my time and we are hoping that we'll be finished by the end of the year. It's really a very emotional, interesting, big project.

LADIPO MANYIKA: We're looking forward to that. It's a really important and timely film. Xoliswa, you are based in South Africa and you've traveled a lot. Just to dream for a second, if you were to leave the continent for a period of time and move anywhere else in the world, what would you make documentaries on?

SITHOLE: Thank you for asking me. The first thing I would really like is to get a Radcliffe Fellowship. I don't want fellowships where I am going to get two cents. I'm too old for that. Radcliffe has resources and the biggest, biggest archive in the world – women's archive. I'm really interested in women's archived stories. I also was inspired by a guy called [David] Shipler, who wrote a book called *The Working Poor*. I really would like to do a documentary series on poverty in America. But I would like to link the rise of capitalism and the rise of poverty in America. I do believe that we need to have spaces where Africans can go in and give a reverse gaze.

We cannot continue having a situation whereby white people come here from America, from England and elsewhere and tell the stories, our stories. I want to go and tell the American story, and I'll probably win a triple Peabody. Who knows? That's just me. I really would. I feel like I need a change. I wouldn't mind being in somewhere like America for about four years. And also there are so many interesting things that are happening as well in terms of the space of television.

One of the documentaries I've always wanted to do is to look at the activism of Black people in the liberation of this country. I'm talking about Black people in America, Black activists. People who were very instrumental in participating in the dismantling of apartheid. So then, you can actually look at the relationship between the civil rights movement and their relationship with South Africa. That's a big project. But that's the other project. I think me being here, I can do it, of course, but I think, as an artist, you need to go somewhere. And then, after America, I want to go and live in India because I love India. For me, India is incredibly fascinating as a country. So, yes, I've told everyone my wish.

LADIPO MANYIKA: There are so many more chapters in your story, Xoliswa. We're very excited to see them unfold. Your name, Xoliswa, means 'I give you my peace'. How do you find peace these days?

SITHOLE: You know what? I pray a lot. I am enjoying my daughter so much. She's giving me so much peace. I'm in pain a lot of the time because of what is happening. One in six people have lost their jobs through Covid. We are losing people all the time. And, when Covid happened, when kids have to go on holiday, school holiday, what happens to those poor children who actually cannot access the school lunches? The rates of poverty. It's just a very, very, very painful and confusing time. But, we keep on. We keep on. You keep bearing witness. You keep fighting and you keep fighting. And, that's all. How do I find peace? I don't know. How do people find peace during this time? I watch stuff. I've started doing yoga. I'm enjoying that. And I talk to friends when it's all too much.

4.

WOLE SOYINKA

In Conversation

Wole Soyinka was awarded the Nobel Prize in Literature, in 1986. Born in Abeokuta, Nigeria, in 1934, he is a novelist, playwright, poet, biographer and political activist. His prolific body of writing spans more than forty works, including his debut novel, The Interpreters *(1965), his plays* Death and the King's Horseman *(1975) and* The Lion and the Jewel *(1962) and a childhood memoir,* Aké *(1981). Soyinka was twice jailed in Nigeria for his criticism of the Nigerian government. One of these imprisonments included a year and ten months in solitary confinement, which is the subject of his memoir,* The Man Died: Prison Notes of Wole Soyinka *(1971). Soyinka is a professor of Comparative Literature and holds positions as professor emeritus at Obafemi Awolowo University, a Hutchins Fellow at Harvard University and an Honorary Fellow at Churchill College, Cambridge. He is the recipient of numerous honors and awards.*

SARAH LADIPO MANYIKA: Let's start with a story from your memoir, *You Must Set Forth at Dawn*. The story begins as follows: 'Once upon a time, Wole Soyinka partook of a trans-Atlantic heist, which involved stealing a piece of art.' Will you tell us this story and what it says about the person you are?

WOLE SOYINKA: You know, that word 'steal' – I don't like it. I went to *recover* the property of my own people. One that has enormous historical significance, spiritual significance, contemporary socio-political significance. But what matters is that the history about the disappearance of this piece of art has always been fraught with contradiction. This particular piece of work was the symbol of my own university on its crest. But it was not the authentic picture, the painting of the original work. And so, as normal, curious people and academics, we undertook the mission of trying to find out where the authentic piece of art was.

There was a substitute, which for me was an insult. Every time I looked at it in the Ife Museum, I frankly felt like puking because I knew what the original was like – a beautiful piece of work, classic proportions and so on. Finally, we got information about where it was and who had stolen it (now there's the word 'stolen') out of Nigeria. So we went on a . . . Well, you wouldn't call it a normal mission of recovery, but we did what we could with the facilities at hand. And it ended in a big fuss because what we pursued when we went into that country [Brazil] turned out to be a replica, not the original. So, mud in our faces, but it was something we couldn't live without doing, it's as elementary as that.

LADIPO MANYIKA: The story of art being stolen from the continent of Africa is a familiar one. Your search to recover it took you all the way to Brazil and London.

SOYINKA: Well, I had also become some kind of collector. And how did I become a collector? I don't really believe in hoarding to start with. But I grew up watching people – and this included even some of my colleagues – loot, arrange the expatriation of works of art under various covers. Sometimes, when they were leaving, their suitcases would bulge with pieces of treasured art which the Nigerian museum had not acquired somehow. And so, I began, as a kind of personal consolation, to buy myself a work of art here and there within my means. In addition, a work of art itself is not just a piece of aesthetic work for admiration, it's history, it's race, it's family, it's community.

And seeing this bequest, this part of us just disappearing like that – and additionally, even more insultingly – being disparaged by the self-vaunting religions of the world, Christianity and Islam, who condemned these works as fetishistic pieces, primitive etc. while they were taking them out, while they were 'legitimately looting' these pieces as compensation for the raid on Benin [1897], for instance. After the raid, the British then looted the palace and all the various art institutions and said this was to compensate them for blistering the Benin Kingdom. They took these works of art back, distributed them, sold them in Europe.

I grew up with this history. These are the precipitates of a people's spirituality. In the process, that meant that even the spiritual network that bound the Black people together was just being shredded to pieces. So, this was beyond just a piece of work to be admired. This piece of work, incidentally, was the image on one of the Nigerian stamps for a long while. And to see this being advertised around the whole world as what the African genius had produced, it hurt. I'm explaining why there was no hesitation about my going on that recovery mission.

LADIPO MANYIKA: You are the son of an Anglican minister. I too am the daughter of an Anglican minister. You are the son of an entrepreneur, activist mother and your cousin, Fela Kuti, is the legendary Nigerian musician. Can you take us back to your childhood and tell us about what of this, if any, might have prepared or shaped you to become the storyteller you are?

SOYINKA: Well, I have inherited certain genes obviously, and creative genes in the music and theatrical direction. My father was a small-time musician, he played the organ. And we have, within the family, converted Christians who transcribed Yoruba music of the Orisha and sort of donated that music in a way to the Christian religion. This trait especially runs through my grandfather, who was an out-and-out Orisha worshiper to begin with, before the poor man was converted to Christianity. I was able to observe him and to see his closeness to nature. In him and his colleagues, I saw a different system of existence, of appreciation of phenomena from that of Christianity, in which I was raised. And for some reason or the other, I preferred that right from childhood.

So, even though I was a chorister for some time – I had nothing against Christian music, I sang lustily with everybody else – it didn't take long before I found myself alienated from that religion. And in school, I thereupon repudiated quite early Christianity as a system of spirituality. I was able to relate to the spiritual being outside Christianity. Finally, I jettisoned it altogether. So that's a background, very artistic in terms of inheritance. I grew up, of course, in an atmosphere of storytelling, masquerades going through the streets, the poetry, Ijala, Yoruba poetry, etc. So, you could say that I already had the silver spoon stuck in my throat, right from childhood.

LADIPO MANYIKA: Your latest novel, *Chronicles From the Land of the Happiest People On Earth,* an ironic title in itself, is your third novel and the first in forty-eight years. Many of the themes explored in this novel are explored in your earlier works, including your memoirs and plays in particular, especially *Madmen and Specialists*. Your book is a savage satire of a novel. It's a whodunit of sorts that includes a secret trade in body parts.

It's also the story of lifelong friendships. I found it to be a novel that moves to the beats of Fela Kuti and, in visual terms, it made me think of William Hogarth's painting of eighteenth century London and of Yinka Shonibare's more contemporary images. It also had a particular personal resonance because I grew up in Jos, one of the main locations for this novel. The novelist Ben Okri said of this novel: 'This is a novel written at the end of an artist's tether. It has gone beyond satire. It is a last dance macabre.' Professor Soyinka, was this book written at the end of your tether?

SOYINKA: Ben Okri, when I see him, I'm going to hammer his head because that particular quotation keeps cropping up and I can understand why. To some extent it is true. I've explored this theme, as you remarked, through various genres, including poetry, which in the course of reading I found myself uncharacteristically breaking down. It was as bad as that, when I attempted to read the *Humanist Ode for Chibok, Leah* I could not complete it. So, this thing has gone beyond mere poetizing, it's gone beyond fodder for creative transformation, for creative mauling, reconfiguring of realities, even beyond a prospectus for survival. So, Ben is absolutely spot on there. At the same time, however, it is not at the end of one's tether for the simple reason that there is a challenge implicitly embedded in it. When there's a challenge, it means you are actually saying that this is not the end of the story; that it's sufficient to be able to hold up a distorting mirror in an unaccustomed way to a community of which one is a part and from whose existence one takes one's own definition, has done for decades. And so, that element of challenge, which I hope is apparent there, means that one hasn't really given up on the nation, on the people, even if one thinks it's about time one bowed out.

LADIPO MANYIKA: There is a Yoruba phrase 'T'ágbà bá ńdé, à á y'ógun jà' that you use in your memoir, *You Must Set Forth* *at Dawn*. Can you translate the phrase and how it applies to you, or not.

SOYINKA: It's a phrase I've summoned to the end of my sanity several times. I've said, look, I've labored along this line for so long, nothing really has changed and I'm getting old. I've become old and yet nothing has changed, and so why should I despair? Isn't there a Yoruba proverb which says, 'T'ágbà bá ńdé, à á y'ógun jà', which means, literally, when one gets to the elderly status, one ceases conflict. One moves away from conflict. I try to apply that to myself numerous times. I found in the end that I'm not quite as old as I feel. And also that there is my personal entitlement to a piece of that earth in which I was born. The more degraded it is, the more I feel obliged to sanitize it to some extent, to make it possible for me to continue to exist within it, with a sense of honor, with an element of contribution to its very survival. So, I'm afraid that very wise saying just never sat well on me, not for very long, unfortunately. Let me stress this: I wish I could actually follow the wisdom in that proverb. I really wish I could.

LADIPO MANYIKA: So, roughly translated, if we are older, we cease to indulge in battles, but that's not happening for you. You said you don't feel old, how old do you feel, Professor Soyinka?

SOYINKA: It's embarrassing. One should learn to be one's age and grow up gracefully. I'm almost ashamed to admit how old I am, given the things I still get into. I don't feel my age. I can't put a figure on it. Each time I recollect how old I am, I feel embarrassed.

LADIPO MANYIKA: In your latest novel you use all kinds of humor – from humor through the language, situational humor and with your characters. And, of course, a lot of the humor is quite dark. You refer to the character Uriah Heep a couple of times, or at least this is a character that's in one of your character's minds. Uriah Heep is an unctuous, sycophantic, awful character in *David Copperfield*. When did you first came across Charles Dickens's novel and how do you think about humor in your own work?

SOYINKA: One of the main authors in my father's small library – he was a school teacher, a headmaster – was Charles Dickens, side by side with Euripides's *Medea*, which left quite an impression on me, and of course Charles Lamb, a potboiler of Shakespeare plays. But Dickens, for me, is just one of the most unbelievable, remarkable fiction writers the world has ever produced. I think his characterizations are grossly underrated. And Uriah Heep has always stuck in my head. For what reason? I knew him, I could recognize him. From childhood, I always said 'that's Uriah Heep' even though I didn't say exactly Uriah Heep. With my siblings, each time a Uriah Heep came to the house, we made sure we were eavesdropping. We were sure to be entertained, disgusted, made to feel superior, comparing him to other beings who flocked around the house.

So, I knew Uriah. That's why he keeps popping up. Part of the problem of our society till today is that we have not yet tamed the Uriah Heeps. They're all over the place. Very often very wealthy, but even when they're poor, they're quite content to remain impoverished. Always subservient because they knew they could rely on a daily bread by Uriah Heepism, whether to the immediate recipient or to any other one who happens to come along to displace that source of livelihood. And Uriah Heeps don't have to occupy official positions. No, in fact they're the most dangerous people in the world because they'll also suck up to you. They'll come to you and say, 'Oh yes, we know what you're doing. We actually take your side, we believe in what you're doing. But, you know, you misunderstand this person. We know he tortures people and so on, but he's also mending the roads, so go easy.' They're all over the place! So, Uriah Heep, he's been a companion of my existence since childhood.

LADIPO MANYIKA: I'm smiling because I think *David Copperfield* is the only novel that I read in childhood that I can recite a line or two from. One line being: 'There can be no greater disparity in marriage than the unsuitability of mind and purpose.' So, that's what stuck in my head from a book that contains Uriah Heep.

The great writer James Baldwin wrote in *Notes of a Native Son*: 'I love America more than any other country in the world. And exactly for this reason, I insist on the right to criticize her perpetually.' Is that something that resonates with you for Nigeria?

SOYINKA: No. I'll tell you why. The sense of national belonging and appropriation, which even the post-slavery generations of the United States have, is something which is missing in Nigeria. We could have had it, but it derailed along the way for numerous reasons. The sense of a cohesive entity to which one can dedicate not just mind, but spirit, is something which I've observed in many of my colleagues, many people all over the world, even after civil wars, fratricidal internal butchering and so on. They come back and they defend that entity. You can see it even in the way they sing their national anthems. Look at their faces, when they hear their national anthem played, you can see them retreat into their interior being. It's there, you can watch it. And in their various activities, their concession of positivity. And, of course, even the receptivity of criticism of their country is based on love.

I accept Nigeria, I accept it as my workspace, as a bequest – it came one way or the other, but didn't come about in a way that it would ever make me say, 'I'm ready to die for this nation.' No, there's always been something tacky, something unnatural, contrived about Nigeria. And people can say what they like. They can shout from the top of the hills and the depths of the ocean, I'm talking about Nigerians. Especially when they've been in power, when they're in power and use expressions like, 'This nation, the indivisibility of this nation is non-negotiable, etc.' I listen to them, I watch them. Some of them are those who contributed so deeply, so effectively to the disintegration that is happening to that nation. So, I don't believe them to start with. I look at my position and I know that, yes, I love the people and, somehow, I've arrived at a kind of dichotomy between people, humanity and nation along the way. Maybe it's a long story, maybe short, maybe it is just a moment, but I'm more concerned about and totally committed to, the humanity within it. But that whole notion of Nigeria as something which one feels viscerally – I'm sorry, I lost that visceral connection ages ago and I don't deceive myself about it.

LADIPO MANYIKA: I hear what you're saying and it's hard to hear, especially as we're speaking on the eve of Nigeria's sixty-first anniversary of its independence. You have me thinking about my own feelings about Nigeria, even though I've been out of the country for a long time. It's hard.

SOYINKA: The irony is this, that I can't stand people bad-mouthing Nigeria. I rise to the best Nigeria when I hear people bad-mouthing it. And I say, what about you? What's good in your country? Don't we have Nigerians in NASA, producing spare parts for your . . . I go to town on it! It's habit.

LADIPO MANYIKA: You've been a tireless campaigner against tyranny and injustice, not just in Nigeria but around the world. In your Nobel lecture, you spoke of apartheid in South Africa and ended the lecture by asking the world, 'How can you stand by and watch what's happening?' And in your poetry, I think of 'Telephone Conversation', you're sort of railing a bit against British housing discrimination and racism. Civil rights in America are something that you have spoken and written about too. You've also always said that Africa, for you, is not limited to the continent. You have your eye on the world.

And, as I'm thinking about the world today, it is probably an understatement to say that the world is in an 'interesting' state. You grew up at a time of anti-colonial movements and, in a way, it almost looks like we've come full circle. We're still talking about anti-colonialism movements of sorts, taking down statues, renaming things. You went through the civil rights period in America and in the last year or so people keep talking about 'racial reckoning' in America. So, I wonder, is what we are experiencing the same or different from decades earlier?

SOYINKA: Oh, not just different but dissociated. Sometimes it's hard for me to find a continuum, but then of course, it's there. We know it's there. We also know of the positive lines of development, which have been embarked upon to pull Nigeria back from where it was being pushed, not where it ended up and so on. When I wrote my independence play, for instance, in 1960, it was supposed to be the official play for independence, but it was removed. It was rejected because those powers that be at the time felt it was too negative, that this was supposed to be the season of joy, euphoria. And the signs were already there. I already saw the signs of a jettisoning of the principles, the fervor that led to the independence. It was there when, as we met as students, the first-generation leaders among them, we saw that all they understood about independence was they themselves stepping in the shoes of the colonizers; that's all.

That independence play, which the government at the time felt was too threatening, was actually a challenge. It was a positive statement. It recognized and accepted an entity that deserved to be developed, deserved to be amplified, heightened along its positive virtues. And, therefore, I recalled history and said, please take warning even from your own views, it hasn't always been a smooth passage and there are those ogres, monsters waiting to drag this nation down. And I've confessed that in my generation, at least part of it with which I interacted in a profound way, we saw our mission as salvaging, as just liberating Africa. We didn't even think in Nigeria terms. This is something which I think I don't stress sufficiently: that at the beginning we didn't even think of Nigeria as a separate entity.

As students in the UK, we eagerly sought out and interacted with the 'first generation' nationalists when they came on Independence negotiations with the British. It was easy to discern that the emerging Nigerian nation was in deep trouble. A handful of them were of course truly motivated and focused. Others, it was clear, were nationalists only as cynical inheritors of the shoes of the departing imperators. That compelled us to start turning our sights inwards. From an obsession with the primacy of liberating apartheid South Africa and other bastions of settler colonialism, we concluded that we had to shift focus to the internal successors to the existing mandate.

As far back as I recall – which is all the way back to primary school lessons on something called the Slave Trade – I have never been able to absorb the notion of an African continent defined solely by saline waters. It was both an intuitive and objective reaction. This has affected much of my political thinking and relationship with the Black presence in the diaspora, their cultural retentions from Africa and their socio-political struggles, especially in racist enclaves such as the USA. There was also the practical aspect: their potential contribution to the mother continent. As we matured into responsible positions locally, we made efforts to seduce them into returning home and injecting their modern, specialist knowledge into our own nations.

One particular effort was the formation of the Association of African Scientists and Researchers – as a companion movement to the Union of Writers of the African Peoples. That scientific unit was headed by Professor Cheikh Anta Diop of Senegal and partnered by the Institute of International Affairs in Lagos in the 1970s. I recall traveling through Latin America and the

Caribbean, meeting intellectuals and technocrats and exhorting them to 'come home'.

Africa, for me, is not just the continent. I am much closer to Africans in the diaspora than to Arabs who occupy the same landmass. It could not possibly be otherwise. And this is without calling on the historic reality that Africans endured slavery from across the Sahara just as brutally as from across the Atlantic. Culture reigns supreme.

LADIPO MANYIKA: Friendship has always seemed to be something really important to you. We see this in both your fiction and non-fiction, and your latest novel has friendship at its center. The last memoir you wrote, *You Must Set Forth at Dawn*, was a homage to Femi Johnson, and your latest novel is also dedicated to him, Dele Giwa and Bola Ige. You've had so many interesting friendships across the years – from the poet Christopher Okigbo to scholar Professor Henry Louis Gates, Jr, and to your fellow Nobel laureates, Bertrand Russell and Toni Morrison.

A few years ago, I had the opportunity to interview Toni Morrison in her home. In her bathroom there are many amazing photographs, one of which was of her with you – a lovely black-and-white photograph. I mentioned this to Toni as we sat down, saying, 'Oh, I've just seen one of my countrymen—' you see, my Nigerian pride '—I've just seen Professor Wole Soyinka in your bathroom.' She said, 'Oh yeah, we used to go to Paris and we'd go and have meetings and talk – elegant talk – and solve world problems. And Soyinka always knew how to solve everything.' And then the two of us said in unison, 'He still does.' Then she responded, mimicking a deep voice, 'Yes, yes! In that voice he has.' So, in that deep voice you have, can you tell us a story about Toni Morrison?

SOYINKA: Well, first I came to Toni Morrison through her works and I said, 'This really is genius writing.' I cannot recall when we first met, probably because when we met eventually it was like I knew her already, like we'd already met. But from the very first-time moment, we bonded. There's no question at all about that. And I set about trying to bring her to Nigeria right away to meet other writers. And then we'd go out together. And she was responsible for an expression which left such an impression on me. She said, 'I'm going to take you out to this restaurant. The cooking there, it'll knock your socks off.' I'd never heard that expression in my life. I said, 'What?' She said, 'It will knock your socks off!' Well, maybe because in Africa we wear sandals most of the time, who wears socks? Only the gentry!

It'll knock your socks off, and that image was something that came from her language. It was her language and it endeared me. And more than that, however, was her sensibility toward the problems of the African continent. She was very much involved. She'd ask questions, sort of how could that be going on, kind of questions. Genuine concern. And so I saw, as we say in Nigeria, she was another country woman, but a very, very close one. Friendship to me is what saves one's sanity, friendship is seeking nothing, no advantage from the other person, but always knowing that it is there, that it's assistance if you need it. And you simultaneously are ready any time. It's almost a mystical thing. Those who have experienced genuine friendship should appreciate how very lucky they are, because it's not often, to actually say this is a genuine friend. I have had some very deep friendships with people, like Femi Johnson, who you mentioned.

LADIPO MANYIKA: Speaking of friendship, I've brought in [to the zoom conversation as a surprise] one of your brothers, Dr Henry Louis Gates, Jr!

HENRY LOUIS GATES, JR: Thank you so much, Sarah. This has been riveting. You asked Wole questions that I'd never heard him asked before, and the answers were fresh and enlightening.

I love the story of the attempt to reappropriate the classic work of art from Brazil. I know that story. I heard it at the time. I've heard it twenty times, but I never heard it better than I heard it today. And it's true. It's a wonder this man's not in a Brazilian prison. But Wole, my very serious question is, what was the name of the restaurant where Toni Morrison took you to knock your socks off? And what wine did you drink when your socks were being knocked off?

SOYINKA: First thing I have to tell you is that you should be ashamed of yourself. This is pay-back time; friends don't do that. Because I appeared as a mystery guest on your conversation with Sarah. Now you forced your way into this one. I'll deal with you later on! Now, the question, Toni Morrison's idea of sock knocking was . . . The restaurant was a bit of a disappointment. And I told her, number one, they didn't use peppers. That was the main problem. It was an African restaurant and the food was probably good, academically, yes, but no peppers. Now, Skip, can you imagine somebody knocking my socks off without any peppers?

GATES: For shame!

SOYINKA: Toni fell down on that. But at least she left me the expression. So, I'm grateful to her.

GATES: On Monday, Wole and I will be having dinner in New York. And, Wole, I want you to pick the restaurant that Toni should have picked. And I want to unveil something, if you can bear with me, Sarah. I've never shown this on camera before, but in that cabinet, that brown door is full of nothing but chili sauces introduced to me by my professor at the University of Cambridge, Wole Soyinka. [Gates stands up and walks to the cupboard.] I'm going to unveil it right now. Chilies! [Pulls out a jar and returns.]

SOYINKA: I think I know that one. Yes.

GATES: Akabanga! From Rwanda. This is nuclear fume!

SOYINKA: I know, I get a regular supply now.

GATES: You gave it to me! You brought it to me. It's burning my head. Yes, it's burning my fingers. Right now, I'm on fire.

SOYINKA: It has triggered the alarm in luggage at some airports, in which the person carrying it was detained. That's true!

GATES: Let me tell you, it's triggered off some alarms in other locales.

LADIPO MANYIKA: You two!

GATES: I'm in the kitchen of my house, as you can see. And right under me is a wine cellar. It is dedicated to my professor who introduced me to wine. My generation didn't drink wine. I'm the class of '73. We got inebriated in more vaporous ways. So, I go off to Cambridge and Soyinka introduced me to wine and chili peppers and Indian food, all at the same time. So my mouth is on fire. I'm getting drunk. I'm trying to understand these chilies and that's the real education. That's the real story of our friendship, without a doubt.

SOYINKA: Right on!

CURATORS

If you want to disempower people, you want to enslave people,
metaphysically, you rob them of memory, you rob them of continuity.

– Henry Louis Gates, Jr

5.

HENRY LOUIS GATES, JR

In Conversation

Henry Louis Gates, Jr, is the Alphonse Fletcher University Professor and Director of the Hutchins Center for African and African American Research at Harvard University. Emmy and Peabody award-winning filmmaker, literary scholar, journalist, cultural critic and institution builder, Professor Gates's most recent books are Stony the Road: Reconstruction, White Supremacy, and the Rise of Jim Crow *(2019) and* The Black Church: This Is Our Story, This Is Our Song *(2021). He has also produced and hosted more than twenty documentary films, most recently* The Black Church *(2021) on PBS and* Black Art: In the Absence of Light *(2021) for HBO.* Finding Your Roots, *his groundbreaking genealogy and genetics series, is now in its eighth season on PBS.*

April 9, 2021

SARAH LADIPO MANYIKA: Skip, as we're speaking in the context of a museum, I just have to begin by asking you, what is the image we see behind you?

HENRY LOUIS GATES, JR: That is a painting by the African American artist Jonathan Green from North Carolina, who lives now in South Carolina. And it was chosen by my older daughter, Maggie, when she was nine years old. We were deciding whether to move to Duke University from Cornell in the late 1980s. So we went down to live there for a semester because I'd never lived in the South before. They talked about how liberal it was, but compared to what? But we decided to give it a try.

And I read the Raleigh, North Carolina, newspaper. And it said there was an opening on Sunday by an artist I'd never heard of called Jonathan Green. And I took them, just the three of us, and I said that they could pick a painting and, whatever they picked, I would buy because I wanted them to become collectors. I bought my first four pieces of African art when I was nineteen years old in Dar es Salaam. And, as you know – you've been to my home – I collect African art largely under the tutelage of my mentor at Cambridge, Wole Soyinka. He's taught me so much about African art, particularly Yoruba art and Beninian art. I also collect African American art (I'm on the board of the Studio Museum in Harlem and the Whitney). So that's Jonathan Green. And yet you can see he's very much influenced by Kerry James Marshall, with the blackface, and Romare Bearden, with the sort of collage-like composition – but thank you for asking.

LADIPO MANYIKA: Now I recall that you grew up in a small town called Piedmont in West Virginia. Tell us about your early years.

GATES: I was born in 1950 in Piedmont, West Virginia, which is halfway between Pittsburgh and Washington DC in the Allegheny mountains on the Potomac river. It's not exactly known as a major center for African American culture! It's in the Allegheny mountains – I'm a country boy, I grew up hunting and fishing. The first day of deer season is a holiday, and then people go and shoot things. I never enjoyed that, but I loved to fish, and I still love to fish.

I've been interested in my own family history, my own genealogy, since I was nine years old, when we buried my father's father, Edward St Lawrence Gates. And my father showed us my great-great-grandmother Jane Gates's obituary and her sepia photograph, which is upstairs in our family history room now. The next day, the day after my grandfather's funeral, I asked my father to buy me a composition book. And that night in front of our little twelve-inch black-and-white TV, I interviewed my parents about what, only later, I would learn is called one's genealogy, one's family tree.

I was able to go back to my great-great-grandmother Jane Gates on my father's line and to my great-great-grandparents on my mother's line, but I really wanted to find out where I was from in Africa. And so, you could say, after 1977 I had a bad case of *Roots* envy. I envied Alex Haley; I wanted to find out. And the irony is, after we invented the series that's now known as *Finding Your Roots* and traced my ancestry, it turns out that my family has lived within a thirty-mile radius of where I was born for 200 years.

I descend from three sets of free people of color, two sets on my mother's side, one set on my father's side. And two sets of my fourth great-grandparents were freed by the American Revolution, and the third set on my father's side were freed in 1823. And one of those fourth great-grandfathers fought in the American Revolution – a Black man named John Redman, whom I've written about. Because of him, my brother, Dr Paul Gates – who is an oral surgeon – and I were inducted into the

Sons of the American Revolution, which is not exactly crawling with Black people.

So, the whole time I'm looking across the Atlantic for Kunta Kinte, and my roots are right under my feet. And it was very liberating. I have deep roots in this curious little area that is in the mountains, and it's not in the urban North and it's not in the deep South. I think my ancestors were freed so early because there was very little use for enslaved people in this region. There are no tobacco fields, no cotton, there's no sugar. So, for whatever reason, they became free.

My town of 2,500 people is an Irish/Italian paper mill town. My father worked at the paper mill for thirty-seven years. The year I was born I think there were about 350 Black people, most of them my cousins. After the famous 1954 Supreme Court case, *Brown v. Board of Education,* that ordered, with all deliberate speed (which means never), the desegregation of schools, my predominantly white Appalachian County integrated without a peep, not one civil rights march, a year later in 1955. I started at the white school, as we called it, in 1956. So, I've always gone to an integrated school and, unlike the memoirs of Richard Wright and other Black people, I was not discriminated against in school.

Like my brother, who is six grades ahead of me, I was always well treated. The school embraced our ideals of a meritocracy. It sounds corny, but they really did. And I was one of the two smartest kids in the class, and they treated me like that. So, I was very blessed. I had a great childhood and I've had a great education since.

LADIPO MANYIKA: You were one of the smartest kids, but you did not fulfill your parents' dream, or at least your mother's dream, of becoming a doctor or even a lawyer. So, what went wrong?

GATES: My daddy wanted me to be a lawyer, my mama a doctor. For my mother, every Christmas I got a stethoscope; birthday – a dissecting kit. When I was growing up, smart little Black girls and boys were meant to be doctors and if you couldn't get into med school, then a lawyer, and maybe a minister somewhere down the road.

For my mom, in heaven there was a Father, Son, the Holy Ghost and a medical doctor sitting right next to the Holy Ghost. And I was terrified! Even when I went to Cambridge, I majored in history. I was a scholar in the House in History at Yale, and I got a Mellon Fellowship to go to Cambridge where, just by accident, I was going to get a second degree and then come back and go to medical school or law school. And, just as fate would have it, I ran into two Africans who changed my life. One was Wole Soyinka. I didn't know how to say his name. I thought he was Polish when I saw it.

LADIPO MANYIKA: Have you done his roots?

GATES: No, no. His hair's too long for me to do his roots! He's like Cornel West; every barber I know says, 'If you get Professor Soyinka in here, I'll give you $500. If you get Cornel West in here, I'll give you $1,000.' But no, I wish he would let me do his roots.

The other person I met was Kwame Anthony Appiah. Anthony was a second year at Clare College, and Wole was in exile because Nigerian governments have a way of just trying to cancel him. And I don't mean in the way you cancel culture; I'm talking about transitioning him to the land of the ancestors – so he's always finding refuge somewhere. Think about that confluence; what a lucky person I am. I happened to get a fellowship, I'm the first Black person to get a Mellon Fellowship from Yale. I go to this college I'd never heard of, Clare College. I had wanted to be a Rhodes scholar. I had wanted to go to Oxford or Cambridge. I wanted to go to Harvard, Yale or Princeton. I'm not going to apologize for that or pretend that I didn't because they were synonymous with elite education. My father's first cousin, his mother was a Gates (the sister of my grandfather), he graduated from Harvard Law School in 1949 and his wife was a Black woman who got a Ph.D. in comparative literature from Harvard in 1955. So the Ivy League was very much in my head.

But somehow in adolescence, I began to learn about Oxford and Cambridge and Rhodes Scholars, and I applied for all these fellowships. And, Sarah, I lost the first six fellowships. I was Black, I was from West Virginia. I was a junior Phi Beta Kappa. I was graduating Summa. How was I not going to get these fellowships? I must have just been an asshole or something in these interviews. I lost all these fellowships and I was down to the last fellowship and I just decided to go in there and be myself because I wasn't going to get it anyway.

It was one of the happiest days of my life when I got the phone call, I got the fellowship. So, I end up at Clare in October of 1973. Everybody at Clare was white except for two other Black people and everybody kept saying, 'Have you met Anthony Appiah, have you met Anthony Appiah?' I don't know about white people in England, but when white Americans say that, the person has to be Black. They never ask you if you met Prince Harry. They ask if you met Meghan Markle, right?

So, I see this Black guy walking through Old Court at Clare and I walked up to him and I said, 'I don't know anything about you, but your name must be Anthony Appiah.' And he almost died. He said, 'How'd you know?' I said, 'It had to be you because you're the other one.'

I decided that I would really like to study African literature, because this was a free degree. It's a second BA, which turns into an MA in the Oxbridge fashion after five years – you send them five pounds and they send you a Master's. And they said, 'Oh, there's this African guy who is an Extraordinary Fellow visiting Churchill College' – named of course for Winston Churchill. And his name was Wole Soyinka. I'd never heard of this brother.

In those days we didn't even have telephones. So you had to write a letter to the professor, put it in the post and wait for a written response. And he agreed to see me . . . and the rest, as they say, is history. And he knew Anthony's father, Joe Appiah, who is like the John Adams of Ghana. He and Kwame Nkrumah were roommates in London. And the two of them took me out for an Indian meal after about a month. And they said, 'We brought you here to tell you something: you are not going to be a doctor. You are going to be a professor. You were put on this earth to teach literature. So wake up, you're going to teach African literature and you're going to build African and African American Studies.'

It took me two years before I could tell my mother and father that I had changed course. I even took tutorial supervision, as we called it at Cambridge, in biology, in inorganic chemistry and in physics, in addition to courses in the English faculty, because I was still going to be a doctor! And thank God I met Soyinka and Anthony . . . and here we are today.

LADIPO MANYIKA: That's a wonderful story. I want to back up a little because you did have a little bit more medical exposure when you traveled to the continent of Africa. You worked, I believe, in an Anglican Mission Hospital for a year. You also hitch-hiked across the equator from one ocean to the other!

GATES: I did indeed. When I was ten years old, that was a great year of African independence. And, for reasons that nobody knows, we used to have a Coleman Family Reunion in my mother's family and give these funny prizes. And one was the 'I ain't left nothing back in Africa' award, and my father got it every year. He had no interest in going back to Africa and that was true for many African Americans at that time. Not all of them, obviously. When I was ten, I was smitten.

In school, we had a current affairs course and we had a great teacher, Mr McKenney. He put up a current-events map each week and would have eight or nine circles on it. It was a map of the world, a flat map. And, that year, I think nineteen countries on the continent of Africa became independent. I became intrigued by the African continent and I memorized the names of countries, the capitals and the presidents. Lumumba, Tshombe, Nyerere, Kenyatta. They were just so lyrical. And, of course, Kwame Nkrumah. Sudan was first in 1956, Ghana second in '57 and Nigeria in 1960. It was marvelous. I would listen to the evening news and however they said the name, that's how I would say the name.

And about the same time I read an essay in *Reader's Digest*. Remember *Reader's Digest*? There was an article about an African boy who basically walked across the equator, having been 'saved' by these missionaries, and ended up in the United States. So, I wanted to go to Africa and at the end of my sophomore year at Yale – that was 1969–1970 – the year culminated with the big Mayday strike. All the American universities went on strike after Nixon and Kissinger invaded Cambodia. But Yale went on strike to protest of the way the Black Panthers were being harassed by the police and persecuted. Bobby Seale was on trial, a block from Calhoun College where my dorm room was. So we went on strike for the Panthers in the middle of April, then the whole world did.

Then I went to Harvard Summer School to take pre-med courses, because Yale didn't have summer school. At Yale, I was in a program called Five Year BA, for which twelve people were chosen (it would take five years because one would take a year off and work). You had to work in what we used to call the third world, the developing world. And I picked Tanzania because our Episcopal church in the Diocese of West Virginia had a sister diocese in central Tanganyika, as it used to be called.

So, in 1970, I ended up in a mission hospital in the village of Kilimatinde, which was about four hours by Land Rover from Dar es Salaam back then. And I turned twenty in that village. It was a 120-bed hospital for 50,000 people. There was no running water. We had kerosene torches, we called them. I lived with European missionaries, Australians and one Irish female doctor. They housed me in an old German prison because Tanganyika was a German colony and there was a German cemetery there. I arrived there in August of 1970 and stayed there in that village until December. I left for Dar es Salaam and then decided I wanted to sail to Zanzibar. You could go down to the dock and basically for a dollar, seven shillings at that time, you could just get on a fishing boat, a dhow, and you'd sail overnight to Zanzibar.

And I met this white guy on the boat who had just graduated from Harvard and he said his fantasy had been to hitch-hike from Cape to Cairo, like the railway proposed by Cecil Rhodes. He had gone to what's now Namibia, Southwest Africa, to help SWAPO [the South West Africa People's Organization] and it had taken the South African secret police about fifteen seconds to figure out he was there and kick him out. Dar es Salaam was a refuge for all of the revolutionary groups because Nyerere provided them with resources and that's why this man was there. And we flipped a coin, because I had said, 'No, I want to hitch-hike across the equator.' I won, and it took us two months.

We started in Dar, we went to Mombasa and then to Nairobi, to Kampala. We were in Kampala a couple days after Idi Amin's coup, when the Bugandans were celebrating their liberation from Obote because Obote was going to nationalize all their land. Then down to Kigali, and then Goma, and then six days on the back of a beer truck to Kisangani, and then we sailed all the way down the Congo river. And I got severe amoebic dysentery. They thought I was going to die, but I made it. And I was nursed back to health by some Catholic nuns in Kinshasa, and then I flew to Lagos. That was in February or March of 1971, my first visit to my beloved Nigeria. Then I flew to Accra because the whole goal was to make a pilgrimage to the grave of W. E. B. Du Bois. And he was buried outside of the castle at that time, before they moved him to the mausoleum where his remains are now housed. I took a photograph, and I had to beg a guard to let me through the chain. I told him I had hitch-hiked all the way across to Africa to see Du Bois, who was my hero. And the guard said,

'OK' – so I took a photograph, which hangs on the wall in the director's office of the Hutchins Center, just about three blocks from my home here in Harvard Square. And so, by the time I was twenty, I had visited six African countries.

And when I came back to Yale, everybody had big afros, they had dashikis, and people were talking a bunch of trash about our African ancestors. They were essentializing Africa and being reductive. They didn't know what they were talking about! Their whole knowledge of Africa came from Janheinz Jahn's book *Muntu*, which is very reductive in its conclusions. And nobody could tell me about Africa then, I had been there. And then I end up at Clare two years later, and there is the future Nobel Laureate. We had no idea in 1973. And there's the greatest African philosopher in history, the budding genius, Kwame Anthony Appiah. How can I not thank God every day for the life I've lived?

LADIPO MANYIKA: So, Skip, you see, this is why we are going to be here eight days because your storytelling is incredible and your life interweaves with all these amazing moments and points and people in history. There's also such breadth and depth and diversity to your work, that it almost defies description. Whether we're looking at some of your seminal work, like *The Signifying Monkey*, your work on Zora Neale Hurston and many different kinds of artists and writers, to the forgotten works you have unearthed and brought to our attention, to your films.

Through all of your work, what's particularly fascinating to me, Skip, is your curatorial instinct and we see this in your institution building, in the Hutchins Center. You've got everything from the Hiphop Archive to the Cooper Gallery of African and African American Art. Your home itself is like a museum! What guides you as a curator?

GATES: I've been interviewed hundreds and hundreds of times, at least, and no one's ever asked me that question. So

I need to think about it. I think one never knows one's entire motivations. Why are you, you? Who one is? But I would say I have a short attention span. I get bored easily, and I'm a curious person. And if you add all those up, they come out me. I'm an entrepreneur, there's no question that it's part of my DNA. I think all intellectuals are entrepreneurs. To think of the plot of a novel, in your case, and then to write it – that is, to have an idea and then to see it embodied in the world – I think that's what entrepreneurs do. So I think all intellectuals have that trait. They just don't turn it into financing and brick and mortar – into something in three dimensions.

I didn't study African American Studies; I don't have a degree in African and African American Studies. I have a BA in History, American political history. A Ph.D. in English Language and Literature. But I took several courses in what we broadly call Black Studies at Yale. And one of the things I realized is that each successive generation of our people had to reinvent the wheel. If you want to disempower people, you want to enslave people, metaphysically, you rob them of memory, you rob them of continuity. And that caused me an enormous amount of grief and frustration. And I would say, 'If only Booker T. Washington and Du Bois could have taken two steps back and figured out, "Look, we can beat them with a one, two punch."' There's more than enough pie to go around. Martin and Malcolm. Now, we partly romanticize, partly have wishful thinking, that they were moving closer together, which is undoubtedly true. But if they could have figured out behind closed doors, 'Look, Malcolm will go out and scare the white man to death, Martin will come clean up, pick up the pieces,' right? There had been so much hatred within the group.

And we were taught the 'One Negro Syndrome', as we used to call it. James Baldwin had to destroy Richard Wright. Ellison had to destroy Baldwin and Wright. There was only going to be one and it's either you or me. And that's what the Battle Royal scene in *Invisible Man* is all about. Well, I decided that if I ever ended up in this field, I wanted to conceive of and complete foundational projects on which subsequent generations could build, so that never again did anyone have to do these things.

And if you study the history of disciplines when you're a student, you think God or Plato invented all the disciplines – philosophy, anthropology or chemistry. But each discipline has a history created by human beings. So I began to study the history of certain disciplines and then viewed African and African American Studies. It's just another discipline, so we weren't reinventing the wheel. And fate then put me in a position to completely, from the ground up, build African and African American Studies at Harvard with the help of Anthony Appiah, the first person that I hired. Now, we have forty-one professors.

It is this foundation that was behind my motivation for editing the *Encyclopedia Africana*, which I did with Anthony and with Wole as the Chair of the Board. And we did it with Bill Gates and *Encarta Africana*. I'm very proud of that. President Bill Clinton put it in a time capsule and a hundred years from now it'll be opened, and it'll be such primitive technology, I'm sure. But if you want to see Bessie Smith, click on Bessie, she's singing from 1925. It was great!

We're doing dictionaries. Oxford University Press asked me just last week if I was interested in editing a Black version of the Oxford English Dictionary. The words that Black people have created, like 'cool' and 'whatever, be that way sometime' and 'get down'. And that had been a fantasy of mine after editing the *Encyclopedia Africana*, a Black version of Britannica to do what James Murray did for the English language, or Samuel Johnson. One of my prized possessions is a first edition of Samuel Johnson's dictionary from 1755.

So that's what I want to do. Because the only way that we can progress as a people is if your children, your son's generation and my granddaughter's generation don't have to start all over. Now, with the *Norton Anthology of African American Literature* – which I'm very, very proud of and edited with ten of my colleagues – if you don't like our canon, you can edit it. You can modify it, but you don't have to start from the beginning anymore. There's none of that. And that's why I do what I do. And I think that my curiosity comes from the fact that I was raised 'in the village'.

LADIPO MANYIKA: Skip, you're a great curator of people. And, by way of example, I want to talk about your PBS series *Finding Your Roots*. The great actor and playwright Anna Deavere Smith and Senator Cory Booker [two of the people in this collection], have been a part of that series. And you've just had such interesting guests. You've had everyone from Nancy Pelosi to Marco Rubio, from John Lewis to John McCain. You have also featured some non-Americans: Richard Branson and so forth. Can you speak for a bit about whether this changes the way that people, your audience and guests, see America and/or see their place within America?

GATES: I thank you very much for your kind words. I love making this series. And I got the idea after a Black geneticist in the year 2000 wrote me and said, 'Dear Dr Gates, have you ever seen *Roots*?' And I was thinking, 'What an idiot, who does he think I am, everybody's seen *Roots*!' He said, 'Well, we can now do what Alex Haley claimed to do in a test tube on your mother's mother's mother's line.' And I couldn't believe it. And he said, 'We're looking for guinea pigs, volunteers among African American men and nobody will say yes.' And I soon learned why, and I'll tell you in a minute.

So, I called this guy, Dr Rick Kittles down at Howard University, and offered to fly him up immediately, which he did. He came to my home in Cambridge. And I told him that, unbeknownst to him, I'd been interested in my own family tree, as I mentioned, since I was nine years old. And that I'd been to Africa and that I wanted to know about my African roots. And so I volunteered. They took my blood – and that was the painful part. And that's why nobody else was dumb enough to agree to be a guinea pig.

But they did my mitochondrial DNA, which is your genetic fingerprint or signature that you get from your mother's mother's mother's mother's line. And for most African Americans obviously, if you think about it, or most new world Black people, that would go straight to Africa. Because if you have white ancestry, it will come from the father's line because of rape, cajoled sexuality, however you want to put it. So, they did my DNA and said that I was from Nubia.

Now, all African Americans want to either be Nubians or they want to be Zulus. Zulus because of Shaka Zulu, the warrior – he kicked the white man in the behind. Nubian because they're the Black pharaohs of the Nile, twenty-fifth dynasty. People argue about what color the Egyptians were, but there's no doubt about the twenty-fifth dynasty, which was between 725 BC and 650 BC: they were Black. We have found statues they made of themselves and they were black-Black people, and no doubt about that. But the Nubians were mixed. So were the Egyptians.

So, I got my certificate of Nubianality, and I showed it to Anthony Appiah and he looked at it, he said, 'What a ton of rubbish.' And I said, 'You just jealous.' Because Anthony's uncle was the Asantehene, the King of the Asantes. But I knew deep down that he was right, because Nubia ran between what is now Khartoum and the Aswan Dam, more or less. So, what did my ancestors do – walk across the Sahara desert so that they could jump on a slave ship bound for Alabama so they could pick cotton for free?! You'd never do that. It turned out that Rick Kittles was being kind because he wanted me to have my African ethnic ancestry. I am one in the five per cent of African Americans who descend from a white great-great-grandfather, and I knew that. The man who fathered Jane Gates's children was a white man, because all her children looked white, and my Y-DNA goes straight to Ireland. So, there's no question about that. He was just anonymous, but now we have actually found his identity – which we'll reveal next season – purely through DNA and triangulation.

But, on my mother's side, I descend from a white woman who, in colonial times, slept with a Black enslaved man. So, my mitochondrial DNA does not go to Nubia, it goes straight to the United Kingdom. So, if a Martian came down and just looked at my Y-DNA, which is your father's father's line, and mitochondrial DNA, which is your mother mother's line, I'm white! But in my ad mixture I'm fifty per cent Sub-Saharan African and fifty per cent European, which means if you had an ideally populated family tree of my ancestors, half would be white and half would be Black.

The average African American is twenty-four-point-eight per cent white or European. They have never tested an African American – any of the three major commercial DNA companies – who is one hundred per cent African. That's quite astonishing. However, they wanted to check themselves because they thought maybe there was something wrong with the test. They have tested plenty of Africans who were one hundred per cent Sub-Saharan African. And that just shows you the extent of sexual exploitation in the slave trade and under the regime of slavery.

But I always ask my guests at the end of a 'reveal' (which takes about four hours to film. And what you see on TV is thirty minutes from that four hours): 'Does anything that we've shared today change your view of America, American history and your relation to it?' And everyone says, 'Yes.' It's a way of telling a history by inserting an individual. It appeals to the voyeur part of each of us. You're looking over the shoulder of a famous person and watching their ancestors inserted into an historical period which makes it much more vivid. Whether it's the Crimean War or the War of 1812 or the American Revolution or the Civil War, World War One or World War Two, or whatever.

And it shows that we're all immigrants in this country, our African ancestors came here in chains. They were forced immigrants, but they were immigrants, nonetheless. Even the Native Americans migrated here 15,000 years ago across the Bering Strait. So, literally, we're all migrants. And at the level of the genome, we're ninety-nine-point-nine per cent the same. That is a political message of *Finding Your Roots*. And I like doing it because I like history. It's mind blowing, what you can find.

Genealogists are geniuses and they turn up these amazing documents using federal census records and estate records and tax and baptism records from little parish churches in Cuba, for example: just writing down little Sarah was born today and her father is Giuseppi and her mother is Maria. Digitization has made the series possible, but not everything has been digitized. As you know, the Mormons – the Church of Jesus Christ of Latter-day Saints – have a belief that they can find your ancestors and baptize them. And so they have been collecting genealogical records since 1839.

Because of them, we have this fantastic, digitized database that has been licensed through Ancestry.com. Full disclosure: they are the leading sponsor for *Finding Your Roots*. So you can do a lot of this work just from your computer, wherever you are in the world, but there's a lot that has not been digitized. So we send researchers to wherever your ancestors were from. In your case, we'd send them to Lagos, or we'd send them to England, to whatever village your ancestors were from.

And I have learned so much about world history. We just featured Tony Shalhoub and, of course, we know about the Armenian genocide in 1915, but his ancestor was killed in a warm-up for that genocide in 1895 when the Turks, the Ottomans, killed 50,000 Armenians in 1895, and they crucified this person upside down according to the newspaper report. Just things like that you learn on everybody's family tree. So it has a very political function as we see the slumbering beast of white supremacy rearing its ugly head in America, brought on without doubt by the election of the first Black president.

LADIPO MANYIKA: Well, and let's come to that. *Finding Your Roots* is a powerful series, as you were outlining, and you've touched on white supremacy which allows me to jump to your next, most recent series on the Black Church, which is just—

GATES: Amen.

LADIPO MANYIKA: Amen! Has the Lord put a song in your heart to sing to us today because that's one thing I love about you, your singing voice. And, as you know, I'm a pastor's daughter.

GATES: I know that. You're a preacher's kid, a PK. You're Anglican, I trust?

LADIPO MANYIKA: Absolutely. So this series, as with all of your films, tells the small stories and it tells the bigger stories. It tells the story of America. There are so many things that I would love to discuss about each of your series. But in this one, in particular, you highlight how African American churches have been a refuge for African Americans who have been targeted over time by white supremacists.

And your series before this was looking at the Reconstruction period and the rise of white supremacy in response to that. How far has America come since Reconstruction, indeed since the civil rights movement, and up to this moment of supposed racial reckoning?

GATES: Well, it's a marvelous question. There are people who actually believe we were better off under segregation, but I think that's an oversimplification and rose-colored glasses. And there's no question that we're better off today than we were a hundred years ago. Since Dr King was killed, the Black middle-class has doubled, the Black upper-middle-class has quadrupled. We're having this conversation because of *Brown v. Board*. Otherwise, we wouldn't be having this conversation. Now, I would have gone to college. Three generations of my family went to Howard, starting with my great-aunt Pansy in 1909, but I wouldn't have gone to the Ivy League. It would've been highly unlikely.

So, we've had a tremendous amount of progress: the first Black president and almost fifty Congress men and women, including my classmate, Sheila Jackson Lee from Barbara Jordan's District in Houston and Black men in the Senate, most recently Reverend Raphael Warnock. There's no question that we've made an enormous amount of progress, but there also is no question that white supremacy is alive and well.

I tell my students at Harvard, in my lecture course Introduction to African American Studies, that there are two streams constantly flowing under the floorboards of Western culture. One is antisemitism and one is anti-Black racism. No matter what happens, no matter what you see above ground, they are there and those floorboards can be lifted up and those forces dippered out and poured into vessels any time. And we see that happening. There are pogroms going back to the Middle Ages. Anti-Black racism is as old as interracial contact and is fundamentally tied with economics, as you well know; both are, antisemitism is as well.

As the expectations for future economic growth have diminished for white Americans, this has been directly proportional to the rise of white supremacy. It's one thing to welcome women and people of color into historically white male institutions, such as Yale or Harvard, or Oxford and Cambridge, or whatever the institution. It's one thing to do that if you have a full economy, as we did in the late 1960s when we thought we could do guns and butter; that we could solve the problems of poverty in America with great society and win the Vietnam war, both of which were stupid and silly ideas. And we should never have been in Vietnam in the first place. But we had full employment. But when the economy shrinks, all of a sudden, if there's only this much liquid in this glass, I'm going to take a long look at you and a long look at this glass and decide how much we're going to share and who's going to be able to drink from the glass.

That's an oversimplified comparison, of course, but that's the way it is. So that when people are threatened economically, they lash out and they need to demonize. Demagogues like Donald Trump manipulate those fears using the tropes of white supremacy.

People used to ask me: 'Was Donald Trump a racist when he was running?' I'd say, 'Well, I never met him. I'll give him the benefit of the doubt, but there's no question he's a genius at manipulating the tropes of white supremacy.' Well, hello, anybody listening, he's a racist. Pure and simple. If he had won [again], it would've been like the end of Reconstruction. He has done so many things to turn the clock back and voter suppression would've been mounted as successfully (as they're trying to do in Georgia) as they were able to do at the end of Reconstruction. I'll give you one quick example.

In 1890, there were 130,000 Black men registered to vote in Louisiana. Louisiana, South Carolina and Mississippi were majority Black states and Florida, Alabama and Georgia were almost majority Black states until 1910. After voter suppression through the writing of new state constitutional conventions, the number of Black men registered to vote in Louisiana by 1904 was reduced precisely from 130,000 to 1,342. That's amazing. They just took away the right to vote because that was a key to Black power. And ninety per cent of all Black people lived in the Southern states, in the former Confederacy.

So, the problems that we face now are economic inequalities across the color line and the ethnic line, but these exacerbate racism and the rise of white supremacy. We have to solve the problem of inequality in order sufficiently to solve the problem of anti-Black racism. And I hope that Joe Biden and Kamala Harris (who is a dear friend, someone I admire very, very much and who I hope will be the next president of the United States after Biden), God willing, have two terms.

Their programs, it seems to me as an outsider and a non-expert, are targeting structural inequality, because no matter how many Silicon Valley billionaires are giving tens or hundreds of millions of dollars of charity in our Black Lives Matter moment, in our post-George Floyd moment, that is like a drop in the ocean. That is not going to solve systemic racism that is 300 or 400 years old. I'm sorry, it's just not. If these people gave as much money as they're giving now every year, it would be a beginning, but one-time donations, even of a $100m, it's just not enough. Just not enough.

6.

MARGARET BUSBY

On Meeting

March 7, 2019

It's cold and gray outside, but inside the Paul Webley Wing of London University's School of Oriental and African Studies (SOAS) it's all sparkle and warmth. For a moment, I stand by the entrance watching the crowd abuzz with laughter, music and chatter as photographers and a film crew circle the room. Here are mothers, daughters, granddaughters and aunties rocking pantsuits, evening gowns, kente, tie-dye, ankara, turbans, tresses, locks, hijab and afros of all curl textures, lengths and colors. We have gathered in our scores on this eve of International Women's Day, some traveling from as far as America and Nigeria for the launch of the much-anticipated book *New Daughters of Africa: An International Anthology of Writing by Women of African Descent*. As the room fills, excitement builds.

In one corner, I see the legendary activist Angela Davis speaking with Cassava Republic's pioneering publisher, Bibi Bakare-Yusuf. In another, I see Children's Laureate Malorie

Blackman and Bernardine Evaristo – not yet a Booker Prize winner, but already a household name to us. I recognize podcaster Sarah Ozo-Irabor, Ugandan novelist Goretti Kyomuhendo and Yvonne Bailey-Smith, mother to another contributor, novelist Zadie Smith. While not all 200 contributors are here, those who are reflect the anthology's rich diversity.

Twenty-seven years earlier, in 1992, a similar gathering took place – not as large as tonight's, but equally momentous, for the launch of *Daughters of Africa: An International Anthology of Words and Writings by Women of African Descent from the Ancient Egyptian to the Present*. Like its sequel, the original anthology is a big, fat, thunking book bursting at the spine with stories from across centuries, nations and literary genres. It features landmark pieces and author-firsts, ranging from eighteenth-century Lucy Terry to twentieth-century Flora Nwapa, who, in the late 1960s, was the first African woman novelist to achieve international acclaim.

Though I lived in London then, I did not attend the 1992 launch, but as a daughter of Africa I have treasured that first anthology and taken it with me across continents from Europe to Africa and America. It sits on my shelves right behind my computer, always visible – a taliswoman. When I was invited to contribute a piece to its sequel, I was both ecstatic and terrified. It felt like the most important collection I would ever be asked to contribute to. I worried about not being good enough. But here I am in *New Daughters of Africa* alongside famous writers, lesser-known writers, some once forgotten.

The time has come for the evening's speeches. We gather in a large circle, several rows deep, craning our necks to see. First a welcome from SOAS's Vice Chancellor, Baroness Valerie Amos, followed by Candida Lacey, publisher of the anthology and commissioning editor of the first anthology. Lacey praises the vision and hard work of the editor. She is followed by Fareda Banda, Chair of SOAS's Center for African Studies, who thanks contributors for waiving their fees, which has enabled the creation of a new SOAS scholarship. And now the editor herself will speak – the woman known as the 'doyenne of Black British publishing' and a 'literary supernova', and after whom the scholarship is named – Margaret Busby.

There's a new round of applause with claps, whoops and ululation, then silence as we strain to catch her words. Quickly, someone turns up the mic, and I hear her paying tribute to Andrea Levy, a beloved contributor best known for her novel *Small Island*, who died of cancer just weeks earlier. Today would have been Andrea's sixty-third birthday, and Margaret dedicates the evening to her memory. Margaret speaks for just a few minutes before stepping back. In the noisy excitement that follows, contributors gathering for photographs, Margaret almost disappears. But soon she stands front and center as we fan around her, some of the taller audience members kneeling by her feet.

'CALL ME MARGARET'

It's early afternoon when I arrive at the house in Clerkenwell. Luke, Margaret's partner, answers the door with a warm smile, but we do not shake hands. This is March 2020, the early days of Covid-19, and we are being careful. I wash my hands and return to the front room with its sunlit wooden floors and many bookshelves. Margaret is dressed in a blue-and-white floral top worn over a black polo neck and black trousers, and wears three gold bangles given to her by her mother. Fond of necklaces with large pendants, today she is wearing a favorite heart-shaped adinkra symbol – Sankofa, signifying the importance of learning from the past. Margaret is a proud 'five-foot-two-and-a-half', slight in frame and of that tribe of women whose age is hard to determine. 'As old as my tongue, a little older than my teeth,' she quips. I know she's in her seventies, but physically, with her shy, girly smile, she could pass for decades younger.

Luke, from whose home Margaret is working today, fetches us water and before he leaves asks how much time we'll need. Margaret guesses that our 'little chat' won't take long given that she's not that interesting. Luke and I laugh, playing along – yes, that's right, Margaret, you're not interesting at all! I pull up a seat opposite Margaret, who sits in a leather settee next to a pile of papers and books. She twists slightly to face me. 'I'm comfortable,' she reassures me, peering coyly from beneath the brim of her loose afro. 'As comfortable as I ever am focusing on myself. That's what makes me uncomfortable!' When Margaret speaks, she sometimes shuts her eyes or looks down for a few moments, but this apparent shyness doesn't get in the way of her talking. Margaret revels in recollection, and keeps her laptop handy for sharing quotes, photographs and letters. Occasionally, when she misses something I've said, I speak a little louder. The more we speak, the more I marvel at how much she remembers – everything from dates to street addresses to people's names. It reminds me of our first meeting.

We first met in March 2015, in Lagos, Nigeria, for the award ceremony of the pan-African Etisalat Prize for Literature. At the time, Margaret was a patron of the prize and I was the jury chair. I noticed that in large groups Margaret was quiet, and tended to avoid the spotlight, but when we met as a small group for dinner she became chatty. I was struck then, as I am now, by her recall and by her frequent interweaving of fascinating historical asides and her close attention to detail. As a patron of the Etisalat Prize, Margaret was one of the VIPs, but no task was beneath her. She was always quick to respond to email and paid close attention to marketing materials and publicity around the prize, often volunteering to copy-edit press releases.

Margaret is meticulous and scholarly when referencing history but also playful in her storytelling – she laughs a lot, breaks into song and mimics accents. Words are her passion. 'Guess which three words I first learned to spell,' she asks. 'You can't guess!' she teases. 'Necessary, fascinating and picturesque!'

Words, she explains, that have almost become a metaphor for life. 'Life must be necessary, fascinating and picturesque,' she smiles. The more I learn about Margaret's life and her family, the more these words seem apt.

Margaret is writing a piece on her parents' life for a forthcoming book on healthcare professionals from the Windrush and pre-Windrush era. She shares parts of it with me, including a letter from her father's best friend upon his death. In it her father is described as having 'a natural dignity which went with a certain shyness', and an 'exceeding kindness of nature' – both of which strike me as good descriptions for Margaret too. Four days earlier, Margaret and I shared a stage at the London School of Economics (LSE) where we spoke about *New Daughters of Africa*. On stage, Margaret surprised me by remembering that it was my birthday and announcing it, and, in the question-and-answer session that followed our talks, Margaret frequently deferred to me. She was the star, but she made me feel like an equal.

How does it feel, I ask, in the wake of the publication of *New Daughters of Africa*, to finally be receiving more attention for your work? 'Well, I'm not sure that I'm getting that much attention,' she replies. 'I think the anthology is deservedly getting attention,' she adds, 'and that's the reason I did it – because over the decades I've just seen so little attention given to writers, writers who deserve attention.' She tells me that she lives by a Greek saying that one should plant trees under which one will never sit. I feel a twinge of sadness, thinking that she deserves much more attention, but Margaret doesn't dwell on this. Still, I wonder, does some part of her feel disappointed?

As we talk and laugh, there are a few things that Margaret shares with me only on condition that I use discretion in how much I reveal. There is the story, for example, of a certain amore who 'neglected' to tell her that he was married and had a child. When I press Margaret on any other romantic liaisons before or after her marriage to the late jazz musician Lionel Grigson, all she says, with just a hint of a smile, is that her 'type' has always been someone whose name begins with the letter 'L'.

We have been talking for over an hour when Luke returns and asks if we'd like something to eat or drink. Margaret says she's fine. 'You sure you don't want me to warm you up a roti?' he tries again. I smile, happy to see her being fussed over by a partner who seems kind and attentive. Margaret and I speak for another hour before I bring the conversation to a close. I could have continued for hours, but I know how busy she is. Before I leave, Margaret looks me in the eye and says she hopes our conversation has been worthwhile. I am stunned, not by her modesty which I'm now used to, but by the fact that these words are almost identical to those used by her friend, the late Toni Morrison, when I spoke with her in her home three years earlier. Not for the first time do I think, birds of a feather.

ORIGINS

Margaret's maternal grandmother came from the Gold Coast (now Ghana), raised ten children, including four sets of twins, and lived to the grand old age of ninety-nine. Her husband, Margaret's maternal grandfather – George James Christian – who came from the island of Dominica, traveled to England in 1899 to study law at Gray's Inn. It would have been rare in those days to find a Black man studying at Gray's Inn, and also rare for a West Indian man to emigrate to the Gold Coast, as he did in 1902. George was a pan-Africanist, and one of just thirty-seven delegates at the first Pan-African Conference in 1900. It is to these extraordinary parents that Margaret's mother, Sarah Helena Christian, was born, in Sekondi, the Gold Coast, in 1906.

Like her father, Sarah traveled to England where she studied nursing in the 1920s. She was headhunted for a so-called 'European appointment' – usually reserved for white people – back in the Gold Coast, where she returned as nursing sister to the prestigious Prince of Wales College and School, now known as Achimota School. At the time, students of the school included Kwame Nkrumah, who would become Ghana's first president, and Edward Akufo-Addo, another of Ghana's founding fathers. With her well-paying European appointment, which included first-class passage to and from England, Sarah helped many of her extended family, including a stepsister's four children, to study in Britain. One of these would be the mother of Moira Stuart, Britain's first Black female broadcaster and Margaret's cousin.

Margaret's father, George Alfred Busby, was born in Barbados in 1899 and grew up in Trinidad, where he won a coveted Island Scholarship to study medicine in Britain – a scholarship that would be delayed for two years until the end of World War One. George began his studies at Edinburgh University, then transferred to Dublin where he was better able to save on his scholarship money and support his siblings back home. He worked as a GP for a few years in the poor, working-class area of Walthamstow, in London, before emigrating in 1929 to the Gold Coast. There, he established a clinic in a poor rural community where he remained for fifty years.

Margaret, the youngest of three children, was born in the Gold Coast in 1944, and spent her early years in the rural town of Suhum, where her father worked as a doctor and her mother as a nurse. Some of her earliest childhood memories include helping her father in his dispensary and reading his medical books. She describes her father as 'taciturn' and not overly demonstrative, whereas her mother, a stylish woman who married in her mid-thirties, which was considered late for the times, came from a line of strong and independent woman, and was quick to express her emotions. The Busby parents led a simple life, saving for their children's education. Margaret remembers her mother having one good dress that she washed each night in order to wear again the next day. Her mother also emptied her husband's pockets each night to prevent him from giving away all his coins to the poor, as he was prone to do.

Margaret was only five years old when she left in 1950 with her siblings – sister Eileen and brother George – to study in England. It was not easy for Margaret's parents to find a school that would accept Black children at that time. One headmistress said, 'Well, we'd love to have them, but it's the parents of the other girls . . .' While George went to a boys' school, Margaret and her sister went first to a school in the Lake District and then to Charters Towers School, an international girls' boarding school in the sleepy seaside town of Bexhill-on-Sea. Many of Margaret's memories of her parents at this time come from their letters. Her mother wrote frequently, inquiring about school, ordering birthday cakes for her children, asking for dress measurements, all the while attempting to shield her children from the financial strain and sacrifice of keeping them at boarding schools.

The Busby children could not afford to return to Ghana during the holidays, so most school vacations were spent in a holiday home or visiting an aunt in Paris. The holiday home in Sussex was run by Verily Anderson, who wrote a book about the place called *Beware of Children* (1958), which was turned into the film *No Kidding* (1960), featuring two 'African girls' named Margaret and Eileen.

Margaret was bright and always the youngest in her class. She sat O-levels at fourteen, two sets of A-levels at sixteen, and then spent a year at a Cambridge college called Lady Margaret House so as not to be too young before attending university. At seventeen, Margaret attended Bedford College, one of the founding institutions of Royal Holloway, University of London, to read English. She graduated at twenty.

Over the years, Margaret has written about her family history in a number of articles, including a piece for BBC Radio 3 that describes a return to Ghana in 1999. There, in an honor bestowed by the community, she was enstooled in the Fante tradition, following in the footsteps of her maternal grandmother. 'This is where I was born,' she writes. 'It is impossible not to feel history weighing heavily on my shoulders. This is where my mother's people come from, where my father's people left from a perilous one-way journey four hundred years ago.' In that 1999 return, like her foremothers, Margaret was given a new name and bestowed an honor. She was made Nana Akua Ackon of No. 1 Asafo Company (Bentsir) of Oguaa Traditional Area (Cape Coast) – a warrior chief.

A MOST BRITISH PUBLISHER

In 1992, when the first *Daughters of Africa* anthology was published, I was working in the London headquarters of Penguin Books. At the time, Penguin was one of the world's largest and most reputable publishing houses, and yet of the hundreds of books it published each year I found very few – in catalogues or on the shelves – by Black authors, or even featuring Black people. I met only one other Black employee beyond those who cleaned or guarded the premises, and while Penguin employed many women, senior management was dominated by upper-middle-class men. If this was the state of British publishing in the 1990s, then what would it have taken for a young Black woman to start her own publishing house back in the 1960s?

As Margaret tells it, on May 14, 1965, while in her final year at university, she attended a friend's party in London. There she met Clive Allison, who, she discovered, shared her love of literature and poetry. Clive had been President of Oxford University's Poetry Society while Margaret was editor of her Bedford College magazine. By the end of the evening, they had decided to set up a publishing company. They borrowed money from friends and found jobs to support themselves while working on books in the evenings and weekends. Margaret found a day job at Cresset Press, but not without difficulty in the largely white, male and upper-middle-class publishing industry. She remembers one receptionist skeptically announcing, 'There's a Black girl here who says she's got an interview.'

Margaret and Clive named their company Allison & Busby, and decided that their first books would be cheap, affordable paperback poetry books. Clive did the marketing and Margaret the editing. Margaret had become Britain's first Black woman publisher, and, at the age of twenty, was also one of its youngest. Initially Allison & Busby had no distribution outlets, so Margaret and Clive sold their first three poetry books out of the back of a van on the Kings Road. But even in these early days of cobbling things together, their work was noticed and praised. The *Times Educational Supplement* called them 'a brave new imprint' while *Books & Bookmen* praised 'three excellent titles . . . they hold their own in any company.'

While initial press for Allison & Busby was positive, it also reflected the gender and racial biases of the time. The *Evening Standard* of September 15, 1969 features Margaret in a long-sleeve, thigh-high dress, sitting on the boot of a car, legs crossed. She is referred to simply as 'married to jazzman Lionel Grigson' and as having worked for Cresset Press. There's no photo of Clive, but he's the one whose words are quoted. A *Sunday Mirror* article from around the same time features a headshot of Margaret with the caption 'girl from Ghana starts a publishing firm', and within the article Margaret is described as 'a fascinating girl. Not only because she looks so good. The way she slots into English society intrigues me.'

Margaret and Clive took the plunge to become full-time publishers in 1969 on discovering a first novel called *The Spook Who Sat by the Door* – rejected by every other publisher the author had tried. Written by African American Sam Greenlee, it is the story of a Black man, Dan Freeman, hired by the CIA to allay accusations of racial discrimination, who then uses his training to organize inner-city 'freedom fighters'. Published by Allison & Busby with little more than what Margaret calls 'youthful enthusiasm', the novel went on to sell over one million copies internationally. Excerpts were used in a national paper, translation rights were sold to Germany, Italy, France, Holland,

Sweden, Japan and Finland, and in 1973 the book was made into a film directed by Ivan Dixon, with a soundtrack by jazz great Herbie Hancock. The novel has since become something of a classic. In July 2020, I came across it highlighted by the *New York Times*: 'more than 50 years after it was published, the book feels thrillingly incendiary, as if it, like its hero, were only pretending to play by the rules while actually providing a blueprint for revolution.'

Allison & Busby prided themselves on being unconventional and punching above their weight. They published writers of all ethnicities and backgrounds, including Anthony Burgess and J. G. Ballard, a novel by the international footballer Derek Dougan, as well as an eighty-five-year-old first-time novelist, Katharine Moore, and non-fiction works by historian philosopher C. L. R. James, which Margaret brought out of obscurity. They also published poetry, socio-political books and modern fictional works that had gone out of print. Margaret often says that the biggest compliment someone paid to Allison & Busby was that 'you never knew what they were going to publish next, but you knew it was going to be interesting.'

Allison & Busby books and their authors also won many prizes. Nigerian-born novelist Buchi Emecheta won the 1978 *New Statesman* Jock Campbell Award; authors Michael Moorcock and Roy A. K. Heath won the *Guardian* Fiction Prize in two successive years, 1977 and 1978; Maurice Nyagumbo, cabinet minister from newly independent Zimbabwe, won the 1980 Martin Luther King Memorial Prize for his autobiography; and Clive Sinclair's short stories won the 1981 Somerset Maugham Award. Margaret seems to have been adored by her authors, with several dedicating their work to her, and others (George Lamming and C. L. R. James included) writing moving letters of thanks, copies of which I find in the personal digital archives that Margaret shares with me.

While working as publisher, Margaret took on many additional projects. She hosted a program for the BBC Africa

Service called *Break for Women*, in which she interviewed African women coming through London. She wrote for newspapers and journals. Her first published piece, 'Skin Deep', written for the *New Statesman* in 1967, was on how it felt to be Black in England. It ran on the same page as a review for a book by Enoch Powell who, two years later, would give his infamous 'Rivers of Blood' speech inflaming anti-immigrant sentiment. In the early 1980s, Margaret was a founding member of Penumbra Productions, a group of London creatives representative of the three main Black communities living in Britain – African, Asian and Caribbean. They produced six films for Channel 4 based on lectures by C. L. R. James. Margaret was also a founding member of Greater Access to Publishing (GAP), which campaigned for greater diversity in the publishing industry.

When I ask Margaret about any publishing role models she might have had when starting out, she mentions the South African writer and editor Noni Jabavu who had published several autobiographical books in the early 1960s. Jabavu was a regular reviewer and contributor to the British press, and the first Black person and woman to be an editor of a literary magazine – the *New Strand*. Over time, there would be other writer-editors, such as Toni Morrison and Alice Walker, to serve as inspiration, but they came later.

Margaret and Clive ran Allison & Busby for twenty years, publishing hundreds of books and inspiring many other small independent publishers. But publishing is not an easy business, and after financial struggles Margaret and Clive decided that it was time to move on. In 1987 the company was acquired by W. H. Allen Ltd. Margaret went on to become a freelance editor, reviewer and critic. She also served as a judge for many literary prizes, most recently chairing Britain's most prestigious literary prize, the Booker, which made history in September 2020 with a shortlist that included four authors of color and four debut novelists.

Having learnt so much about Allison & Busby, I am curious to see what has happened since. On Allison & Busby's current website, I am surprised to find no mention of the company's history or its eponymous founders. And while there is mention of some of the authors from Allison & Busby's backlist – Katharine Moore, Jack Trevor Story, Budd Schulberg and Colin MacInnes – the latter listed under 'A&B Classics' – none of its pioneering Black authors are mentioned.

HER WORLD, OUR WORLD

In 2004, fifty writers of Caribbean, Asian and African descent gathered for a photograph at the British Library. The photograph, inspired by the famous photograph of American jazz musicians taken in New York in 1958, *A Great Day in Harlem*, was called *A Great Day in London*. In the 2004 photograph, Margaret stands almost hidden in the upper left-hand corner, behind literary critic Maya Jaggi and in front of novelist Lawrence Scott and poet Linton Kwesi Johnson. Almost everyone in the picture is either a friend, a colleague or an author whom Margaret has published or mentored over the years – all pioneering Black and Asian writers involved in publishing or the arts. Margaret's connections within the Black arts scene extend around the world.

Among the articles and photographs that Margaret shares with me in March is a letter she received from the Nobel Laureate Wole Soyinka, dated December 15, 1975, on the letterhead of *Transition* magazine, sent from Accra, Ghana. Soyinka is writing in response to a letter in which Margaret takes him to task for including few women in his anthology, *Poems of Black Africa*. He promises to do better. 'I know that in the next edition I will especially search for poetry by women.' This, I discover, became the impetus for Margaret to compile her anthology, *Daughters of Africa*. And in that anthology Toni

Morrison features prominently – one year before she became the first Black woman to win a Nobel Prize.

When I had a chance to meet and interview Morrison in 2017, I wrote to Margaret asking what Morrison was like. Margaret responded by sending me a video of an interview she did with Morrison in February 1988. In it a young-looking, soft-spoken Margaret speaks with poise and insight about the literary context and importance of Morrison's work. The interview had been hurriedly made after another TV interview between the two of them was dropped over concerns about poor audience size. One month later, Morrison won a Pulitzer Prize. Margaret jokes about being in great demand between 1992 and 1993, when Morrison and then Walcott won the Nobel Prize, because 'none of the mainstream literary critics seemed to have read either of them at that point.'

The more I learn about Margaret, the more I realize that her life has indeed been 'necessary, fascinating and picturesque'. Margaret seems to have been in touch with every prominent figure in Black literature, art and music from across the world – a veritable pan-African who's who of the twentieth and early twenty-first century. My curiosity grows, and we begin what becomes an ongoing and sometimes daily email exchange. Margaret eventually sends me a virtual album labelled: A&B/ MB (assorted book jackets, cuttings, letters, photos). It takes me hours to work through the hundreds of images included. As I pore over them, I keep thinking that her archives need to be properly stored and protected in a national archive, especially so when she tells me the reason she has scanned so many images is due to a leak in her roof!

In one undated black-and-white photograph Margaret stands with her cousin Moira Stuart, speaking with American novelist and essayist James Baldwin. At a small cocktail party, Baldwin is holding a drink, talking, while Margaret and Moira gaze at him with looks of enthrallment. Baldwin appears in several of Margaret's pictures, including photographs taken in the early

1980s at the Black Book Fair in London. In these latter pictures are more friends of Margaret's: Guyanese artist Aubrey Williams; John La Rose, founder of New Beacon Books; Jamaican dub poet Linton Kwesi Johnson; American pianist Randy Weston.

In another photograph, this one in color, Margaret is sitting next to Nina Simone – both are smoking at a small table crowded with wine bottles and glasses. They are at Ronnie Scott's Jazz Club on a night when Nina is performing. Margaret had met Nina one year earlier, in 1984, at Trinidad's Piarco Airport following Carnival. Margaret had been taken to the airport by her friend and novelist Earl Lovelace, and, as the plane to London was delayed, the three of them passed several hours together – Nina trying to persuade Earl to help her with her autobiography. Back in London, Margaret stayed in touch with Nina who, according to Margaret, was, at times, 'scarily mad'.

Many other musicians appear in Margaret's album. At the 1969 book launch party of *The Spook Who Sat by the Door*, jazz musician Roland Kirk has his arm threaded through Margaret's. In another, the great Manu Dibango sits at a piano backstage at the Barbican. Paul Simon, Hugh Masekela and Miriam Makeba are in other photos taken in the home of cultural activist Pearl Connor and her husband Joe Mogotsi, of South Africa's singing group the Manhattan Brothers. In one photograph, Hugh Masekela has an arm around Margaret, and they lean in to each other, smiling. Margaret tells of a thriller that Masekela had written which she was helping him with. There's a whole collage of photographs taken over the years of Margaret and her sister Eileen with songwriter and musician Stevie Wonder, dating back to the 1970s. In one, Stevie sits on the floor of Margaret's home next to a record player and a pile of CDs and cassettes. In another, Stevie is in Ghana with Margaret's brother, George. More recently, pictures from 2005 show Margaret and Stevie at Abbey Road Studio after a recording, and at London's O2 Centre in 2008.

There are many other pictures taken backstage at the Barbican, with everyone from jazz vocalists Dianne Reeves, Dee

Dee Bridgewater – Margaret and Dee Dee wearing matching leopard tops – to legendary saxophonist Sonny Rollins. In New York, Margaret is photographed with T.K. Blue at Sweet Basil, and in Cape Town, with South African jazz legend Abdullah Ibrahim after introducing his eighteen-piece band. Despite Margaret's shyness and reserve, I realize by looking through all of her archives just how fundamental a part of Black culture Margaret has been and continues to be – not just in the UK, but around the world.

And then there are photographs of Margaret receiving various honors. In one, she is receiving her OBE from Prince Charles at Buckingham Palace. In another, she has just been initiated into the Alpha Kappa Alpha sorority and is dressed all in white like her fellow sorors. This is the sorority of Rosa Parks, Bernice King, Maya Angelou and Kamala Harris, to name but a few. Margaret describes the sorority's 1998 convention in Chicago, when she and her sorority sisters attended a Gladys Knight concert and sang 'Midnight Train to Georgia', whooping along to the chorus.

Two days before we met in March, Margaret had been in Walthamstow unveiling a blue plaque in honour of her father: Dr George Alfred Busby (1899–1980) – Caribbean Pan-Africanist Walthamstow Physician and Surgeon. Later that same day, Margaret attended the memorial of her friend and publishing giant Sonny Mehta. And in the days before, Margaret volunteers a glimpse into her week:

'Sunday, I went to WOW at the Southbank at the Royal Festival. I was on a panel about Toni Morrison, and then from there I went to a memorial for Mustapha Matura. Trinidadian playwright who died.

'Saturday was at LSE with you.

'Friday was the *London Review* bookshop conversation between Lorna Goodison and Linton Kwesi Johnson and then we had supper after.

'Thursday was a Booker meeting between noon and two. Then a taxi to the Ivy, Victoria, to have lunch with Lorna Goodison and Linton Kwesi Johnson and various friends because Lorna had just come back from Buckingham Palace where she got the Queen's Royal Medal for poetry, and it was taxi back to the BFI for a screening of a Toni Morrison documentary which was wonderful and emotional . . .'

Margaret is constantly in demand and always busy, and yet somehow she never appears to run out of energy. She turns up to support old friends, she participates in events grand and small and brings others along whenever there is occasion to do so. Most recently Margaret has been doing interviews, photoshoots and filming – many relating to her role as Chair for the Booker Prize. In her emails she includes the names of her photographers and filmmakers with links to their Wikipedia entries, some of which I suspect she might have written herself. Margaret has written hundreds of Wikipedia entries in her ongoing efforts to fill in the gaps and flag unsung heroes. She urges me to do the same.

Margaret has taken to the new age of Zoom virtual events, including a guest appearance on the pan-African virtual literary festival, Afrolit Sans Frontieres. In other emails, she tells me about a 'brilliant jazz education initiative' called Tomorrow's Warriors, for which she is a trustee. She mentions writers who have recently sent her their manuscripts – there's a novel from Yvonne Bailey-Smith – 'watch this space' – and a memoir from Barbara Masekela. Meanwhile, Margaret is busy completing a new piece on her family history. Sadly, around this time I also learn of the death of Margaret's beloved sister Eileen Busby Keita. Margaret sends me her moving tribute, as well as an album of family photos.

Having read many of Margaret's writings, I suggest that she put together a book of her collected essays. 'A book of my pieces?' Margaret responds. 'I nominate you as editor!' which is just the sort of thing Margaret does. Smiling, I find myself reaching for *New Daughters of Africa* and Margaret's introduction:

> *My ambition was and is to shine a light on as many as possible of the deserving, whether or not they are acknowledged or lauded by the gatekeepers, who traditionally single out a privileged few, seemingly never too many to rock the boat. But the boat is going nowhere if it is content to drift in stagnating water.*

7.

ANNA DEAVERE SMITH

In Conversation

Anna Deavere Smith is an actress, playwright, teacher and author who has been credited with having created a new form of theater. Her work combines the journalistic technique of interviewing her subjects with the art of interpreting their words through performance. She has created over fifteen one-person shows based on hundreds of interviews. Plays include Fires in the Mirror *(1993, runner-up for the Pulitzer Prize),* Twilight: Los Angeles, 1992 *(1994, nominated for two Tony Awards),* House Arrest *(2003) and* Let Me Down Easy *(2014). Her most recent play and film,* Notes From the Field *(2015), looks at the vulnerability of youth, inequality, the criminal justice system and contemporary activism. Smith has appeared on television series, including* For The People, black-ish, Nurse Jackie *and* The West Wing. *President Obama awarded Anna the National Humanities Medal in 2013. Additional honors include the prestigious MacArthur Award, the Dorothy and Lillian Gish Prize for achievement in the arts, the George Polk Career Award in Journalism, the Dean's Medal from the Stanford University Medical School, two Tony nominations and several honorary degrees. She is university professor at NYU's Tisch School of the Arts.*

September 14, 2020

SARAH LADIPO MANYIKA: Anna, of all the honors you have received, which one has meant the most to you?

ANNA DEAVERE SMITH: Well, they all do. Certainly, the National Medal for Humanities was a big deal. I was able to take my niece to the White House for the first time, very festive, but I was also surprised and honored about the Stanford School of Medicine. And that particularly means something to me because that was as a result of my play *Let Me Down Easy*, which was loosely about healthcare, more generally about the resilience of the human body, and more specifically about death. You just don't say those kinds of things when you're trying to sell a play. But that the play meant something to Phil Pizzo, who was the Head of the Medical School at the time, and that I had a chance to meet very interesting doctors and make friends there meant a lot to me.

And so, I basically think of myself as a clown, and I don't mean that to seem self-deprecating. Anybody who knows about the tradition of a clown – if you think about a French clown, an Italian clown, and I'm sure there's an African clown that you can tell me about – knows it's not silly. A clown is less interested in pathology and sort of more interested in mythologies, but nonetheless, to be taken 'seriously' when I'm writing a play about life and death by people who really deal with life and death on a daily basis meant a lot.

LADIPO MANYIKA: You brought up Africa. I'd love to hear more about your connection to the African diaspora. I know that you had a very special experience when you were with Professor Henry Louis Gates, Jr, on his program, *Finding Your Roots*, with your genealogy.

SMITH: Well, Dr Gates's show, in my case, was mostly about the United States, and very much about one of my relatives in

Gettysburg. But I remember, soon after that, whether I called you, whether you saw the show, I was very excited that I had roots in Nigeria, and you welcomed me as an Igbo sister and that meant a lot to me. I often think about the many trips I've taken to Africa, one trip to write *Let Me Down Easy,* but also, I dated a Nigerian man when I was in college, in school in London, and that was very exciting to me to go to events with him. I remember going to a Nigerian wedding, for instance.

And I do think that Tunde Omolegbe, that was his name, had a lot to do with my understanding of myself, not just as a part of the African diaspora, but as a woman, and particularly as a Negro woman, a colored woman, a Black woman. If he's anywhere out there in the stratosphere, thank you.

I also traveled to South Africa right after apartheid fell, and then more trips after that. I went to Rwanda ten years after the genocide, Uganda, Kenya, just to go through the airport, and Senegal, then Morocco, other parts. So it's been powerful. It was important to me to touch down in Africa, and so I have now done so on a variety of occasions. I haven't yet been to Nigeria.

LADIPO MANYIKA: You mean Tunde didn't get you out there?

SMITH: No. No, no.

LADIPO MANYIKA: Tell us about your great-great-uncle that you found out about for the first time on *Finding Your Roots.* And what was the impact of learning about him on your work?

SMITH: Well, my uncle, my great-great-uncle, Basil Biggs—

LADIPO MANYIKA: A great name.

SMITH: Yeah. And he, it turns out, I found out on *Finding Your Roots,* was a veterinarian in Gettysburg, a man of the community, a race man, I bet. That expression, 'Race woman, race man', those of us who are trying to uplift the race, I'm one. And then he got the contract to bury the dead after the Civil War, and so he organized that.

The thing that's so interesting about this is that I have a cousin named Basil. I had an uncle, the late Biggs Fraser Smith. When we would go to Gettysburg several times a year, we would see Aunt Hannah Biggs. We would visit my aunt Julia. No one told us, no one. We played in the battlefield, no one told us. And sadly, when my family saw the *Finding Your Roots* episode, my mother and father weren't alive.

The impact of the details uncovered by *Finding Your Roots* was extraordinary. Basil Biggs was only one story. I learned some things about my mother's side; in particular, one of my ancestors there had an oyster house – I guess he would've been also my great-great-something – he too was a race man.

And so, I think the first impact on my work is that my interest in community, my interest in having art be in the world and not in an Eiffel Tower, the fact of my being a race woman is not of my doing. I'm coming from a long line of people like that. And then the other thing that helped me understand is, I've always been an Americanist and I've set out in my work to learn as much about America as I can. My eighteen plays are all under an umbrella of *On the Road: A Search for American Character*. But people don't always think of us African American artists as truly American.

Still, I'm a walking critique. Since college, when I walk in a room, I'm an evident critique of the United States of America and its racism, and people don't quite know, am I going to be friendly about it? Am I going to be demanding about it? What am I going to be? But my showing up is a critique. And yet, I'm profoundly American, and this is a part of what I was able to really feel in the *Roots* episode.

LADIPO MANYIKA: I've heard you say many times that as a dramatist, you like catastrophe. We've got a fair amount of catastrophe right now. How's that going for you as a dramatist?

SMITH: I'm just starting a new project now about girls, which is a follow-up to *Notes From the Field*, which was about the school-to-prison pipeline. I decided that I want to see, understand a broader ecosystem of how poverty affects children, and how it robs them of their joy, their education, lots of things, maybe their sexual freedom. Whatever it is, it takes something away from them. And I certainly talked to girls among the 250 people I talked to when I wrote *Notes From the Field*, but I want to really look in close.

So, this work has certainly been delayed [by Covid-19] in terms of going into the field to meet people, but I'm really hoping to learn how they see this in their unofficial language. We hear all of the smart people, all of the academics, all of the journalists. I can't wait to get there and hear what's going on, as far as they're concerned. It's very, very, very upside down. It's different than other upside-down moments. Obviously, the pandemic has kind of frozen us in place. I don't have the mobility that I've previously had.

So, the good thing about upside-downness is everything is shaken out. If you can think of it like dropping a bag of groceries, and then there they are, splayed out on the street for everybody to see, and then you have to arrange it back. And it may not, likely will not be arranged back the same way.

The best that could happen now is that we will rearrange this in a positive way. We won't solve all the problems. We won't take away racism. We won't fix healthcare. We won't do a lot of things people are hoping we're going to do, but some people are taking a hold of this malleable moment. I heard somebody use that phrase the other day, I found it was a very good phrase. Some people will take a hold of that malleable moment and do something while the window is open.

My experience is that the window closes too quickly. And I wonder how you feel too, Sarah, given the fact that part of your heritage is Nigerian. You've lived in different places in Africa. When people say this moment is unprecedented, I feel it undermines history in a way. Let's just think about what it must have been like in the continent of Africa as colonialism began to fall country by country.

LADIPO MANYIKA: One of the things that I love about you, Anna, is your focus on words. You are a student of words, and this word, 'unprecedented', I think is an important one. In many ways, I feel that we shouldn't be surprised about a lot of the things that we're facing. It's not as if they're popping up out of the blue. There is a lot to learn from history.

Speaking of history, do you remember the very first performance you gave? Do you remember someone saying, 'You could be an actor!' How did it all start?

SMITH: Well, my mother tells the story, although I don't remember it, I think it was in first grade and she was delighted I think, and God bless my mother. She was not the type of mother who would come rushing backstage and say, 'Oh, my God, everybody was looking at you!' A lot of actors had that kind of mother, but I didn't. It could have been because there were five of us and she didn't want anybody to feel more attention than the other. She was real. She showed up for everything, but she was very low-key. However, she was quite delighted to tell people about me in the first grade, playing a troll. I don't even know the play, and she herself would say, 'Oh, I can remember you singing, "I'm a troll, fol-de-rol."'

LADIPO MANYIKA: Oh, you were singing. You started off singing!

SMITH: I can't sing, but I guess I sang. But whatever it was, I certainly seemed to have put myself in it with no inhibition. However, I didn't really think about being an actor until well after I was out of college, and I sort of tripped over an acting class in an excellent conservatory, the American Conservatory

Theater, and then through a series of accidents I ended up becoming an actor.

It was a very profound moment in my life. Everything happened quickly. Nothing has happened as quickly since that time.

LADIPO MANYIKA: Was it a smooth ride?

SMITH: No. It was more like I went to their Summer Training Congress and then I was going to go back to what I was doing. But I got a call that the head of the school wanted to see me, and he said, 'Well, you may not want to do this, but there's a place for you here.'

Then I called my friend, Diane Salinger, and said, 'He said there's a place for me there. Should I take it?' 'What are you talking about? Of course, you should take it!' And my friend, the late Chuck Selber, 'What are you talking about? Of course, you should take it! Come over here. I have dinner for you!' And he made me dinner, which was a big piece of honeydew melon with a blob of peanut butter. He was from New Orleans. He said, 'I knew you'd be hungry.' It was just one of the best congratulatory dinners.

So, I went to the first year, I came back the second year. There was one Black woman in the company. She quit. They put me in there, but I was really doing just background stuff, and there's been nothing easy about my career. I'd just give that encouragement to people who are out there watching, who are artists of any kind or doing anything that is difficult.

It was not easy. It's just that fortune stepped in to make a way for me. I've mentioned to you already, Sarah, Michael J. Sandel's book, *The Tyranny of Merit*, which leads us to believe that if we get there, it's of our own doing, we get what we deserve. But in a conversation between Sandel and another political philosopher, Jackson Lears, Lears says, 'No, you get what you get.'

So, I think that in this case, I understand that I am not here, to the extent that I'm anywhere, my achievements are not of my own doing, and that sometimes the door opened. Was that luck? Was that God? I don't know. I didn't ask for it. It was unbidden, but it was a gift.

LADIPO MANYIKA: You have worked in film, on the stage, and in TV. Of those three mediums, do you have a favorite?

SMITH: I don't have a favorite. There are different demands in each format. And in each of these professions, because of the pandemic, there are going to be extraordinary transformations, extraordinary things we cannot imagine, as we sort of solve this problem about how to do our work, a work that requires extraordinary intimacy – and it requires intimacy quickly.

So, for example, maybe when you think of intimacy you think, 'Oh, well yeah, a love scene. OK. That's that.' But even my work in the theater, where people call something a one-person show (and on Sunday, I'm going to start teaching a class at NYU on one-person shows), it's not a one-person show. I don't know if you've ever been in any of my rehearsal halls. It's an incredibly, incredibly intimate experience with the director, with the people I invite in as conversants. They fight, I listen, I go home. I rewrite the play. Sometimes they're tough on me. Sometimes they're not, but it's really an intimate thing.

And so we are all taken away from these intimate environments in which we make our work, and how we're going to come out of it, it's going to be different. I don't have a favorite. Of course, I like doing my own work. I develop my own work. It allows me to meet lots and lots of people and learn things, but I also enjoy the community of television and movie-making.

LADIPO MANYIKA: You created a new form of theater – documentary theater – in which you do extensive interviews with people. And then you pull out a few characters and you present on stage, verbal portraits that speak to American society. You've said your work has been in search of the American character. Can you tell us more about that and, in particular, in relation to your latest play, *Notes From the Field*?

SMITH: Lots of people remind us – I think of Obama, for one – that part of American character is dissent. Lots of people remind us that democracy is a process, is an experiment toward a perfect union. What are the things that help that and what are the things that make that impossible?

And so, in the case of *Notes From the Field*, I was interested in those things that keep kids, our kids of color for the most part, but I'm sure poor white kids as well, from making it through the joyous experience of learning, of getting the light switched on, about something that's going to make you curious for the rest of your life, 'What happened?'

I learned a lot about that and in the midst of it, there were the riots in Baltimore, my hometown. My hometown being a place I was going to go. I had made a plan to go to four geographic areas. So I went to Northern California, Stockton, and the Yurok, Indian tribe, Native American tribe. They called themselves Indians very often. Philly, South Carolina. I went up and down what was called the Corridor of Shame because the schools are so bad. And then I went to Baltimore, and it just happened that I had, again, that window, that wasn't about me. Just happened that I had to delay my trip. So then when did I end up in Baltimore? Right on the heels of the riot after the killing of Freddie Gray.

And so then, in making this world, this ecosystem of the story of kids who can't make it, I included the Baltimore riots. I also included the coming down of the Confederate flag by Bree Newsome in Charleston, South Carolina, after those hideous murders. So, that's briefly what it's about. As you can see, there's never really one sentence.

LADIPO MANYIKA: So, Anna, starting with *Fires in the Mirror* and then *Twilight*, all the way through now to *Notes From the Field*, there are issues, things that ail America, that keep coming up over and over again. And there's a character in *Notes From the Field* that says something to the effect of, 'I am tired of being tired.'

Do you feel like that?

SMITH: I don't feel like that. I'm a hope-aholic. I think somewhere, probably before college and before acting school, I can't tell you where at all, I understood that this was going to be a big project, not my work, but that I was going to be living in a big project. I certainly started to glean that when Martin Luther King was killed. I was at a school – a women's college unfortunately named Beaver College – and when I arrived there were seven Black women. I think one of them is actually tuning in, Karen McKee Krisberg. Of the seven, there were three upperclassmen. And then us in this freshman class because schools like Beaver, as my counselor told my mother, that year were looking for nice Negro girls like Anna, so off I go. And we were nothing alike in many ways.

So, I think we were a little bit self-conscious about each other. It's not like they had a party when we arrived. There was no Black Students Union or anything like that. But when Martin Luther King was murdered, that's the moment we came together, and we were the Beaver College Blacks. And we certainly weren't walking critiques, but then we quickly became walking critiques and we managed to get the first African American teacher, and we managed to get a Black Studies class.

I don't know if that's when I entered the world of the not-yet-perfect-union, or if it was earlier. So, I understand that this is a big, big project and I don't feel hopeless. As I've mentioned, I'm a hope-aholic. And one of the reasons that I go to catastrophic places to do my work is because I remember a long, long time ago, long time ago, interviewing a pediatric cancer surgeon.

And I said, 'Well, why cancer?' And he said, 'Because I get to do bigger operations.'

And so, I'm in the midst of a big operation. I don't expect it to be right. Maybe when people feel hopeless, they're expecting it to be right. It's not right.

LADIPO MANYIKA: Anna, can you give us a taste of one of your characters from *Notes From the Field*?

SMITH: Sure. So, this is kind of like asking an opera singer, 'Could you sing?' Just to say, this is made for theater. These are actual real words, actual, exact, real words, and I'll be reading, so the words will definitely be exact, of Kevin Moore, who took the video of Freddie Gray, who was beaten by Baltimore Police. And it was believed, universally almost, that he was killed while in police custody, or at least died while in police custody. So this is word for word from Kevin Moore, who I interviewed in Baltimore when I went down there right after the riots that followed the death of Freddie Gray:

> The screams [are] what woke me out of my *sleep*. The *screamin'*. I'm like, well, 'What's all this screaming?' And then they came to pull me up, like, 'Dude, they tasin' him, they tasin' him! I'm like, Wooh!' [*High-pitched.*] So I jumped up and threw some clothes on and went out to see what was going on, you know. And then I came out that way, and I'm like, 'Holy shit!' You know what I'm saying?
>
> They had him all bent up and he was handcuffed and, like, facedown on his stomach. But they had the— the heels of his *feet* like almost in his back? And he was handcuffed at the time. And they had the knee in the neck, and that pretty much explains the three cracked vertebrae and crushed lernix [*pronunciation of* larynx], eighty per cent of his spinal cord being severed and

stuff. And then when they picked him up, I had to zoom in to get a closer look on his face. You could see the *pain* in his face, you know what I'm saying? But then they pulled around on Mount Street and pulled him out *again!* To put leg shackles on him. You put leg shackles on a man that could barely walk to the paddy wagon? That don't make sense to me. And I've never known a-a-a on-the-beat officer to carry leg shackles in— on their person or in a van, that's something that you do when you're going to another compound or when you're being transported to the court or something like that. They don't put leg shackles on you outside, they just don't do it! You know, so you put leg shackles on a man that can't walk. You know. Then you toss him in the back of a paddy wagon like a dead animal. You know what I'm saying? Then you don't even put a seat belt on him. So basically, he's handcuffed, shackled, sliding back and forth in a steel cage, basically. 'Cause that's what— it's not *padded* back there. I don't know why everybody seems to say, 'Oh, oh, uh it's a pad— it's padded.' *No*, it's not padded! It's about— it's— it's about as padded as v— the outside of that van.

It's *ridiculous* how bad they hurt that man. I mean, come on, a crushed lernix? Can you do that to yourself? Three cracked vertebrae? Can you do that to yourself? Can you sever eighty per cent of your own spinal cord? You know what I'm saying? In the back of a wagon, shackled and handcuffed, no less? I wish you could just see how they had him. So I'm like, 'Man, this shit is just crazy, man. They just don't care anymore!' Man, I just feel like we need to *record* it. You know what'm saying? We need to get this word out that this thing is— is happening. This is the only weapon that we *have* that's actually . . . the camera's the only thing that we have that can actually protect us, that's *not* illegal, you know what I'm saying? But in— in the same sense, these guys could feel threatened or, 'Oh, well, I mistook this camera for a gun.' You know what I'm saying? So that's what I'm sayin'! [Like I said,] I haven't really filmed anything before, or been known for filmin', you know what I'm saying?

But *that* time I was like, man, 'Somebody has to *see* this.' You know what I mean? 'I have to *film* this.' When I touched back down around, I just basically called every news station that I could and just got that video out there! You know, mainstream thirteen, forty-five, uh, eleven, *New York Times, Russia Today.* [*Laughs.*] I don't even speak *Russian* but, you know, I did the interview.

[*Answering a question.*] No, it was actually, [I took it with] my phone! [*Laughs.*] And . . . I had some brothers from Ferguson, and they came out and supported me. Yeah, and they actually spent the night in my house! My brothers from Ferguson, they took me to *Best* Buy. And brought me four cameras. Basically *arming* me! It's a movement. It's not gonna stop here.

[*Answering a question.*] Eye contact. This *story* [of Freddie Gray's eye contact] was with the— the *whole story* since it be— since it happened. That's how the officers, I guess, wrote the paperwork: That [Freddie] made eye contact. And he looked suspicious. Oh, 'And that gave us probable cause to' . . . do whatever. We know the truth, y'know what I'm saying? Just a glance. The eye contact thing, that— it— it— it— it— sets off, it's like a trigger. That's all it takes in Baltimore, is just a glance.

[*He sits down somewhere – a step, a curb, a box. He starts to cry.*]

Have you ever been to a place where . . . [*six-second pause*] . . . you don't *feel* tired – you *tired* of being tired. You know'm saying? Where you *fed* up. And it's nothing else left. And you can't get any lower? [*He listens to an*

155

answer.] *Past* that. You know? So . . . That's where I've been. [*He listens to a question.*]

Gotta keep climbing. You gotta keep fightin'. You gotta keep climbing. You gotta keep praying. You gotta keep doing all'v the things that you know can make you stronger because in the end [*a deep inward breath*], you just gonna need all the strength that you can to muster to git yourself from that hole, it's like a bunch of crabs trying to pull you back. You know what I'm saying? It's like *quicksand*. And you fighting and you fighting you just sinking faster and faster. You know.

And I hate it that Baltimore is going through such harsh times right now. The fact that my children might have to fight this fight, you know? I'm not gonna be here forever. You know'm saying? Then how do I train my children to deal with this, you know what I'm saying?

[*He stands up listens, listens to a question from the interviewer/audience.*]

The leaders? Right now, man, the leaders are looking pretty assholeish. Uh. Look. It's— it's just so much the leaders can do. You know what I'm sayin'? It's only so mu— so much they can say. But at the end of the day the leaders gonna make up their minds. They're gonna *do* what they wanna *do*, you know what'm saying, so . . . we have to make it better, not wait *around* for *them* to make it better. These people are tired and— and— and they want *answers*. And it seems like the only way they can get answers, to them, is if they cost the city money!

LADIPO MANYIKA: You've just given us a sense of how you embody characters and you tell a profound story through the words of your characters. Anna, you performed *Notes From the Field* in England. You're a great observer of America, and you are also just a great observer of the world. When you were in London, we were messaging each other and you said that you went to a different church every day. Can you talk about why you chose to do that?

SMITH: I often say I'm not a church woman, but being in the presence of where many people have prayed is a very powerful experience, and it is sort of a unifying experience.

When I'm performing, in particular, I find that when I can go to that energetic source where people have been praying, and some people have been suffering, and some people have been learning, it's really just so centering. In America, there are not many churches that are open anymore during the day, and all over London, churches are open in the day. I'm an Episcopalian and I went to many of them, and it was a really important part of conditioning myself to meet the audiences every night.

LADIPO MANYIKA: I've often said to you, Anna, that I think you're an artist ahead of your time. Your book *Talk to Me* includes many conversations you had with people in Washington. And one of your plays was around presidencies and leadership and it was not well reviewed at the time that it came out. Do you think America is ready for that play right now?

SMITH: When I don't do well, mainly I'm upset that people spent money on me and it didn't come through. *House Arrest* was the name of the play, and it was a huge project. I interviewed 520 people. I went on both [Bob] Dole and [Bill] Clinton's campaign trail, could not have done it without extraordinary support from the theater. And the chairman of the board at the time was a man named Riley Temple, an extraordinary man. And the day that the review came out, we went to breakfast together at the Four Seasons in Washington. And he's a really cool man who understands artists, but I remember him saying, and naming the critic, 'That [name of critic] is terrible.'

And so, as it turns out, we met again at the Four Seasons on the day of the inauguration of Trump. And we sat there and he said, 'Now is the time for *House Arrest.* Now's the time,' because it's about presidents and the press, and it's about American history, and it's about the flaws. And so I think, if anybody wants to do a production, please do. You can get the script through Dramatists Play Service.

LADIPO MANYIKA: I love your book, *Letters to a Young Artist,* with advice and thoughts about being an artist. Would you give the same advice today?

SMITH: Well, yes. The book is written to a fictitious high school student. It isn't clear whether it's a boy or a girl, the race is not clear. My editor, LuAnn Walther called me and said, 'I think you have a younger audience than you know.' And I said, 'Well, what about something like Rilke's *Letters to a Young Poet*?'

And so I'm talking to this one specific kid that I've made up in my mind. And one of the things I keep stressing in the book is that art has its place in the world, and that we as artists are sort of universalist, even as we are in particular. If I were doing *Letters to a Young Artist,* volume 2, I would talk a lot about making something new. And I would talk a lot about the termites in the house, in institutions where art is created and presented. And I would talk all about opportunity.

And, in fact, when I teach and start on Sunday, teaching at NYU, I'm going to be encouraging my students, even as the class is called one-person shows, to really look at the termites in the house as opportunities to make new structures around which we can make new things, new kinds of support.

So, I would really talk about just throwing it away so you can look and see what's good, and rebuild arts 'Institutions', as we know them.

LADIPO MANYIKA: That's beautiful. I'll remember that . . . In closing, a few quick questions. If there's anything you could change about the way that people see or think of the African diaspora, what would it be?

SMITH: It's much more diverse than you can possibly imagine.

LADIPO MANYIKA: And who is your favorite artist from the African diaspora?

SMITH: That is a really, really, really hard question. Of course, we all revere Wole Soyinka, right? But I was also incredibly influenced by Barney Simon of the Market Theater in South Africa, because that theater really was speaking directly to apartheid, and speaking to the world, and was a very important part of bringing apartheid down. So, I'd say the Market Theater.

LADIPO MANYIKA: And who do you feel is the most under-appreciated artist?

SMITH: I don't know that this individual is under-appreciated, but I don't think I feel her getting the full glory that she deserves, and that is Ntozake Shange. And if for no other reason that when my African American women students get up to perform, they're almost always – and how many years are we after *For Colored Girls* [*Who Have Considered Suicide / When the Rainbow is Enuf*]? Forty! They weren't even alive – talking in the same rhythms that she first spoke in that play, *For Colored Girls*.

So, I think we need to have a Ntozake Shange Street, if we don't have one. And San Francisco's a perfect place for it, because a lot of the play was created in bars of San Francisco. And it's also the type of city that would get it, that we need a Ntozake Shange Street, or at least a Ntozake Shange Way.

8.

WILLARD HARRIS

On Meeting – A Century of Us

My second novel follows the adventures of Dr Morayo Da Silva, a flamboyant, sensual woman dancing on the edge of old age. I initially envisaged my character as being in her eighties, but, given the exuberant life I imagined for her, I was talked into lowering her age. In the novel, she's seventy-four, which is still a stretch for some readers. Then I met Mrs Harris.

We were seated next to each other at a nail salon, each of us getting mani-pedis. She spoke with a slight Southern drawl, wore her hair in a neat afro, and looked smart in tailored black trousers and a lavender pink sweater. She appeared impeccably groomed with an eye for fashion. I thought I'd met a real-life Morayo, a fabulous older woman in her seventies, until Mrs Harris mentioned a seventy-fifth reunion. Puzzled, I wondered if she'd misspoken. Leaning towards me, she whispered, 'I'm ninety-six and turnin' ninety-seven next month.' Stunned, I just had to know more.

Mrs Harris, I discovered, was the first African American Director of Nurses at a major San Francisco hospital in 1964. She had long since retired from nursing but still worked part-time as a proctor, 'a security guard' she joked, making sure the students 'don't cheat'. The seventy-fifth reunion had been for her alma mater, Meharry Medical College of Nursing, from which she had graduated in 1941. She was a member of their legacy group and also active with her college sorority, Delta Sigma Theta ('Deltas') where she chaired the Arts and Letters Committee. She also served as a church lay minister, did water aerobics twice a week, and had started piano lessons to help with arthritis in her fingers.

On the day after we got our nails done, on the eve of the 2016 presidential election, Mrs Harris worked all day as a volunteer, managing our local poll station. She'd seen a lot in her lifetime and continued to keep herself politically and socially informed and engaged. A few weeks later, she was up at 5:00am, taking an elderly friend, a decade younger than she, to the hospital.

Mrs Harris had promptly declared me her 'new best friend'. She insisted I call her Willard, and asked if I'd like to join her and a friend for an early morning walk – laps around Kezar Stadium. She drove there from her house. She explained that walking with others kept her motivated, but what soon emerged was that her rich social life seemed just as important as the exercise itself. She had friends and family near and far. A grandson and great-grandchildren lived in Germany. Email was how she suggested we stay in touch.

And perhaps it was because Willard kept herself so busy that she didn't appear anxious about things I would have expected her to worry about. Teeth extractions, for example. The day after her dental surgery, I phoned to see how she was doing. There was no answer, so I went to her house and left a small gift by the front door. I thought she might have been sleeping. She explained later in an email:

Dear Sarah – how sweet of you!!!! – I will surely enjoy, beginning with tonight (teeth or no teeth). I went shopping –

bought a new bathing suit, top to match (blue) and a pair of
BOOTS (now that it has stopped raining – who knows it may
rain again).
    Willard

Willard's age didn't seem to stop her from seizing life or being open to new things. She was quick to laugh at herself, joking about things like not getting a tattoo, only because she'd heard it hurts, or having taken swimming lessons in every town she'd lived in – from Jackson, Tennessee, to New York and San Francisco – yet still not knowing how to swim. And no, she wasn't 'bout to let me write her life's story because she had 'too many secrets', including the fact that her gentleman friend didn't know she was older than him. And so it was that we would sometimes roar with laughter, 'Just like two crazy women,' she said, after we discussed what I should wear to a fancy dinner party rather than the occasion itself. 'Stand up there and look pretty, like Michelle! And make me proud!' she exclaimed, triggering a new round of laughter. And in a manner that reminds me of some of my African relatives, she calls my husband *her* husband and when I'm traveling, she'll phone him to see that he's OK. She'll cook for him too – gumbo, banana bread or her legendary deviled eggs.

Willard wasn't prone to giving advice, but when I asked what she'd tell a younger self she immediately replied: 'Not to sweat the small things' and 'To live every day like this is the last day of your life, because it could be!' She was also quick to push back whenever I described her as exceptional. 'I'm still learning,' she told me early on. 'Trying to decide which bridges to cross and which bridges to burn.' Our conversations were peppered with what Willard liked to call her 'sayings' – too blessed to be stressed; don't take your pain in advance; nobody's gonna die if you say no; no such thing as error, just opportunities for learning. After each of these, Willard would invariably add: 'I don't always practice what I say, but I think about it!'

—

In her 100th year and just before the pandemic, Willard was still driving and working. One of her jobs included checking people's IDs at San Francisco's largest tech conference, Dreamforce, which saw over 170,000 attendees during the week she worked. She continued to keep busy with her church, her sorority and her piano lessons, which now included recitals. In 2020, a few weeks shy of her 101st birthday, Willard had every intention of continuing to work at the poll station on election day. She'd been watching the presidential debates and was worried about Donald J. Trump getting a second term. As the election date drew near, her children urged her not to work at the polls that year, not because of Covid but for fears of possible election violence. For the first time in over a decade, Willard did not work at the polling station.

During the first year of Covid lockdown, Willard and I kept socially distanced and stayed in touch by phone and email. I remember her complaining about wasting too much time playing 'silly games' on her phone. But from what I could gather, she led a busy Zoom life, which included senior bingo, stationary bike classes and church services. She was also tech savvy enough to know when she needed to reinstall her browser to support new versions of Zoom. In the summer of 2021, we decided to start walking every week, if our schedules permitted, hers being busier than mine.

Our route is a half mile loop up and down the gentle hills of our neighborhood. Willard wears a soft cap to keep her head warm and a sweatshirt, usually the mocha-colored one with the five Olympic rings, which she jokes is probably older than I. She uses a cane now which gives a steady beat to our walk. Tap-tap-tap. In the first few months, Willard only allowed me to take her hand when we crossed the street, but these days I hold her hand the whole way and she laughs at how she previously didn't want it. Willard does most of the talking, never seeming to run out of breath, but between blocks she pauses for a few moments to rest her back against a wall or tree trunk. Frequently, we're stopped by neighbors or passersby who smile and then look at Willard in disbelief when they find out, because I can't resist telling them, just how old she is.

On our walks we exchange family news and talk about current events. In the early months we spoke about Covid and the various medical updates. Willard wanted to know how my family was dealing with Covid in England and how things were for my mother-in-law in Zimbabwe. More recently, we've been talking about the war in Ukraine. Willard is pleased with how Biden is leading and lending support to Ukraine and hopes he'll keep firm and not send 'our boys' to war. We've also spoken about *Roe v. Wade* and the looming possibility of this landmark ruling being overturned. 'If they take that away from us, what else are they going to take from us?' Willard mulls.

Willard is fond of the daytime talk show *The View*, so sometimes our conversations are prompted by what was discussed on the show. This includes celebrity news from the 'umh-umh-umh' of the Will Smith slap to . . . 'Why is it that people is hatin' on Viola Davis [over her portrayal of Michelle Obama in a new TV series]?' But mainly what we talk about are the ordinary things of life: the life and times of Willard's pet goldfish; the antics of Domino, her daughter's puppy who ate a stick of butter, then got a hold of Willard's false teeth and started chewing on those too! We also talk about books. Willard lends me one written by her dentist, on the importance of being one's own healthcare advocate, while I give Willard a copy of *Caste* by Isabel Wilkerson. And, now that Lent is over, Willard has returned to her beloved morning ritual of drinking coffee with a splash of Korbel's brandy. I ask if this is the secret to her longevity. Willard laughs, then reminds me that, 'The good Lord must have reason to keep me alive.'

At the end of March 2022, Willard is in the news, featured on the front cover of San Francisco's Recreation & Parks summer newsletter. In the photograph she's standing in the shallow end of her beloved Rossi swimming pool holding up the hand of one of San Francisco's Recreation & Parks Commissioners. The accompanying article is entitled: *Oldest Recreation Participant Returns to Her Favorite Class* with the following description:

> *Willard Harris nimbly climbed up the stairs of the recently renovated Rossi Pool to make a return to her favorite, Aqua Yoga. Harris is the oldest recreation participant in our system, who was born in 1919 and turned 102 this past December. She had not been to the pool since it closed for renovation in 2019, but religiously attended the class prior to the closure. Once in the water, she greeted old friends, and new participants. She moved as spryly as anyone else in the pool, completing the whole class even after a three-year hiatus.*

Willard has agreed to donate her brain to medical science, and she's now the subject of two longevity studies. Every few months she's interviewed by a researcher. When I ask what sorts of questions and tests they give her, I'm impressed by the detail with which she remembers the various memory, cognitive and physical testing. She adds that she's truthful when they ask if she's noticed any changes. 'I say, yes. I have noticed that my memory is not as good, yet I'm better than my daughter.' She chuckles, then quips, 'She can't remember sh*t!'

It's Willard's daughter who urges me to ask her mother about her early life, but the most interesting glimpses into the past come unprompted. On more than one occasion, especially when we pass other walkers, Willard mentions how 'back in the day' she used to have to step off the pavement for white people. It's at moments like this that I feel transported back to Ann

Petry's 1946 novel, *The Street*, or to one of Zora Neale Hurston's short stories, with Willard as the spunky main character. The name Willard, she explains, was given to her by her mother who named her after a prize fighter, Jess Willard – a very racist, bigoted white man, she adds. Willard never met her father and her mother died from TB at the age of thirty. Several years later, the aunt looking after Willard also died. Willard did not have an easy childhood, further marked by colorism. Her skin was deemed too dark.

Our walks always end with some minutes of sitting on Willard's stoop. It's here one day that we go over a speech Willard is to give to the Meharry Medical College Nurses Legacy Group. I learn from her speech that part of her nurse's training was done at Homer G. Phillips Hospital in St Louis, which was, at the time, the only public hospital for African American nurses in a city with segregated facilities. I also learn that, in 1941, she was named the best all-round nurse of her class. I reassure Willard that she doesn't have to memorize her three-page speech. 'Oh, but I wanted to show off with the speech and memorize it so that people could be so impressed,' she says, reminding me that this is what she did with her one hundredth birthday speech. She agrees eventually that it's not necessary, adding, 'Why stress myself?'

I'm in London on the day Willard gives her speech and, when I tune in virtually, she's looking resplendent in her double string of pearls. She's sitting in front of her dining-room cabinet with a sign at the top that reads *Love You More*, the words she uses to end our phone calls. 'Looking good!' I type in private chat and then catch the flicker of a smile when she reads it.

A few weeks later, it's Willard's turn to give me advice on my writing as we sit on her stoop. I'm writing the introduction to my forthcoming book and feeling particularly despondent in the wake of a recent racially motivated shooting in Buffalo. I ask if she thinks America has made much progress around race in her lifetime. 'Yes!' Willard insists, reminding me that to have had a Black president and to have Black congressmen and women is a big deal. Such things, she repeats, were unheard of in her day. And, lest I forget, education is no longer segregated and the same for housing. She tells me that when she first moved to San Francisco, in 1957, the woman next door wouldn't speak to her because she was Black.

'Don't you think we've come a long ways?' Willard asks, earnestly. And as she gives me a long probing look, I know that I cannot afford to despair, especially not when I consider what Willard and her generation endured and how hard they fought for change. Before I can respond she lists more examples of progress made and reminds me that even interracial marriages and same sex marriages were completely unheard of back in her time. "Course some of those white folks have not gotten over it yet,' she adds, wryly. 'But I don't think any Black person can disagree with me that we've come a long way and that we've still got a ways to go.'

CHANGEMAKERS

My ambition was and is to shine a light on as many as possible of the deserving, whether or not they are acknowledged or lauded by the gatekeepers, who traditionally single out a privileged few, seemingly never too many to rock the boat. But the boat is going nowhere if it is content to drift in stagnating water.

– Margaret Busby,
New Daughters of Africa: An International Anthology of Writing by Women of African Descent, 2019

9.

MICHELLE OBAMA

On Meeting

FROM A DISTANCE

When I caught my first glimpse of her, looking so tall and elegant in her pink silk blouse and dark skirt, I held my breath. It was my first time in the same room as her. I was enthralled, but also worried that she might trip, coming down the grand staircase in high heels without holding the banister as she waved. In this moment, I realized that I'd been holding these twin emotions – admiration and concern for her – from the very beginning.

'Four more years!' someone cried, as the President announced this would be their last Christmas in the White House. 'But we will still celebrate Christmas,' the President laughed, 'and maybe, next time, we'll come to your house.' Unappeased, people turned to the subject of their hopes and started chanting her name: 'Michelle! Michelle!' We stood on tiptoe, hoping for a clearer view above the sea of hands raised high with phones.

We'd seen Michelle Obama on the front covers of magazines, we'd heard her give speeches, we'd watched her dance, and we'd counted all those push-ups on *The Ellen DeGeneres Show*. The 'we' that was in awe seemed to include everyone I talked to, from Lagos to London, from Rome to Bangalore. Even in conversation with complete strangers, we would talk about her – about our favorite images, a cherished moment, her poise and how she made us feel, seeing her in 'that role', in 'that place' – the White House, the People's House, the nickname embraced by the Obamas. We did not know her personally other than what was presented to us, yet we spoke of her with a first-name familiarity, as though she were one of us.

We'd also heard and felt annoyed by the many who mocked her, in the never-ending diatribe of sexist and racist jabs. This 'daily diminishment' as the poet Claudia Rankine has aptly named it, ranged from digs at her physique and her clothing (how dare she wear sleeveless dresses!), to taking her words out of context so as to make her sound unpatriotic. Through her embrace of technology @FLOTUS (the first First Lady with a Twitter presence) and her many initiatives, including well-being and healthy eating, there was plenty from which to guess at what she was like. But she was also famously guarded. We knew that as a Black woman in America she faced more scrutiny than any other previous First Lady. There was ~~little~~ no room for her to make mistakes.

I've thought about Michelle Obama more than any previous First Lady, perhaps because I felt a greater sense of kinship with her than with her predecessors. We were both Black, close in age, had children at the same time, and, despite our own achievements, were known as 'the wife of' – with all the baggage that notion carried. I admired her and marveled at how she'd survived eight years with such grace. That alone felt like a feat. I've often looked at pictures of her and wondered: When you walked out on stage that night, in November 2008, and saw the thousands cheering and crying at the news of your husband's election, was it electrifying or terrifying to watch behind bulletproof glass – arms outstretched to you and your family?

When you stepped into the White House and greeted many of the Black staff in that historically white White House, what was that like, really? Did the White House feel like a home, a fortress, or a prison? Your glam shots, the dancing shots – were they as effortless as they looked? Hair? Oh, the questions we could ask about hair!

Now I was seeing the First Lady, for the first time, unmediated by cameras or other people editing or packaging her. We were physically close, yet she remained an enigma. I'd hoped she might speak but, on this occasion, she chose not to. As I looked around the room, I wondered what everyone else was thinking. That year, I'd been reading essay submissions for an anthology of writings by women of color, many of whom referenced the Obama family as a source of hope and inspiration. The essays came from women of all ages and backgrounds just like those around me now. As we stood looking at her together, I found myself joined by characters that had followed me to the People's House from my bookshelves back home. These included Toni Morrison's characters – Pecola, Golden, Sethe, Beloved, Cee, Sweetness and Bride – all dotted around the room in a house once built by slaves, a house they could never have imagined being invited to as guests, let alone standing as equals with those who were white.

Sethe, Beloved and friends had arrived with me earlier, through the East Gate, to stand with my husband and I in a slow-moving line with other guests, bracing the cold between checkpoints. We were a diverse group – Black, white, brown, young and old – that looked like America. Arriving at the East Wing, we checked in coats and wandered through brightly lit corridors, past giant nutcrackers and heavily decorated Christmas trees. A Marine Corps band played holiday music while uniformed staff carried silver trays and platters, replenishing food-laden tables. Now, here we were in the presence of a First Couple that looked like us. And not only were they Black, but the First Lady was dark skinned – the skin tone that has historically borne the brunt of racial discrimination (just ask Pecola and Bride) – yet here she stood, a woman of irrefutable beauty and grace in a room chanting her name.

As my husband and I left, along with America and history's characters, we stopped to look back at the White House from the side gate. 'Take a good long look,' said someone, 'because we may never be back. We'll never see this many people like us in the White House again.'

IN PERSON

In the summer of 2017, racial tension was again running high in America and culminated in the white nationalist rally in Charlottesville, which left one person dead and many injured. At the time, we were on a family vacation in Martha's Vineyard where, just a few days after Charlottesville, we attended the annual Hutchins Forum hosted by Professor Henry Louis Gates, Jr, and moderated by Charlayne Hunter-Gault, a warrior for racial and gender equity in America and abroad. The theme for that year's public forum was 'Race and Racism in the Age of Trump'. The debate had been heated, and I felt despondent and fearful for the safety of my teenage son who sat with us through the debate that afternoon. What would it take for people to understand just how bad things were? When would people really start to care about Black lives? All this with my son next to me brought back the heaviness that had led me several years earlier to write an essay on my fears for young Black men in America.

As always with these things, I tried not to burden my son with my concerns for his safety, and especially not on an evening when he was invited to a send-off for some kids his age starting college in the fall. It was an indoor bowling party that looked and sounded like thousands of other parties that might have taken place across the country that summer, but because it was being hosted by the former First Family, there was no way our son could affect an attitude of cool indifference. He was excited, and we were excited for him.

Later that evening, when we drove to join our son in Oak Bluffs, known historically as the Black haven on the island, a group of young people with a sprinkling of parents were still bowling and enjoying themselves. Hip hop's summer hits (Kendrick, The Weeknd, Migos) were playing, heads were bopping and bodies swaying, food was still laid out, and people were laughing and talking while those bowling were teasing and trash-talking. Most were everyday people and mainly African Americans. I could not help but be lifted and thrilled by the bright, beautiful, college-bound students.

My husband, who had been appointed to a White House advisory council by President Obama, introduced me to him. We exchanged greetings and spoke briefly before he was off – intent, it seemed, on winning his game, which had noticeably improved since his early campaign days when he'd been mocked for 'dainty' bowling. While I watched the children bowling and having fun, I spoke with the poet Elizabeth Alexander, whose recent memoir, *The Light of the World* – on life with her late husband, an artist born in Eritrea – had greatly moved me. I was so consumed with our conversation that I didn't notice Mrs Obama sitting behind us. When my husband interrupted us to introduce me to her, I was startled.

As we shook hands, I started to stammer, trying to explain that I was even more excited to meet her than her husband. In my attempt to be deferential, I could hear myself coming across as awkward and gushing. She smiled kindly, politely, at what I felt were my flubbed-up first few minutes of meeting. There she was, tall, goddess-like, with hair tumbling down her shoulders. She had big eyes and long eyelashes. She wore clear lip gloss and a wrist full of colorful bangles. She was even more striking in person than in her pictures. I was seeing Mrs Obama for the first time in her self-described role as 'mom-in-chief' among her close friends, many from Chicago with children the same age as hers. They danced, laughed together, and occasionally bowled, all the while watching over the fine young ones they'd raised. It made me happy to see Mrs Obama and her family looking relaxed and at home, doing things that people do with ordinary friends.

Soon we were interrupted by a parade of young people that came to hug Mrs Obama and thank her as they said their goodbyes. I noted the reverence with which young people approached her and the ease of their interactions, the kind that one has with a favorite, cool aunt who knows exactly how to connect. She looked at them, as she'd looked at me, straight in the eye, holding their gaze. These were the lucky ones, many of whom were young men like my son. But even for the lucky ones, outside of these cocooned walls lay the real world with all its special complications waiting for them. For now, celebrating with our children before sending them out into the world, I tried to keep these anxious thoughts to myself, but wondered what she would have thought had I shared them. I did later learn what she thought about these issues in her book.

My second meeting with Mrs Obama took place one year later, at another late summer bowling party. She greeted me with a hug, and this time I felt comfortable enough to call her by her first name. As we spoke, one of the women serving food brought a specially prepared plate of spicy shrimp for Michelle to sample. I don't know if Michelle had requested this or if it was just something the woman knew she liked. Either way, Michelle was attentive and appreciative. Acknowledging those working behind the scenes – from chefs to aides and secret service – is, as I would later notice in her book, something she always does.

I felt at ease talking with her and comfortable enough to be myself and ask about her forthcoming book. I felt a sense of kinship around our shared interest in the importance of women's stories. I also sensed that, when I spoke about my own experience as a writer, she listened with genuine interest. Her genuineness was something that even those who'd never met her could feel. I was reminded of this recently when my twelve-year-old goddaughter, Tenjiwe, who lives in Johannesburg, described Michelle Obama as 'a person who means what she says, unlike other famous people who will not do what they say.' I told Michelle that I expected her book would do well in America and also internationally. She nodded, seeming appreciative of my enthusiasm, but not flattered by it. I wondered if she was wary of setting her expectations too high – perhaps like any writer awaiting the release of a first book, she felt a mix of excitement and trepidation.

I met Michelle again at a Family and Friends book reception which I'd been invited to by our mutual friend, Michele Norris. The two Michelles would later be in conversation together on stage. The reception was small – no more than two dozen of us, including a five-year-old princess in white tutu ready to twirl and play. By then, I'd read *Becoming* and enjoyed it so much that I'd also listened to the audiobook read by Michelle. When Michelle made her way to where I stood with my husband and our friends, we were eager to congratulate her and talk about the book.

We asked about everything from what it was like to have recorded the book for audio (she'd used a pillow to muffle any stomach sounds), to her writing process (collaborative, working with a small team), to what she might write next. She didn't say what might come next, but nodded to one of her team when I suggested writing for young people.

I asked her if there had been a point in the writing when she'd made a long list of all the nasty things people had said about her, just as a way of getting it off her chest. I was struck by how little mention there is of the nastiness in her book. She smiled, in what I took to be an acknowledging that she had revisited all of it. But as she didn't dwell on it, I got the feeling that retaliation and keeping score wasn't her style, and I admired this.

We carried on, all of us, talking as writers do, and possibly for too long. Soon her assistant was pulling her away to meet others, but before she left she urged us to continue giving feedback and suggestions. In being so open to feedback and new ideas, it struck me that she was continuing to embody the title of her book. 'Becoming' means that one is never done – that there is room for personal growth, with the implication that one can always do better. In this respect, Michelle reminded me of my friend and neighbor Mrs Harris, who started piano lessons in her nineties, and who continues to show me that she is still learning and becoming.

MICHELLE ROBINSON

'If you wanna know Michelle Obama, you've got to know that little girl Michelle Robinson in all her contexts,' said Michelle, on stage at a book tour stop. 'You can't judge me unless you know all of that. You can't revere me unless you know all of my bumps and bruises.' And so it is that the first third of *Becoming* covers Michelle's childhood starting in the South Side of Chicago where she lived in a tiny apartment with mom, dad and brother.

While *Becoming* is a moving family memoir, it is also a story of race and inheritance. Michelle's family flight from Jim Crow South to Chicago could easily have been one of the stories chronicled in Isabel Wilkerson's historical opus, *The Warmth of Other Suns: The Epic Story of America's Great Migration*. Not only is Michelle's family story (on both sides of the family) one of migration from the South to the North, but it's also the story of racial discrimination in the segregated North. Sometimes, no amount of striving can overcome the odds stacked against one. Michelle writes about her grandfather, Dandy, a scholarly man, who had to abandon his dreams of attending college, as well as lesser dreams, in the face of discriminatory work practices on account of his skin color. He eventually became a postal worker who lived, as Michelle describes it, 'with the bitter residue of his own dashed dreams'. Racial discrimination was pervasive in Michelle's family past and its present. 'The color of our skin made us vulnerable,' she writes. Whether it was her family car being keyed when they visited a white neighborhood, or the police officer who assumed her brother had stolen his brand-new bike, or Michelle's white dorm mate whose family moved her out so she wouldn't have to room with Black people, race, as Michelle writes, 'was a thing we'd always have to navigate.' Her college experience at the elite, majority-white institution of Princeton – where the burden of assimilation was placed on Black students – was also a part of this story of race.

Had I been reading about Michelle's childhood from my childhood home in Jos, Nigeria, I might have been surprised to hear of the persistence of racial profiling and discrimination in America. Nigeria had its own challenges, but has no history of apartheid and no established tradition of societies structured along racial lines, so, in contrast to Michelle, I didn't experience race as a defining element of my upbringing or identity. And as a child, much of what I gleaned about America from its music and TV was positive. In 1978, I wrote to President Jimmy Carter's daughter, Amy, curious to know what life was like in the White House. She was the same age as me and, at the time, her father's name was frequently mentioned in adult conversation, as Nigeria was transitioning from the Westminster style of government to an American-style presidential system. As a girl, I didn't think twice about wanting to be pen pals with Amy. I wonder now, had I been a young Black girl from Chicago's South Side, would I have been as enamored? Indeed, would a letter from Chicago's South Side have been answered as quickly as mine was, coming as it did from a foreign country?

I found myself pondering Michelle's school photographs which showed the shift from an ethnically diverse kindergarten classroom to one that became predominantly Black by fifth grade – the result of white flight. This change in classroom demographics mirrored mine, except that at the American missionary school that I attended in Nigeria, where previously few Black students had once been accepted, the shift signaled progress rather than decline.

I was surprised by the degree to which I saw aspects of my childhood in Michelle's story. Perhaps this is the power of her story, in that it allows us to see aspects of ourselves in it. Listening to the responses of many who have read her book, I know that I am not alone. While others may see different things, for me, thousands of miles away from Chicago's South Side, and only five years younger than Michelle, I too grew up 'to the sound of striving' from where we lived in a tiny two-bedroom apartment (the size of the two-car garage over which it sat) on Naraguta Avenue in Jos, Nigeria. Like Mr Robinson, my father – a vicar – worked at the same job for many years and my mother stayed at home with the children.

I saw myself in her personality traits and, in particular, the extent to which she worried about being good enough. 'Are you good enough?' runs like a refrain throughout her book. This is a sentiment that many young girls and women have experienced – many of us with accompanying stories of the low expectations placed upon us based on gender and/or race. Michelle writes about her guidance counselor, who doubted whether she was 'Princeton material', noting that 'failure is a feeling long before it's an actual result.' I too experienced something similar when I'd moved to England and was attending a sixth form college. I was not encouraged to apply to Oxford and Cambridge. Instead, I was directed by the school's careers office to one of the 'caring professions' – not a doctor as I'd once dreamt of being, but a nurse or teacher. Michelle's story, while deeply rooted in the American story, speaks to experiences that are universal. It speaks to the universal challenges that women and young girls continue to face around the world, as well as to those of less privileged backgrounds where one encounters, to use Michelle's words, the 'universal challenge of squaring who you are with where you come from'.

As I read, I found additional connections to my own life. In

1991, Michelle visited Kenya with her then boyfriend, Barack Obama, the 'strange mix-of-everything man'. Because I'd lived in Kenya several years earlier and because I'd read *Dreams from My Father*, in which Barack writes of his first visits to his father's home country, I was curious to know how Michelle had found Kenya. I'd hoped she might feel some sort of connection to the country and the continent. But, as she writes, 'It's a curious thing to realize, the in-betweenness one feels being African American in Africa. It gave me a hard-to-explain feeling of sadness, a sense of being unrooted in both lands.' Her response reminded me of James Baldwin's writings, in particular his essay 'Encounter on the Seine', in which he describes the sense of 'alienation' between African Americans and Africans 'over a gulf of three hundred years'. Baldwin, who understood Africa and America well, offers in his writing bridges across this gulf. As Michelle's memoir travels around the world, I believe it too has the potential to bridge this gulf.

After living in Kenya, I moved as a teenager to Islington in London. As such, Michelle's visit to Islington's Elizabeth Garrett Anderson School, a mile from where I once lived, was of particular interest to me. The school includes many working-class students and recent immigrants. And because I could see my teenage self among these students it was easy for me to understand the positive impact of a First Lady's visit. Back in the 1980s and '90s, I used to look to America for everything from Black role models to Black hair products. The only professional Black woman that I saw on TV at that time was Moira Stuart – the first female Black British TV newsreader. While there were other professional Black British women of note, few enjoyed the visibility of their white counterparts. Looking back, it's probably no coincidence that I dreamt of being a newscaster and that the first job I applied for after leaving college was with the BBC. The First Lady's visit must have had a similarly empowering effect on those she met, for, as she notes, the school saw a marked improvement in test scores following her visit.

INSPIRER-IN-CHIEF AND ROCKSTAR

We came in our hundreds to San Jose's SAP arena, fondly known as the 'Shark Tank' for the San Jose Sharks hockey team that plays there. Ushers in white shirts and ties with royal blue blazers directed us to our seats, while uniformed and stone-faced plain-clothes security personnel hovered, ever watchful and alert. The 12,000-plus tickets had apparently sold out within minutes of going on sale and the excitement in the arena was palpable. There were more women than men, and roughly an equal mix of Black, white and brown. Some were dancing to the music, others watching and applauding to the video show and photographs being beamed around the room from many giant screens. Some in the audience clutched hardback books with pale-blue and white covers, the way one might clutch a Bible or a banner, were this a religious revival or convention. Many had come with friends or family, and the looks on people's faces conveyed excitement and anticipation. Music pulsated through the arena – well-loved tunes from the Jackson Five and Aretha Franklin to more contemporary hits from Beyoncé and Ellie Goulding. When Whitney Houston's 'I Wanna Dance With Somebody' came on, I was transported to my student days at the NEC Birmingham, England, thirty years earlier, at concerts with crowds of equal size for performers like Whitney Houston and Sade at the height of their careers.

Ten minutes before start time, the already loud music was raised a notch as a countdown began. At zero, the lights went out and the words *HEY SAN JOSE* flashed across the screens. From backstage came a familiar-sounding woman's voice announcing: 'I'm so happy to be here! I have one question for all of you tonight.' Then, one by one, with strobe lights and high-beam stage lights sweeping across the crowd, came the words *WHO / ARE / YOU / BECOMING* heralding the pre-show. Then came Michele Norris who, in her signature warm radio voice introduced the woman we'd all been waiting for. The stadium erupted with applause and we rose to our feet in our thousands as Michelle Obama strode on stage in a flowing pink silk pant-suit and high heels to the tune of Alicia Keys's 'Girl on Fire'.

Listening to Michelle, I realized just how good she'd become at connecting with her audience. Gone was her once shy nervousness, as well as her tendency of earlier years to speak with the same ponderous 'uhs' her husband was so fond of using. She drew on her sense of humor with playfulness – impersonating others and code-switching. To recall Zadie Smith's poignant essay 'Speaking in Tongues', Barack is not the only Obama that can speak in tongues. Michelle did all sorts of voices – from that of her husband to her mother to her children, and even George W. Bush, as illustrated by the story she began with. George, she recounted, offered her a mint at their most recent encounter at his father's funeral. The mint, she noticed, was an old White House Altoid. 'How long have you had these?' she asked him, to which he'd answered: 'We took a bunch of them before we left.' The audience roared with laughter. Michelle is fond of saying she's 'never been a fan of politics', but this doesn't mean that what she says has no connection to politics. Some of the greatest applause that night came when she gestured to the political, including the way she ended her opening story about Bush: 'We can disagree as people in our politics without demonizing each other. We don't agree on everything, but that doesn't make him any less of a person than me.'

Norris asked about how Michelle first met and fell in love with Barack. Michelle playfully referred to Barack as 'flavorful' and as a 'swervy dude', in contrast to herself. When they first met, she was Barack's advisor at a Chicago law firm and she didn't want to date her advisee: 'I was like, no, no, that'll be too tacky and that's when the white folks will be like, "See, they all love each other."' Michelle kept poking fun at herself when speaking about her and Barack's decision to seek marriage counseling, 'We were going to counseling to fix him,' she said, referring to Barack. 'And then the doctor had the nerve to look over at me, and I'm like, "What are you looking at? I'm fine. I do everything perfectly!"'

She was open about the more difficult times in her life – from the loss of a parent to the loss of her best friend, as well as her own personal struggles around self-worth. 'Find the people that believe in you,' she said, 'and stop paying attention to the few who don't know you and don't care about you and aren't thinking about you.' And, to women in particular, a lesson that I found helpful and have already quoted to girlfriends, she urged us to prioritize ourselves more than we might ordinarily do – to learn how to put ourselves on our calendars first rather than allowing everything else and everyone else to get there first.

Michelle didn't shy away from acknowledging the challenges that young people face, especially those without people to advocate for them, as her mother had done for her. 'One turn of fate, particularly for kids of color, can make the difference from sitting here or sitting in jail,' she said. 'Life is that precarious for so many kids in this country.' Rather than allowing overwhelming systemic failure to lead her to despair, she remained focused on what can and must be done. This, I realized, was important for me to remember when confronting racism in America as well, as when receiving requests for help and mentorship from high school students in my home country of Nigeria.

And then the conversation ended, as it had begun, with a nod to the political. 'Don't let fear be your guide,' she urged. 'That's one of the things that is most frustrating about these times, that that is how leaders are leading now. They're leading with fear.'

Before she left the stage, she stood up to thank the audience for their love and support. 'Let's take care of our babies!' she called out before exiting to her signature song, 'Signed, Sealed, Delivered I'm Yours'. Buoyed by Michelle's message and her call to action, we turned to smile at friends and strangers alike as we inched our way toward the exits. Some were already engaged in animated chatter, revisiting favorite parts of the night's conversation; many of us seemed to be standing taller.

As I looked around at the vast crowds, I wondered if the entrancement I'd witnessed in this arena would be the same in arenas around the world. While traveling in Europe earlier that month, I'd seen stacks of *Becoming* at airports in a number of translations. In France, *Becoming* had the same title in French: *Devenir*. But in Danish and German the translations were slightly different: *Min Historie* and *Meine Geschichte* translated back to English as 'My Story'. In America, Michelle's story had transcended that of former First Lady. I wondered if 'her story' would do the same elsewhere.

As we all streamed out of the arena on a high, I saw a man outside with a makeshift stall. He was selling T-shirts featuring Michelle's off-the-shoulder book cover image. T-shirts were twenty dollars each. I wanted a Small but he only had XXL, XL, L and M. 'Here,' he said, offering me a Medium. He looked my age, African American and, from the smell of the T-shirt tossed in my direction, a heavy smoker. He had one eye out for customers and the other eye out for the police. Life is that precarious, I was thinking, before he turned to me and said, 'It'll shrink to fit.' It struck me, looking at her likeness, that in becoming, Michelle had not shrunk to fit. But the seller had no time to linger. He had shirts to sell and a living to make.

10.

MICHAEL HASTINGS

In Conversation

Lord Michael Hastings of Scarisbrick was Chancellor of Regent's University London from 2016 to 2021 and is now Chairman of SOAS, University of London, and Professor of Leadership at the Jon M Huntsman School of Business, Utah State University. Lord Hastings began his career as a teacher before moving into government service, where he worked on policy to bring employment and development to Britain's inner cities after two rounds of violent race riots in the 1980s. He led policy and communications for the Commission for Racial Equality and founded Crime Concern where he spent twenty-one years as a trustee building safer communities and, in recognition, received a CBE in 2003. He is the former Head of Public Affairs at the BBC and was their first Head of Corporate Social Responsibility. He also served as the Global Head of Citizenship for the international accounting firm KPMG. In 2005, Hastings was conferred with a Life Peerage and sits as an Independent Peer in the House of Lords.

October 9, 2020

SARAH LADIPO MANYIKA: How are you?

MICHAEL HASTINGS: Abundantly, happily, very well. I have found the period during which we've all been struggling with coronavirus and our responses to it actually ironically somewhat of a beautifully orchestrated, restful time, being very purposeful and engaging. But, for any of us who are Black, whether African Americans or Black Brits, we've also had the horrendous pandemic of fury as a result of the horrendous display of mass murders that have gone on, especially in the US, because of police incriminatory and discriminatory shootings. So, you've got the pandemic of disease. You've got the fear that comes from it, and you've got the pandemic of fury. And I have to admit, Sarah, I've really found it emotionally difficult, because you look out on far too many decades of unresolved anguish, and it has beat hard in my heart.

LADIPO MANYIKA: The last time we spoke, when I asked how you were, you spoke of being in a state of 'irritated anxiety', and you highlighted some of the issues we have with leadership around the world. Do you still have that feeling?

HASTINGS: Yes. Irritated anxiety, because I grew up in a period of time – the 1960s, '70s, '80s – where we iconized leadership. We really expected so much from presidents and prime ministers. We expected not just tone-setting for their own nation, but there was such a duty that went beyond the well-off world into the less well-off world. I'm old enough to remember when we used to talk of China as just, 'Oh, those people over there who all wear blue boiler suits and ride bicycles.' That was our image. And now this superpower looms in front of our faces on a day-to-day basis. The world has changed so rapidly, and it's kind of ironic that, just a few years ago, it was President Xi at Davos – the

President of China – being the tone setter, the one who gave the seminal thought on the state of the world. It was very strange, but uplifting and positive.

I'm a great fan of Angela Merkel. I think she has to have been the most outstanding political leader in the democratic world on the planet. I read a profile of her which talks about how she goes shopping with her husband on a Saturday, pays her own bills, doesn't have a government car, and lives simply and purely. And somebody came up to her and said to her, 'Mrs Merkel, I took a photograph of you in that dress a few years ago.' And she said, 'Yes, precisely. I have a duty to serve the German people, not to be a model.'

There are still strong people in our democratic world that we can respect and we can adhere to, but in the US, and in the UK we've let go of too much that we once thought was the heritage we wanted to show off to the countries of Africa, the Caribbean, Asia. 'Look, come and follow the lead of our democratic systems.' And we've seen presidents, and, yes, potential presidents squabbling like children and cats in a sack, and abusive rudeness, and demeaning illogicality, and even prime ministers who wish to break international law in order to make political points. We are in a sour place.

So, yes, I do have great anguish. And part of my duty in Parliament is to make sure that I vote and speak on the things that matter deeply. One of the things I was really glad to vote on this week, and vote positively on, was a motion we brought forward in the House of Lords to ensure that people who are trafficked across Europe, through Europe's non-boundary-ness, into the UK, are not just thrown back, because they've now come from the EU into the UK. We have a duty to protect those who are trafficked, to look after them, to see them as migrants who need proper refugee status. So, the House of Lords took that on as a matter of honor, and I was glad we won that vote. But we've got to stand up for the dignity of the oppressed, and I wish leaders really believed that. That's what makes me anguished.

LADIPO MANYIKA: You have stood up for the dignity of the oppressed throughout your life. Tell us about the House of Lords, your role is as a Lord, and how many Black Lords are there?

HASTINGS: Well, I don't look very Lordly at the moment, because I'm at home. I'm in a Nelson Mandela print shirt. I have six of these, in the different colors that Nelson Mandela would wear. It all funds a charity, the Nelson Mandela Children's Hospital in Johannesburg, so I'm proud to buy them, proud to wear them. And I had the joy to meet him twice when he came through the UK, and I will never forget this one thing that he said, as an iconic leader to a group of us, which was: 'The purpose of life is to plant trees in whose shade another generation will sit.' I have carried that with me always, because that is to invest in the long life of the next community.

The House of Lords, well, we are a great ancient institution, far older than America, as it were, in its current state of life. The House of Lords was there before 1776, and it was kind of there before 1619, depending on which view of history you choose to take. The House of Lords is a Parliament appointed by Her Majesty the Queen. So, we have a bicameral system, much as in the United States where the House of Representatives and, of course, the Senate were modeled on the House of Commons and the House of Lords. The difference is that Senators have to get reelected. In the House of Lords, we never have to go out and get elected because we're appointed by the Sovereign, Her Majesty the Queen. She makes the decisions and appointments. Yes, there are about 800 in total, second largest chamber in the world after China's. Attendance is around about 450 a week, on average, because it is not a job. It is an honor and a responsibility.

The members who choose to take on the mantle of a Baron or a Baroness, who become a Lord at Her Majesty's command, are gifted with the duty to uphold the Constitution, which is invested in the monarchy and the rule of law. We don't have constituents. Elected members in the House of Commons have constituents, and they must deal with constituents' business. We have constitutional business, which involves making sure that law is properly scrutinized, is clear-sighted, that gaps are not missed, like the one over trafficked migrants, which was missed in the House of Commons. We take it up in the House of Lords. And sometimes these things cause conflict between the two chambers, as there is often conflict between the House and the Senate in the US. But that's what you have in the American system. It's meant to be the pursuit of intelligence, insight, wisdom and dignity. That's our job, and if that means voting against what the Democratic House votes against, they can forcibly turn us over if they want, but good argument is important.

So, the role of the House of Lords is to defend what is good about law, uphold the Constitution, protect the public interest, and to represent the Monarch.

LADIPO MANYIKA: You are part of the establishment, but don't come from it.

HASTINGS: Absolutely.

LADIPO MANYIKA: Tell me about your family background and the rich cultural heritage that you come from.

HASTINGS: There are many layers. I'll tell you what I know. In terms of the complexities of my background, my dear father, who died in 1976, was born in Angola. His parents had been missionaries. I understand that they had come from India. They were missionaries in the medical sense, and then also in the spiritual sense, so they built a clinic, they built a school, they built a hospital, and they built a church. And I have amazing pictures of my grandfather's work. Of course, I never met him. He was long dead before ever I was around, but I did meet my grandmother. She was unfortunately senile and not able to really speak to us, so we didn't gain anything from that experience in terms of history and knowledge.

My father was then sent, as was his brother and his sister, from Angola, from Luanda, all the way to England to go to school in Somerset, where they attended school, and then went on to Edinburgh University. All three of them studied medicine. My aunt became a general practitioner, my uncle became a surgeon, and my father became a dental surgeon who then chose to go to Jamaica to practice dental surgery. There were a lot of Indians who had set up shop in the West Indies. And so that's where he went, to a little town called Sav la Mar, and, in the process of looking down my mother's throat, fell in love with whatever was down her throat. I mean, he was a dentist.

LADIPO MANYIKA: I've never heard that one before.

HASTINGS: My mother died in 2010, but she used to tell the story of, 'Your dad just constantly wanted to fix my teeth.' She had a mixed background. Her father was from Panama, and her mother was of Ghanaian heritage, although she was obviously living in Jamaica. So I've got mixes everywhere, and I'm happy to say, I feel like a true pan-African, in the fuller sense of the word.

LADIPO MANYIKA: Earlier in your career, you worked in government service and were instrumental in bringing employment and development to Britain's inner cities. This was around the time of two rounds of violent race riots. Take us back to that time. What was going on?

HASTINGS: Well, in 1981 and 1985 there were two really uncomfortable, long and many-week-lasting rounds of urban riots. Twenty-one UK cities went up in flames – parts of

Liverpool, parts of Manchester, parts of Birmingham, different boroughs and many parts of London, parts of Bristol, parts of Newcastle. It was all over the country. And, in essence, it was the result of long-held Black anguish over unemployment and racial disparity.

Margaret Thatcher was the Prime Minister at the time. The UK absolutely needed to go through an industrial revolution, a modernization. There had to be a significant amount of privatization of state-controlled business. And the UK was bringing in coal from Eastern Europe which was much cheaper than the coal produced in the UK. So there was this huge industrial upheaval going on, and the difficulty of any form of political and economic change is that it creates too many victims, and Black people really did suffer that displaced pain. Too many lost jobs, without hope for the future, and a sense of anguish at a lack of racial freedom boiled over into the streets.

When the riots started again in 1985, there was this incredible fear it was all going to happen again in 1986. It was at that point that I had a phone call. I was a school teacher. It was half term. In those days, phones sat on desks or walls. I was sitting at a desk, and the phone rang, and it was one of Margaret Thatcher's chief advisors. I knew this man, but we hadn't spoken in six years. And he rang up to say that I needed to come in. The Prime Minister needed a job done. So, I did.

I was appointed as a consultant to work with the Department of Employment and to get around to the communities. And as I went around I was building bridges between many broken Black hurting leaders – many coming from faith communities, many others who were just community activists. They had long given up on the dream that they might matter. My job was to show them they mattered, and then to build these relationship bridges with government agents, civil servants who had money. Having the money and not having the relationship doesn't get you very far, because there has to be trust built with broken and angry communities. So that was my job.

I traversed the country for five years. It was wonderful to be able to generate ideas and get the money out of the system and invest in employment and development schemes, many of which are still standing now. I'm just thrilled at the opportunity that we had to broker a peace based on good relationships, and the guts that leadership had, to say, 'Look, come on. Let's just face reality. We might have the money, but we don't have the contacts. Let's bring in someone who's got the contacts.'

LADIPO MANYIKA: Building good relationships and establishing trust is a thread that runs through all of your work. Now, to the matter of Black lives mattering. [Post the George Floyd murder] I have heard over the past months from a fair number of friends in Europe and in London who have been watching what's happening in the States and are appalled by what they're seeing, but, almost at the same time, congratulate themselves for how good things are in Europe and in Britain. Where are we, do you think? And what would you say to someone who says, 'We're all right'?

HASTINGS: I'd say, 'Don't be naive.' I'm sure many people don't know that the UK does track ethnic diversity. You don't get that in France or Germany. It's almost as though everybody in those countries is monochromatically accepted to be the same. So we can map diversity disparities here. We can map inequalities here, but that's not the case across Europe. And, I have to say, the EU has been inadequate on that one. There is really no emphasis in the EU on racial justice, and that is a shocking indictment of such an expensive and major political institution, that it doesn't take this with the seriousness it deserves.

Britain is not where the US is. The US has a kind of ingrained institutional racism, which is extreme. I get it. I understand it, and I see it. *Time* magazine used this phrase: 'America solves its race problems through incarceration and police brutality.' And that has been the messy, uncomfortable story since the 1950s. It's been blatantly obvious. Of course, before that, you were talking about periods of complete racial disengagement, and then you go back into the slavery period before that.

Now, in the UK, Black people can vote the same as anybody else. In Britain, you don't have these kinds of voter delaying tactics which are going on across the US now. You don't have militias, which you have in the US. However, that said, if you are a young Black man in Britain, you are ten times more likely to be stopped by police authorities. And these are government figures. I haven't made these up. They are going to make some assumption that because you are young, Black and male, and probably driving a car they think you shouldn't drive, or just looking a little bit different, that you're either a drug trader or you're carrying a weapon. Now, that results in a searching process in which, according to the UK Home Office's own 2019 figures, eighty-three per cent of stops and searches result in no questionable behavior and no further action. In which case, tens of thousands of young Black men have been made angry and wounded, and in some cases assaulted.

We also have cases here in which police brutality has led to deaths. There was just an example on the news here today. And this is referring to a case from some years back, where a ruling has been brought forward. We do have our cases, but they're not at the percentage levels they are in the US, but any one [case] is unacceptable.

We have too many incidences of disadvantage, and inability to get work. This is an uncomfortable truth. If a young person with a complex African name submits a CV, it is highly likely they may not get an interview. If the same person with the same CV submits the application with a European name, they get an interview. Now, that's what you call deliberate. It's deliberate, but almost hidden racism, because it's based on a set of assumptions. We do have that intolerance, and we have uncomfortable statistics indicating if you're a Black person standing before a court, and a white person is charged with the same crime, and it's the same trial, the Black person will get a sentence four times longer than a white person.

LADIPO MANYIKA: All these statistics are very damning, and they paint the picture. I remember living in London in the 1990s and so many of my Nigerian friends, for employment purposes, were changing their names. They became the equivalent of Joe Bloggs, rather than Tunde so-and-so. We have a long way to go in England, and, as you say, figures are even more alarming in America.

HASTINGS: What the Black Lives Matter movement did from the US to the UK was to make the world understand it is still possible in 2020 to watch a Black man die live on television, in an act of determined, murderous violence by a police officer with three others watching.

Now, I'm sure you know that that particular policeman was released on bail, the bail of a million dollars. Somehow, he managed to find a million dollars to come out. Meanwhile, the family of George Floyd is still in trauma. This is the disparity of injustice, which is so extremely unacceptable. We have too many cases here, which really bother me, of miscarriages of justice. I do a lot of work in prisons, and I meet so many Black prisoners. When I go through their case files, I cannot see how this man has ended up on a life charge. What I see is a series of connected incidentals which, if presented without proper representation and good legal authority, incriminates him, and that is not justice.

LADIPO MANYIKA: Speaking of criminal justice systems, if anyone Googles your name and the House of Lords, they'll see some fantastic pictures of you with Jamie Foxx and Michael B. Jordan, but also Bryan Stevenson, who has devoted his whole life to fighting injustices within the US criminal justice system. You've been very active around prison work and the criminal justice system, in England as well. In addition, for a time you worked for the BBC as Head of Corporate Social Responsibility. What does that mean?

HASTINGS: Well, I was really proud to be the first Head of Corporate Social Responsibility for the BBC, and I carried that mantle into KPMG, where we changed the title to Global Head of Citizenship. What I wanted KPMG, a brilliant professional service institution, to recognize was that this stuff shouldn't be about a little bit of volunteering, and a little bit of money, and some good philanthropy, and a few nice pictures, and some smiles. This stuff should be about business accepting its duty as a citizen.

Barack Obama, when he set the first stone on the Obama Center in Chicago, said that the most important role any of us can have in life is not to be President or Prime Minister, King or Queen, Chief Executive or Chairman, but to be a citizen. I really believe that, as individuals, we must be citizens, and therefore effective in carrying communities and neighbors, involved in the quality of the communities in which we live, and serving the institutions to build those communities. So must companies, because, after all, companies and institutions of public life draw their life from the citizens. They draw their income from the citizens, either directly or by default.

I wanted KPMG to be a citizen. I wanted the BBC to be a citizen. And the wonderful thing is they wanted to be as well. I'm proud of the fact that the BBC put so much effort into supporting children, through its Children in Need annual fundraising program, and supporting Comic Relief through the gifting of air time to enable vast amounts of money to be raised, to fulfill the objectives of the sustainable development goals, and to carry programing that draws out the disorder and distress of society, but then provides solutions.

And for the BBC, I'm proud of someone like David Olusoga's great series on Black Britons before slavery. There's a new series with Samuel Jackson, which is of course a joint BBC-American television production, looking at the reality of Black histories through the centuries, not just because of slavery.

So, that's how great institutions can take on causes. But when it comes to this area of what some would say is corporate responsibility, I'd call it corporate citizenship. I'd refer your readers to no better a CEO than Doug McMillon, the CEO of Walmart. Go onto the Walmart website, and look up a very good short video that tells the story of Walmart's commitment to environmental sustainability, to low carbon and now moving toward no-carbon presence, because of what they do. How they reuse, how they're involved in the circular economy. And Walmart being one of the first employers in America to have a living wage. These are things that business can do to transform people's lives and give them greater economy and freedom. I really believe in that.

I urge every business, too, to look at the Business Roundtable, which is an American institution of over 200 chief executives and leaders of organizations. Two years ago, under Jamie Dimon's leadership, they took on the commitment to define business as an organization that develops the value of the entire community around it, and is prioritized by the stakeholder, and not just by the shareholder.

LADIPO MANYIKA: Michael, another thread that runs through your work is that of an educator. You started off as a teacher, and you're now the Chancellor of Regent's University in London. Talk about education, the importance of education, and how educational institutions are having to pivot in an ever-changing world underscored by what has happened around Covid and in an ever more virtual world.

HASTINGS: A friend of mine put it like this, and he leads many schools: Education needs to be about framing the future, not having a stuck curriculum based on just historicities or the way we used to do it. Now, obviously what has happened this year because of coronavirus everywhere, schools have been closed, and children have been away, and learning has been delayed, and exams have been prevented. All of a sudden, we're having to think differently about how we evaluate learning, but also how do we develop learning?

Sarah, here we are talking to each other through a one-dimensional screen, which obviously not everybody in the world has. But around sixty per cent of people in the world have these one-dimensional mechanisms for being able to receive so much vast knowledge and insight that we can pursue and discover relentlessly through the internet. We can find so many amazing, insightful short films and stories and captivating pieces of information. But the irony of all of that is that it hasn't made us a more learning culture. And the *having* of knowledge is not what causes education. It's the wanting to receive knowledge that causes education. So people need to be focused on what the future will represent.

And here's one dimension of the future. The United Nations and the World Economic Forum recently published some interesting population figures which showed that the second largest country by population in the world in 2100 is not going to be India or China. It's going to be Nigeria, with 791 million people! The continent of Africa, with four billion people. Now, come on, as the world is changing, so the reality of Black lives will be everywhere, and the need to move away from a monochrome way of thinking into a multidimensional, international way of understanding.

The World Economic Forum publishes a set of skills which are necessary for future success, either as an entrepreneur, or as a business person, or just somebody interested in leading change in the world. And the number one on the top of those skills is being able to have complex, defined solutions and think about complex problems. Now, when you think about it, in how many schools do children get pushed to think about complex problems and find solutions? But actually, in an increasingly entrepreneurial and diversifying world, that's exactly what we need. We need to be able to think our way through not just the applications of technology, but how do we make the world work for the different sectors who are going to be either displaced by artificial intelligence, or automation, or robotics. What do people do with this innate need to work, and the energy that they have? Obviously, for some people, expressions of creativity and art will be natural. For other people, there has to be an increasing release of those gifts toward either caring services, or to agriculture, or to innovation.

I discovered recently that as a result of, ironically, a great cataclysmic event in the early 1800s, we got the bicycle. There was a volcano in Indonesia which caused a massive blackout of the sun for many months. There were snowfalls in Sydney, when there never were, and in New York in summer, and the consequence of this was that people couldn't feed their horses. Because they couldn't feed their horses, a German inventor went and invented the bicycle. Now we have bicycles everywhere. We're so grateful for it. So out of extreme circumstances can come great innovation. We need to remember that.

If learning is about the future, it's about innovation, it's about possibilities, and it's about humanity, and it's about understanding complex things, and finding solutions, and applying the mind to the full potential of our ability to think emotionally, as well as our ability to think cognitively; that's proper education. Now, we can gain so much curriculum content by television, YouTube, content online and by good reading. Our structures of education are orientated around things we can pick up now by the internet. So we need to change our learning into discovering how to think, innovate and apply. Looking at complexity, finding solutions and building humanity.

LADIPO MANYIKA: I love the bicycle example. I think we need more 'bicycles' than ever these days. Michael, in this world in which there's so much turmoil, what is it that grounds you?

HASTINGS: I'm glad you asked me that question, because it's really important. I begin my day, every day, reading from the scriptures. I believe in Jesus, and I follow him. I have done so ever since I was fourteen years of age, and I made a faith commitment to follow who Jesus is, to know him, to love him, and to know the truth of the scriptures. So I read the Bible every morning and I will keep going until my last day. I discover so much to reflect on positively, because I'm wanting to hear wisdom.

And I love reading books. As you mentioned, I am a Stephen R. Covey Professor of Leadership, so I do read Stephen's books. *The 7 Habits of Highly Effective People.* I'm reading *The 8th Habit* at the moment, on greatness. I read one of his son's books recently, on the speed of trust. I read the *Economist.* I read the *Financial Times.* I read *The Times* newspaper. I read *Time* magazine. I read the *New Statesman* every week. I'm keeping my mind vibrant and alert, but I really need that space every morning where I can pull away and find the peace of God, and really learn. Actually, it's in reflecting on the goodness of God that I'm grateful, hugely grateful. In seeking to hear the whispers of God that I'm energized. As he leads and gives me opportunity, I'm glad to follow. That's how I'm motivated.

You know what else I'm motivated by? I'm so motivated by people who long to change their lives and put the energy into changing their lives. If I can serve them in doing that, that is an enormous joy. And that's why I mentioned the work that we do in prisons, because there are people who you'd think would give up hope. 'Oh, no way.' They are longing, longing to capture their freedom of mind, if not their freedom of physical reality. So it's a blessing to be with transformative people all the time who give me great encouragement.

LADIPO MANYIKA: If you could change anything about the way that people think of the African diaspora, what would it be?

HASTINGS: It'll take a long time to get that mindset of less adequate than, less capable than, less competent than, less possible than, out of the mind of many Europeans and North Americans. It's too well embedded. But you only get there, you only change your mind when there's a combination of two critical things. One is you build relationships with people. You reach across the aisle, literally seek out the other, the different other. I long for that seeking out. For people not just to see the people of the African diaspora as great cultural bearers of heritage from another continent, but actually as phenomenally intelligent academics, economists, medical experts, people who are innovators, technicians, creators, drivers of wealth, supporters of community and hospital workers.

Yes, there is a need to change the narrative. And there is a radical need to embed respect. Because when you get to know people who are different, of different cultures, you learn to love them. When you learn to love them, all those kinds of prejudices just drop away and you don't need to carry them any longer.

There are so many people who want to look at the African continent and say, 'Oh, it's all washed up.' Some people might call it a 'something-hole'. And I have traveled and traversed twelve countries across the continent over these many years, and I've seen it from the poorest, most shambolic places, all the way through to the most immensely sophisticated technological and dignified places across the continent. I'm proud to say there are wonderful countries like Botswana and Rwanda now, which are so strong. Ghana, which is settled and positive, and Kenya, which has now got an effective peace process in place between what were previously disagreeing tribes. To see the energy and creativity there is across the continent is beautiful. Africa's people arc beautiful, and Africa's culture is beautiful. They're also competent, intelligent, capable, strong, insightful, academic, significant. These are real words of change I long to see applied to all of us. We need the wider world out there to give us the time and the dignity to be heard.

11.

EVAN MAWARIRE

On Meeting

April 19, 2016

It's night-time in a small fluorescent-lit church office. A man sits alone, anxious and ashamed. He cannot provide for his family. His rent is due and so are his children's school fees. He has a knack for fixing things, but not this. Not when his country's economy has collapsed. Not when its President – in power for thirty-six years – rules with an iron fist. In the man's office hangs a flag. He reaches for it as he considers the promise that a nation's flag represents. He drapes the flag around him, picks up his phone, and begins recording. Hunched in front of the camera, hands toying with the ends of the flag, words pour out of him with passion and urgency. He ends his lament on a call to action:

'This is the time that a change must happen. Quit standing on the sidelines!'

Posting the video to social media would be preposterous, he knows. People in his country have been beaten, imprisoned and disappeared on the mere suspicion of dissent. But, a few hours later, he does it anyway. He uploads the video to Facebook and tags it: #ThisFlag. By morning, his four-minute video has gone viral and soon virtually everyone with a cellphone in his country, as well as many thousands who have fled the country, will see it. This hitherto unknown man is now a marked man.

#THISFLAG

What Evan Mawarire cannot foresee when he posts his video is that thousands of Zimbabweans will be emboldened to join him in speaking out, many for the first time, on the injustices, corruption and decades-long collapse into poverty of their once prosperous nation. Within weeks, #ThisFlag will give rise to the largest social media movement his country has ever witnessed, and Evan will be called 'the flag guy', heralded far and wide as the spark for Zimbabwe's Arab Spring. In a clever act of subversion, inspired by his act of wearing it, Zimbabweans from all walks of life begin displaying their nation's flag.

Initially, the government appears clueless about the reach and power of social media, with the government Minister of Higher Education dismissing #ThisFlag as a 'pastor's fart in the corridors of power'. At one point, and farcically, the government attempts to ban the flag, but within weeks they realize its power. Evan starts receiving threats that range from anonymous phone calls to blatant physical assaults, which include being accosted by the government Minister of Information. Undeterred, he continues posting his videos – one a day for the month of May, and more in June – which he now narrates both in English and Shona, thereby expanding his audience and reach. At the start of July, Evan narrowly escapes an abduction attempt. He moves to a safe house. Then he takes his social media activism one step further.

Evan calls for peaceful protests in the form of a series of national stay-aways. Under President Robert Mugabe, any form of public protest is banned. And yet, on July 6th, 2016, Evan's call for the first stay-away is, to everyone's surprise, heeded by the entire nation as people stay at home. The nation comes to a standstill and the ruling ZANU-PF Party will almost certainly resort to its usual, brutal playbook. Under Mugabe, opposition leaders and activists are routinely imprisoned, beaten and disappeared – and all for doing far less than bringing a whole nation to a halt. Preparing for the worst, Evan records a video to be released should he be arrested or abducted.

The day after the national shutdown, I land in Zimbabwe for a family visit. The US has issued travel warnings and there is talk of riots, but on our drive from the airport to the northern suburbs of Harare, things appear calm. Visibly, not much has changed since my last visit three years earlier, other than further deterioration of the roads. But there is something new – all the roadside vendors are selling Zimbabwe's national flag. The flag is now on cars, in shop windows, around people's shoulders – it's everywhere. Even more striking is what I hear. Everyone, from relatives to friends and even strangers seem animated with mention of 'the flag guy'. It's the first time in my twenty-four years of visiting Zimbabwe that I've heard Zimbabweans speak so openly, almost fearlessly, in support of someone critical of Mugabe and his ZANU-PF government. What's more, I learn that the flag guy is a pastor.

Over the years, I had been following the rise of Pentecostal preacher-prophets and their megachurches in countries where I once lived: Nigeria and Kenya, as well as Zimbabwe. I'd seen how these preachers enjoyed extravagant lifestyles funded by the tithes and donations of their congregants while many of these same congregants struggled to make ends meet. In Zimbabwe, millions were surviving on food aid. These same preachers often courted the favor of repressive leaders in power, blessing them, and welcoming them into their churches. I had grown disillusioned with such leaders who, to my eyes, were not setting a Christ-like example of humility and service to others. So, to hear of a Pentecostal pastor of a small congregation, who was not only brave enough to speak truth to power but to speak on behalf of ordinary citizens, was both inspiring and exciting.

THE JUNIOR PRESIDENT

When Evan was born, in 1977, Zimbabwe was still Rhodesia and under white, apartheid-style, minority rule. At that time, the Black majority lived either in dense, segregated city townships or in the rural areas labeled *maruzevha* (native reserves). Evan's family lived first in the rural areas and then later moved to Glen Norah, one of the older Black townships on the margins of the capital. As the first-born of six children, Evan was expected to set a good example for his younger siblings, especially so once admitted to Prince Edward School.

I have visited this boys' school on a number of occasions – my husband was one of the first Black students admitted after independence in 1980. Until then, Prince Edward was a whites-only school, steeped in the nation's colonial history from its royal name and famous Jubilee Field to its school motto: *Tot Facienda Parum Factum* (So much to do; So little done) attributed to the imperialist Cecil Rhodes, who named the country after himself. This hundred-year-old school continues to be known for its academic excellence and sporting prowess, with its own astronomy observatory, vast acres of lawns, sports fields and state-of-the-art science labs.

When Evan started at Prince Edward in the early 1990s, this was an exciting time for him and for the country. Zimbabwe was doing well and seemed to be bucking the trend of other African countries. Its President, Robert Mugabe, was lauded at home and abroad as a model for Africa. Yet under the surface all was not well. Unbeknownst to many, a genocide had been committed in Matabeleland in the 1980s reportedly under Mugabe's orders, and the news of this was kept suppressed. Meanwhile, at school, Evan was not faring as well as expected. He performed poorly on his Form Three exams, and his father decided to withdraw him. The fees were high and the family couldn't afford to keep a child who wasn't doing well in an expensive school. To Evan's consternation, he was sent to a Salvation Army mission school under the supervision of a strict disciplinarian uncle.

Charles Clack Secondary School in Magunje could not be more different from Prince Edward. It was located in the rural areas and designed for Black Africans pre-independence. It had no running water, no electricity and only pit latrines for toilets. Cattle routinely wandered the school grounds. But, at Charles Clack, Evan studied hard and did well. He became a school prefect and discovered an interest in civics. He joined the inter-schools competitions for Zimbabwe's Junior Parliament and through this countrywide competition he would ultimately be selected, from students all across the country, as Zimbabwe's Junior President.

THE FIRST ARRESTS

July 12, 2016

Evan has been in hiding for several days when his wife sends urgent word that the police are looking for him. On advice from the Zimbabwe Lawyers for Human Rights (ZLHR) he turns himself in and reports to a police station. Accompanied by a ZLHR lawyer, he is questioned for hours. Then his home is searched. No incriminating evidence is found. Regardless, he's detained and charged for 'inciting public violence and disturbing the peace'. He is thrown into Baghdad – a crowded holding cell in Harare's Central Police station, where two dozen men sit huddled on the concrete floor. It's wintertime. Evan has never been to prison before. The only spot available is next to the open toilet. His blanket, the last remaining one, is stained with fresh feces. Hours later, in the middle of the night, when other prisoners have fallen asleep, two men quietly remove Evan from Baghdad.

He is handcuffed and marched to a basement cell. Here, he is ordered to remove his shoes and sit on the floor. The interrogators play good cop/bad cop. He is asked repeatedly for whom he is working and who funds his media activism. They don't believe him when he says he's acting alone. It's freezing, and Evan soon loses sensation in his bottom and feet. The interrogators ask: What will you do if we send someone to rape your wife while we hold you in jail? How will you feel if we release you to bury your children? When they dump him back in Baghdad, they warn him to watch out for *vamwe vacho vanoda varume* (the men that like men).

July 13, 2016

It's morning and Evan has been awake all night, shivering. He is transported to Rotten Row Magistrates Court. A crowd of several thousand has gathered. Inside, Evan is shuttled between one filthy holding cell and another. Finally, when night falls, he is led into the courtroom which has been opened to hear his special case. His face lights up when he sees his wife. She doesn't look harmed. She isn't under arrest. His lawyer is asked to stand, and alongside him are nearly one hundred more lawyers who have shown up in support. But then comes the pronouncement that his charge has been escalated. He is now being charged with attempting to subvert a constitutionally elected government. He looks visibly shaken. This new charge, akin to treason, carries a twenty-year prison sentence.

Then Evan hears the crowds outside singing – freedom songs and church songs! Like the Biblical battle of Jericho, the metaphorical walls collapse. His lawyers successfully argue that the switch to this second charge is unconstitutional and Evan is released. Now he's outside with a moment of freedom, fresh air and the noise of the crowd. Then the whisper, from one of the guards, that he will be immediately re-arrested. To save him from re-arrest, he's told to go out through the crowds. The crowds in their excitement nearly crush him. They also act temporarily as a shield, but his lawyers know this is not enough. Another safe house, a quick disguise and a fast journey south through a quiet border town into Botswana, and Evan is in exile.

Days after Evan escapes, President Robert Mugabe himself rebukes Evan on national television, questioning whether 'he's a true man of God'. Days later, on July 23rd, the government-sponsored newspaper, the *Herald*, carries the headline: *Mawarire Is No Saint*. The article claims that Evan made up his story of financial woes and that he was in fact 'sponsored by Western governments to distabilise [*sic*] the country'.

When news arrives that Evan is safely out of the country, many Zimbabweans feel relief, but soon there are grumblings. What good is their savior outside? And now that the State had lost its prey, officials are undeterred in their efforts to discredit Evan. Fueled by clever disinformation, people's disappointment grows. Evan is called a 'sellout' and, after the years of war, the pastor knows well what happens to a sellout. Meanwhile, President Mugabe continues to ridicule him in public. It is clear that Evan is not welcome back in the country.

Evan spends the next six months out of Zimbabwe, first in South Africa and then in the US, during which he finds the support to get his family out of the country too. Abroad, his wife gives birth to their third child. Evan is safe, his family is safe, but he is dislocated. He has no job in this place of safety, no friends, no community. He had acted on impulse, impulse born of desperation, and his voice had been the voice of the people, but now he feels rudderless. After discussion with a few close friends, and his lawyers, he decides to return. He knows it's dangerous for him to return to Zimbabwe, but he also doesn't want to abandon the cause. He makes plans to return, telling only a few people the date of his arrival.

February 1, 2017

Evan is met by the authorities as soon as his plane lands. Five men march him away, interrogate him, then turn him over to the police. He is arrested and sent to remand prison. That night, Evan is thrown into a truck and told that he's going to Chikurubi. He's the only prisoner in the truck. His leg irons begin to clatter as his legs shake. The mere mention of Chikurubi (like Robben Island, Rikers or San Quentin) is enough to instill terror. Chikurubi Maximum Security Prison is known for housing the most hardened of criminals, and for its prison violence, overcrowding and disease. It is here, in the years before independence, that the white Rhodesian government used to throw the leaders of the struggle. Evan asks his guard if this is the end. He's imagining being dumped in a ditch or worse. They arrive at Chikurubi – high concrete walls, razor wire, security lights and armed guards everywhere.

Inside, Evan is given a bucket to hold all the possessions he's allowed to take – his Bible, some underwear and a striped prison-issue sweater made by the prison guards' wives. He's placed in the D Wing. D is reserved for the most serious offenders – from murderers to rapists – those serving eight years to life. Now comes his crash course on life in a maximum-security prison – a beating from a prison guard and some unexpected kindness from fellow inmates.

For the next few months, Evan will be in and out of prison in a continuing cycle of arrests, imprisonment and release on stringent bail conditions that include the surrender of his passport as well as the title deeds to his parents' house. This pattern persists until November. Then, the unimaginable happens.

November 14, 2017

Major General Sibusiso Moyo appears in full military fatigues
on Zimbabwe's national TV. He announces that the armed forces
have stepped in to 'pacify a degenerating social and economic
situation in the country'. It is not 'a military take-over' or a coup,
he insists, even as troops appear on the streets of Harare. The
troops block government buildings and occupy the State House.
Within days, Robert Mugabe is forced to step down. And with
him goes his wife – his one-time secretary and hugely unpopular
would-be successor, mocked as the 'The First Shopper' and
'Gucci Grace'.

Two weeks later, Evan's case is finally brought to trial and
he is acquitted of all charges. He becomes a free man as Robert
Mugabe is deposed. The country goes wild with jubilation at
Mugabe's removal – people crying, ululating, dancing, horn-
blaring in the streets. Pastor Evan is amongst them. He's ecstatic
– laughing and crying, as people pose with him to take selfies
with their flags. Flags are everywhere – on cars and buildings
and wrapped around people like superhero capes. Mugabe
is out and his former Vice President-turned rival, Emmerson
Mnangagwa (nicknamed 'the Crocodile' and long suspected of
involvement in the Gukurahundi genocidal killings) is made
interim President. Mnangagwa (also known as 'ED') proclaims
a 'New Zimbabwe' wearing a scarf in Zimbabwe's flag colors.
The fact that Evan was the first to wear the flag as scarf appears
forgotten. The scarf is now called the 'ED Scarf'.

ABROAD

It's early evening in the summer of 2018 and Evan is wearing
jeans and a Stanford university sweatshirt. I notice the
Zimbabwean flag tied around the straps of the backpack he
puts down as he arrives. My husband, who had met Evan two

210

years earlier after Evan had escaped to the US, has invited him to our home in San Francisco for dinner. Two others join us, both Zimbabweans – one is a cousin visiting from out of town and the second an undergraduate at the University of California, Berkeley.

When Evan sees me, his greeting is warm and effusive. 'Hello ma'am, how are you? It's a pleasure to meet you,' he says, smiling broadly as he turns to greet the others. As I watch the ease with which he interacts with the younger student, it's easy to see what made him a popular, humorous youth pastor. 'Wow!' he exclaims enthusiastically when hearing what each of us is doing, even though we are more interested in hearing about him and the situation in Zimbabwe.

We are meeting in the run-up to Zimbabwe's first election following Mugabe's removal from power, and Evan is running for political office. He is running as an independent for a seat in Harare's city council, which is where he feels he can make the most difference to improve people's daily lives. He had been campaigning up until a few weeks prior. But then, as he explains, being offered the prestigious Draper Hills Summer Fellowship at Stanford University was an opportunity he couldn't turn down, as it enabled him to see his family in America whom he hadn't seen in a year and a half. Meanwhile, he remains in close touch with Zimbabwe via phone and social media, and his excitement for the promised hope of this election is palpable.

A few days later, with the election results now in, we meet up with Evan again and this time his mood is subdued. He says his disappointment is not about his own electoral loss, but about the lives of the peaceful protestors and bystanders shot dead on the streets of Harare in the wake of the election. The election has been won by Mnangagwa, the interim President who replaced Mugabe. Mnangagwa is from Mugabe's ZANU-PF party, not the opposition Movement for Democratic Change (MDC). For years, Mugabe had brutally repressed the MDC. He had also cheated the party, most blatantly, out of the 2008 election.

Indignant and angry, Evan sits hunched at the dining table with his muscular forearms braced in a semicircle in front of him – a stance like that of his first #ThisFlag video. Our conversation around the election and the ensuing violence pauses when, after dinner, we attend the first International Congress of Youth Voices, where my son is a delegate. As we listen to the passionate presentations, Evan is visibly heartened. One of the congress mentors is Congressman John Lewis, the much-revered civil rights leader who once worked with Martin Luther King, Jr. When Congressman Lewis speaks of the necessity of getting into what he calls 'good trouble' and 'necessary trouble', his words strike a chord with us all. By the end of the evening, Evan is the first to stand in applause. Soon after, he leaves California to return to Zimbabwe.

IN THE WORDS OF OTHERS

I am now keen to know, with the passage of time, what people think of Evan. In Zimbabwe, I ask everyone who will speak with me – from young to old, Black and white, formally educated or not, rich and poor, professors, students, artists and business leaders. Similarly, I ask Zimbabweans in the diaspora – in South Africa, the UK and the US – many of whom left Zimbabwe either because of the country's economic collapse or simply to escape Mugabe's brutal ruling party. Everyone I ask expresses admiration for what Evan did, or attempted to do. Most, however, only seem to know a small part of his story and few are aware of his ongoing work within civic society, which includes mobilizing for clean water services in the wake of a cholera epidemic.

Of the many who praise Evan, some know him from his church, others from what they have heard or read in the news or social media, and one from a chance encounter at Avondale Shopping Center where, in the car park, they had discovered a shared love of Land Rovers. People describe Evan as a 'good person', as 'grounded', 'level-headed', 'a church man of morals', 'humble' and a man of 'presidential potential'. Several highlight the fact that Evan never set out to be a political leader and that his aim all along was to engage citizens – to start a citizens' movement. He had resisted joining any political party and refused to run for President as many had wanted him to do. Nevertheless, one pan-African businessman suggests that Evan ought to have done a better job of acknowledging the activists that came before him (such as Morgan Tsvangirai, a respected leader of the opposition MDC).

One student says that in a country like Zimbabwe where most people are religious, Evan could have done more to harness the power of the pulpit. Others say that Evan should not have 'run away' from Zimbabwe after his first arrest in 2016. In a heated conversation between a group of Zimbabwean students studying at the University of California, Berkeley, one claims that, had Evan stayed in Zimbabwe just two more weeks in August of 2016, something 'fundamental' would have happened. 'Yeah,' quips another, 'he would have been dead!' Others make the point that so much was beyond Evan's control. Funding was a challenge, says a struggling Harare-based entrepreneur, explaining how difficult it was for Evan to get his message to the rural communities where people, though connected to social media, didn't have funds to buy 'bundles' (data packages) to download his videos.

Many blame ZANU-PF as well as ex-President Mugabe for destroying Evan's credibility by pushing the story that Evan was backed by Western sponsors. Also, as one businessman puts it, Zimbabweans had been conditioned to see their opposition leaders (such as Nelson Chamisa and Tsvangirai) beaten up and, because Evan never appeared to have severe cuts or visible bruising, this made some people suspicious.

—

IN HIS OWN WORDS

When Evan speaks, his passion and oratory skills are reminiscent of other preacher-activists such as Martin Luther King, Jr, and Bishop Desmond Tutu. His speech has a Biblical ring to it when he uses phrases such as 'the least among us', 'those who are heavy laden', or when he references 'widows and orphans', and occasionally he quotes scripture. He has an ear for accents and a natural feel for the poetry and rhythm of language. What is also striking is the conviction and passion conveyed through his words.

Evan becomes particularly animated when he speaks of some of the most marginalized people who have had a lasting impact on his life, including prisoners he met while at Chikurubi.

He is humble when talking about himself, frequently referring to others as brighter and more courageous. Those that he mentions as having inspired him are not the famous people he has sometimes been compared to, but ordinary, everyday people including his parents' pastor and a caretaker at Prince Edward School.

When I ask Evan to describe the events following his first arrest, he does so with a sense of timing and drama that keeps me rapt, sometimes adding deadpan humor at the tensest moments of his story. When being transported – handcuffed in the back of a pickup truck – to his first court appearance, he describes the moment when he asks the heavily armored guards if he might pray with them and, to his surprise, they all lower their weapons and close their eyes. And, when recalling his first stint at the notorious Chikurubi Maximum Security Prison, he describes the way prison guards looked at him as though he were a rare, wild animal caught in a residential area. They were surprised to find him so young and so short.

Evan is not only quick to draw on humor, often poking fun at himself, but he is also candid when chronicling the rollercoaster of emotions felt in the course of his journey. He admits to sobbing uncontrollably and to nearly convulsing on the first night he was interrogated, to struggling to hold back tears when he saw his pregnant wife patiently sitting in court on the following day. Often in the course of conversation, Evan is contemplative, reflecting on what he has learned since the events of 2016 which brought him to national prominence:

One of the things I learned when people responded by calling me a sellout [was] the realization that if you're going to do it, you have to do it out of conviction and not out of the applause or what people want to hear. The way I learned the lesson was that my two major arrests had one very distinct difference. The first had thousands of people gathered there. The second, when I was arrested at the airport, there was nobody. No one! It was a shock but also the penny dropped that if you're going to do this, you can't do it for the crowd because they'll be there when it's exciting, but when it gets tiring, they don't have an obligation to be there at all.

I lost a lot of friends along the way when I started speaking out. I still have one or two but it's a very small circle. I'm in one of these strange situations where you feel like everybody knows you, but you know no one.

One of the fears in the kind of space that I'm in right now is that I would disappoint the people who do love me [. . .] Sometimes I'm caught off guard, I'm not in the space of 'here's the other cheek'. That's why, as a pastor, it has been such a terrible thing for me and I've said to people: 'You know what, I'm not speaking as a pastor. I'm speaking as an ordinary person who has hurts, who has frustrations, who has fears and who is concerned about how they're going to deal with a future that has been messed up by someone who's no longer here.'

When people look at me and my life through the lens of the high moments – the different nominations for prizes and the invitations to speak at these high-level gatherings, or amazing institutions of learning – they don't understand the aspect of cost. *None of that could ever be a replacement or a reward for being away from my kids for three years, missing all of their birthdays. None of that could ever help me explain why my daughter would ask me, after she hadn't seen me for fourteen months, if I'm her dad. So sometimes people see my life through the lens of some of those things and they think that the cost is easy, but it's quite a cost to bear. The prison arrest – and the attempted abductions and threats to life – all put a value on how much I value my family. I'm prepared to die for them, I'm prepared to go to prison for them, so that my children understand what freedom means, what justice is. And it's my hope that my kids will learn earlier in life what it means to fight for what you believe in. In many ways, it started off being about my family, but it has become much bigger. Sometimes I regret it. Many times, I regret it. When I speak in public, I have to find the courage to be brave for everyone else, to not say I've had enough, to not say I can't take it anymore even though I feel like that a number of times. It's just not the thing you say when you happen to be the symbol of hope for everybody else.*

MORE ARRESTS

January 16, 2019

In the dead of night, armed men arrive at Evan's Harare apartment and attempt to abduct him. They assault the caretakers in his block and try ramming down his front door. Unable to get in, they send police to arrest him early the next morning. The arrest is filmed by neighbors and posted online. Evan is remanded and charged with inciting public violence and for being in support of the trade unions who called for peaceful demonstrations protesting the doubling of fuel costs. His charges are later escalated to that of subverting a constitutionally elected government – identical to the charges leveled at him two and a half years earlier. He is thrown back into Chikurubi. This time, he's placed with fifty-three others in a cell measuring just eight by five meters. Many of these inmates had been rounded up in the course of the fuel protests. Some have broken bones, while others have open wounds from police beatings. A few are minors, only sixteen years old.

January 30, 2019

Evan is released on bail. He is suffering from a chest infection. One of the first questions a reporter can be heard asking on a posted video is: 'Were you beaten?' As in 2016, the conditions of his bail are stringent. At each successive court date, Evan's case is kicked down the road. Between January and September 2019, he makes ten court appearances.

Meanwhile, things in Zimbabwe continue to deteriorate. An Amnesty International report published in August describes Mnangagwa's first year in office as marked by a 'systematic and brutal crackdown on human rights including the violent suppression of protests and a witch-hunt against anyone who dared challenge his government.' On August 23rd, Evan writes an op-ed for *Time* magazine describing the depth of the nation's economic hardships and the government's brutal response to those who dare to protest. Then, in September, the unimaginable happens again. Ex-President Robert Mugabe is dead. He was ninety-five years old.

September 6, 2019

On the day Robert Mugabe dies, I am in Cape Town participating in South Africa's Open Book Festival. In a surreal moment, I awake to the news of his death from the animated chatter of Zimbabwean housekeeping staff that I can hear standing outside my hotel room. I understand enough of what they are saying in Shona to guess that something significant has happened. I switch on the TV and that's when I hear Zimbabwean government officials speaking of a deceased Mugabe as though he were a hero – the same officials that had cheered at his ousting less than two years earlier.

Three days later, I fly to Harare. I message Evan to ask if we can meet. I'd like to hear what he makes of Mugabe's passing and of reactions to his death. I'm also concerned for his mental and physical well-being given how long he's been held in limbo and separated from his family and also given the continued hardship of daily life in Zimbabwe. Zimbabwe's economic collapse had not ended in the two years since Mugabe's ousting. My mother-in-law, like so many others in Zimbabwe, has not had running water for months and power outages are now the daily norm. The prices of things – including basic commodities such as bath soap, deodorant and Vaseline – have become prohibitively expensive. Cash is also in short supply. I wonder how Evan is supporting himself, let alone his family of four, *and* responding to the extended family expectations that come with being the eldest son.

AT HOME

I've arranged to meet Evan at Avondale's popular Café Nush. While I wait for him, I try figuring out where best to sit. I am guessing that his movements and meetings are constantly monitored but, still, I'd like to find a spot which is not in full view of everyone.

Evan greets me with his warm smile. It's his choice that we sit outside. He's dressed casually in jeans and a T-shirt bearing Zimbabwe's initials – ZW. There's a tear in the seam of his shirt and he looks thinner. He's been running marathons, he tells me. He is wearing sunglasses, and after we order (a coffee each and a barbecue beef wrap for Evan) he asks if I mind him keeping his shades on. He says his eyes are sensitive to light then, half jokingly, that the sunglasses make him feel invisible, but of course 'they see me,' he adds.

His voice turns serious as we begin to talk about Mugabe. 'The saddest thing in all of this,' he repeats, 'is that whilst [Mugabe] lived, we were forced to be silent, and when he dies we are again forced to be silent. And the least he could have done, the least he could have done,' his voice now getting louder, 'was to die here in Zimbabwe!' Angrily, Evan describes how, as Zimbabwe's hospitals were falling apart, Mugabe received treatment in an expensive hospital in Singapore until his death. Evan tells me that he cannot bring himself to say 'rest in peace' for Mugabe and he's furious with the hypocrisy of those who do.

After a pause, he apologizes for raising his voice. I respond by saying that I'm not surprised by people's hypocrisy, coming as it does from a country so traumatized, until Evan's cold stare stops me short. His voice grows quieter but even more steely as he reminds me of Mugabe's cruelty, which he insists was there from the very beginning. He reminds me of the Gukurahundi genocidal killings of the 1980s and the notorious Fifth Brigade allegedly ordered by Robert Mugabe to commit the atrocities. The death toll estimated by some reports was as high as tens of thousands. '[Mugabe's] death has to be a point of clarity rather than a point of contention!' Evan insists, with a stern, no-time-to-waste demeanor.

As we continue speaking, Evan is even more candid about his emotional state than I remember him being previously. He speaks of how difficult he finds it when strangers tell him what he should do, when they lecture him on how he must not exhibit rage as a pastor. But writing, he tells me, has helped him deal with things. That morning he had written what he felt were a few good pages in the memoir he is working on. And yet, just as he shares what gives him focus, he admits to feeling confused. He describes these feelings with the same fervor and urgency as in his #ThisFlag video, except this time there is no sense of hope:

> *It's like I'm stuck with this thing, this ball of yarn. And I don't know where the start is or the finish anymore. And I feel like I've spent the last two years trying to figure out where is the beginning of it, where is the end of it? And I'm on my own and I'm just frustrated with the thing that I'm trying to unravel and it won't. It just won't unravel. Each time I'm coming to the end of it you just get caught up in another arrest and then you pull it and . . .*

Feeling stuck, he says, makes him question his relevance. He's worn down by those who accuse him of being a sellout. The determination I had heard him express a year earlier – of the need to do things out of self-conviction rather than be swayed by the fickle whims of crowds – seems to have been ground out of him. And with a heavy sigh he acknowledges that those in power have also been successful in baiting and taunting him.

'Up to today,' he says, banging on the table, 'people still say, why did you run away? I feel like saying just F-off! Bloody hell! Not only did I come back and get arrested and spent a whole year in and out of prison and got tried for it. Do you realize that I was tried for this? And then, after all is said and done, I still stayed. If I was a freaking coward like you said I was, the moment I was acquitted, I would have packed up my little bags and left! And never come back! Not only did I stay, but I spoke out again.'

Now his tone is bitter and combative. He admits to being less patient, to swearing where he never used to and to being prone to pouncing on people rather than giving them the benefit of the doubt. He tells me he hasn't been able to speak freely to anyone for a long time. He doesn't trust people to be genuine. He feels that everyone has an angle. As he speaks, I am reminded of the moment in his first video when he wonders whether those who sacrificed for Zimbabwe in years past would feel, in hindsight, that their sacrifice had been worth it. I'm wondering if he feels his sacrifices have been worth it when he tells me:

> *The 2019 arrest, I feel like that was not worth it. I feel like it was because of all these people. I feel like I had to do something, I had to prove that I was still in the game, that I was still committed. Because people, they keep taking. They take, and take, and take, and take!*

As I listen to Evan and watch him, it's almost as if I can see him enmeshed in the ball of yarn, twisting between acknowledging that he's on edge (and not wanting to be) while simultaneously justifying his right to lash out. Now there's no deadpan humor in his narration, only anger and frustration followed by silence, then further outpourings:

> *People seem to be enjoying watching you taking the hard punches. We love it when you're hit hard and you just return a soft answer or you just say something inspirational. And I'm saying: Sometimes I'm fresh out of inspirational quotes. Sometimes I'm caught off guard, I'm not in the space of 'here's the other cheek'.*

Evan flicks away tears from under his sunglasses as he angrily clanks his way through his beef wrap, always careful to be polite and cheery to the workers who wait on our table. Still thinking of what he's said about his last arrest not being worth it, I find myself wanting to reassure him. I tell him he doesn't have to prove his relevance. Surely, he has proven this already. He listens silently before the words pour out again:

> *I can't be a Mandela! I don't feel like being a Mandela! Is that what it means for me to continue to be relevant? Is that what it means for me to continue to be someone that you love, appreciate and trust? Because I don't know if I can sustain*

*that. There are days I can do it, there are! But there are days
and moments when I'm just a human. I'm just a human being.*

He falls silent until he picks up his phone to show me the latest
pictures of his daughters that his wife has sent. In these pictures,
unlike the ones he had shared in 2018 while visiting us in San
Francisco, Evan does not appear. The other day, he says, his
youngest daughter screamed 'Daddy!' so excited was she to see
him on the video call that he couldn't help but burst into tears. He
describes his girls with love and tenderness – one is 'a fireball',
another just started school, and then there's the daughter that
recently Googled him. She told him that she'd figured out he
was a 'YouTuber', that he'd been with the police and that he'd
been in prison – all this before she asked: 'What do you really do,
Daddy?' And here, for one brief moment in the seriousness of
things, Evan's humor returns. 'If I could have taken a commercial
break, that would have been the time to do it,' he laughs.

I ask Evan what he wants. 'That's a really tough question,
but, whatever I do, I don't ever want my girls to go without me.'
Then, after a pause, he returns to my question. 'But if there's
anything you couldn't stop me from doing, it's finding ways to
help people that need it. You can't stop me from that. It's a good
thing. And sometimes, it's what gets me into trouble.'

October 3, 2019

Evan is back in court. His case is once again kicked down the
road. The next court date is scheduled for January 2020.

November 20, 2019

I receive a text message from Evan: *Just come from court and got
some good news. They have withdrawn the charges and will proceed*

by way of summons whenever they are ready. The only downside of it is that the case continues to hang over my head and can be called up anytime.

I text him back, excited to hear this good news. Hours later, I see a post on his Facebook page denouncing a new round of police brutality. Peaceful crowds waiting outside the opposition leader's headquarters had been beaten and tear gassed by police forces.

And so, it continues.

12.

CORY BOOKER

In Conversation

Cory Booker is an American politician, lawyer and author who has served as the junior United States Senator from New Jersey since 2013 and was a candidate for the Democratic nomination in the 2020 US presidential election. As senator, Booker has brought an innovative and consensus-building approach to tackling some of the most difficult problems facing New Jersey and the United States as a whole. Booker notably helped craft the most sweeping set of criminal justice reforms in a generation, the First Step Act, which became US law in December 2018.

December 13th, 2020

SARAH LADIPO MANYIKA: The first time I met you, Cory, was twenty-eight years ago in Oxford. And I was thinking, if I had known at that time what you would go on to do, and if I had said to you, 'Cory, I can see in twenty-eight years' time, 2020, that you will be a US Senator, you will have run for president, you'll be vegan, you will have this amazing girlfriend who is a great actress and even a Jedi in a recent [TV] series . . .' If I had said those three things to you, what would you have laughed at the most, all those years ago?

CORY BOOKER: Well, I became a vegetarian in Oxford and I knew even then I was going to be a vegan, so that wouldn't have surprised me at all. Dating a Jedi would have probably shocked me! But I think that even by then, in 1992, I realized that if you have a great imagination for yourself and the contributions you can make and are willing to take risks, life would always expand your sense of the possible. If you had said to me at eighteen years old that four years later I would be in Oxford meeting incredible people like you, I would've said that's impossible. What would I be doing in England? I feel like I've been on a blessed journey to try to give to the world, but I seem to get such abundance back and it leaves me feeling very humble and sometimes, on some days, unworthy, frankly. So, I'm grateful to be where I am and I just hope I can prove worthy in the years to come.

LADIPO MANYIKA: You have written a wonderful autobiography entitled *United: Thoughts on Finding Common Ground and Advancing the Common Good*. It's your story, and a story of those who have shaped you, who have impacted you. You also quote a lot of my favorite writers, including James Baldwin. In fact, you begin the book with a quote from Baldwin. And the quote is basically: 'Know from whence you come.' If you know where you come from, there's absolutely no limitation to where you can go. Let's start with your parents.

Your father, if I'm remembering correctly, was a salesman for IBM. He rose very quickly through the ranks. I think the move from Washington DC to northern New Jersey was due to professional reasons for both of your parents. And they tried to look for housing. They would go to houses that were advertised as up for sale and then – surprise, surprise – they would get to the house and would be told, 'Oh, the house was sold.' I wonder if you can finish the story for me.

BOOKER: Well, the first part of the story was a very shaping story. I was a baby, barely a few months old. And my parents, after being denied housing, found this incredible group of activists: a Black woman named Lee Porter, a white man named Arthur Lessman, a Jewish man named Marty Friedman. This group of activists just said, 'This is not going to stand.' And we may not be able to change everything, but we're going to do something. And they ended up putting a sting operation together where my parents would go look at a house, be told it was sold, and a white couple would come right behind them and find out the house was for sale. And, in the house I grew up in, my parents were told it was sold, but the white couple put a bid on the house and it was accepted. And on the day of the closing, the white couple didn't show up, but my dad and Marty Friedman did. The real estate agent was so upset that he actually punched my dad's lawyer and they got into a fight as he sicced the dog on my dad. That's how we got into that neighborhood!

My dad had a very different reality – he grew up poor to a single mom, and ended up being taken care of by the community and by an incredible family that became my family, who took him in. His story was one of tough struggle and now he's raising his two kids in affluent suburbs. As he used to say to me, 'Boy, don't you dare walk around this house like you hit a triple. You were born on third base.'

And so, by the time I'm eighteen years old, I'm living a life beyond my dreams. I'm president of my class, on my way to Stanford University as a high school All-American football player, honor roll, all these things. In fact, I still remember finishing all my school – Oxford, Yale, two degrees from Stanford – and my dad is like, 'Boy, you got more degrees than the month of July, but you ain't hot.' Life ain't about the degrees you get, it's about the service you give. Prove yourself. Are you really worthy?

So, the interesting thing is I didn't know the second half of that story until I journeyed into life. As you said, I went to Newark and started working representing tenants, then as city council person and mayor I helped to transform the city, and then on to the Senate. And then I did what a lot of senators do who have a high sense of self-regard: I decided to write this book. That's when I was really shaken because I tried to find the people that had helped my family move in. Lee Porter was easy to find because she's still head of the Fair Housing Council in northern New Jersey. She is ninety-three years old now, incredible soul.

LADIPO MANYIKA: Wow.

BOOKER: She sent me to the lawyer [Arthur Lessman] that had organized everything. And what shook me when I talked to this elderly retired New Jersey judge was a question that wasn't on my list of interview questions, which was just, 'why?' Why would you represent Black families at a time when there were fears of white flight and real estate prices going down? Everybody was afraid of us Black folks. And he just told me the simple story of sitting on his couch on March 7, 1965. The date didn't mean anything to me at that moment. It should have. He said he was watching what most of America was watching. I think it was on CBS – a TV movie called *Judgment at Nuremberg*.

And so here his heart is already being broken up about the horrors of the Holocaust and then they break away from the movie to show a bridge in Alabama called the Edmund Pettus Bridge. And he watches as these marchers, led by a man he didn't know at the time named John Lewis, literally bleed upon that bridge. And he got up with such a force of determination. This young lawyer, who had just started the business and was struggling to make it, said, 'I'm going to go to Alabama.' Then he realized he couldn't afford a plane ticket, or to close this little tiny firm. And then he did something that I think is the secret to the hope of America, which is just an American deciding 'this cannot stand and I'm just going to do the best I can with what I have, where I am.' And he decided he could spare one hour a week to do pro bono work. He called around and he found this young woman named Lee Porter, who said, 'I need help.' And that was 1965.

He said that years later [when] they perfected what they were doing, they developed the sting operation, and then he gets the case file. And he says to me, 'I got a case file for this family and I got them in housing. You know the name on the case file?' I said, 'No, sir.' He goes, 'Cory, it was your parents, Cary and Carolyn Booker.' And so, I'm literally sitting here in this office because of those marchers on Edmund Pettus Bridge, but also because a white guy on a couch 1,000 miles away didn't just sit there. There's this wonderful saying that I take from Angela Davis, but I think many people have said it: It's not enough to say I'm not a racist. If racism exists, you have to be an anti-racist. If sexism exists, homophobia, bigotry of any type, if that's existing in our country, you can't just say I'm not that, you have to be working against it. And he did that and changed the course of my family's destiny. I'm grateful for the question and it still humbles me today.

The first thing I did before I got sworn into this office was to go see John Lewis and sit with him in his office. And it was one of those moments where he was very emotional about what it meant. I'm only the fourth Black person ever popularly elected in the United States Senate. And to sit there with a man that changed my life in a very dramatic way, as well as all of us standing on his shoulders . . . it's just been a meaningful journey to me that I'm still trying to live up to the giants like him.

LADIPO MANYIKA: In your book you talk about these giants like John Lewis and the impact they've had on your life. And you talk about the choices that you have been able to have, thanks to all who have come before you and your parents. You could have been a great athlete. You *were* a great athlete! But you could probably have become a *professional* athlete; you could have definitely worked in a corporate law office. I think you can go on to be a great writer and write many more books. Lots of choices! And you talk about why and how you thought about choices in life. But I want to focus on one choice, Cory, which is your choice to live in a low-income neighborhood. Tell us about this choice.

BOOKER: I think that all of us should blossom where we're planted. And just because you've decided to be a corporate lawyer doesn't mean you can't change the world like Arthur Lessman, who was a private attorney as well. But, for me, I just made a choice as a very young person that I wanted to be a part of communities in struggle. I wanted to be connected to what animates me and what drives me every day. And so, when I came out of law school, and really before that, 1996 to 1997, I picked a place that people told me not to go to, which was a strip of Martin Luther King Boulevard in Newark. I think that was the first time I heard gunshots at night when I'd be sleeping or had people shot in front of where I lived. The first time I saw a drug trade. It was as virulent as that. I just immersed myself in the community and it was the first time I was actually afraid for my life in the sense of being caught in something that was beyond me.

What I found, though, was that, in life, when you step out into darkness and you follow your heart or your values, life is going to send you people to help you. I always say I got my BA from Stanford, but my Ph.D. in the streets of Newark because my professors just started appearing. And the first woman who took me in – a woman named Ms Virginia Jones, who I write about in the book – in one of our first interactions she says to me, 'Describe the neighborhood.' And I described it just like I described it to you. The danger, and the graffiti, and the abandoned buildings. And she just got angry at me. She basically said to me, 'You can't help me.' And I'm like, 'I'm a Yale-trained lawyer, for crying out loud. What do you mean I can't help you?' I was like, all high on myself. And she's like, 'Boy, you need to understand that the world you see outside of you is a reflection of what you have inside of you. And if you're one of these people who only sees problems, and darkness, and despair, then that's all there's ever going to be. But if you're one of those stubborn people who, every time you open your eyes you see hope, you see opportunity, you see love, you see the face of God, then you can be someone who helps me.' And she walked away from me. And I remember coming back to her with a lot less attitude and just realizing that I'm going to learn from this woman.

She was the tenant president of the buildings I would eventually move into in the Central Ward of Newark. I never want to forget the community that first took a chance on me. I still live in that community today, and right down the street from where the projects used to stand. I love my community; I love my neighbors. We don't confuse wealth with worth. I continue to be challenged, and inspired, and driven, and sourced by this community of color where the median income, at the time of the last census, was about $14,000 per household. But it is such a rich place and it so informs the work I do here for our state and our country.

LADIPO MANYIKA: There is a lot that is broken in our society, in our world. There is so much that ails us and you have taken on many issues and continue to do so. How do you think about what to prioritize and what are the priorities for you as a Senator?

BOOKER: Well, I represent people and in my state there are a lot of things to consider. Earlier today I met with the regional planning association about the urgency of infrastructure in the greater New York metropolitan area. The tunnels that connect Manhattan to New Jersey maybe have fifteen years left of life. They're massive projects that will probably amount to one of the biggest infrastructure projects in the country. So, I have to deal with the people I'm representing and the biggest problems we face, whether it's Hurricane Sandy or what have you.

And clearly, we're in a crisis right now of monumental proportions. The third largest mass casualty event [Covid-19 pandemic] in the history of the United States. That means really running at this hard and being in it. I tell my team all the time – life is about purpose, it's not about position. And my purpose has stayed the same since I was that twenty-eight-year-old running for city council. I love my country and yet I feel like we are still so far short of our highest ideals, and I believe that the American dream is real for no one unless it's within the reach of everyone. And so, my purpose here in Washington that drives me, in the same way as when I was a city council person, is to attack those issues that can best help our country be who we say we are. This great experiment, or this great yearning that has yet to be fulfilled. But I believe we are called, especially if we put our hand on our heart and swear an oath: liberty and justice for all. We are sworn to try to do that work. So, a lot of the things I do are about economic justice and opportunity, about environmental justice, about reforming the criminal justice system, as you said in your introduction, and the kind of work that can create a more prosperous society for everyone.

And I believe if Blacks had the same access to capital as whites, who are similarly situated, we'd have about a trillion dollar larger economy overall. We are all going to benefit from creating a more just, inclusive, equitable society. We will increase the abundance and the human flourishing in this country.

LADIPO MANYIKA: 2020 has been a year of racial reckoning and I want to talk about this a little bit more because you talk about this a lot. You've been involved with a commission. You called for a resolution or a truth and reconciliation, which is how I'm interpreting it. How do you feel we can address some of these issues of racial justice and get to a place of healing? The great playwright and actor Anna Deavere Smith said to me she remembers you saying that African Americans must resurrect hope every day. Talk also about the notion of 'resurrecting hope'.

BOOKER: Maybe I'll address the hope question first. As I always say, if America hasn't broken your heart, you don't love her enough. To love someone is to know them. And there is so much heartbreak, so much hurt, so much wretchedness that goes on in our country every day that should be heartbreaking to all of us. And I learned that in Newark the hard way. I really learned what it means to be broken, to be shattered. As I talk about in the book, I witnessed the murder of a teenager, and I'm desperately just trying to stop this kid from bleeding to death. And it was almost like enough was enough. I'd lost an election for mayor in 2002. It would be two more years until I eventually run and win, but I had just seen too much death. I had lived in this community now for seven years or so, with defeat after loss after . . . I was broken. I was just broken.

The inspiration I've always found, that has gotten me through, has been the people who are my elders who somehow, through tragedy, have found a way. Ms Jones, the woman I just told you about, her son was murdered in the building I would move into and yet she never left. And she was one of the most hopeful people, but I know that hope was scarred, and wounded, and injured, and probably died. And she resurrected it for all of us. I remember that day after that kid got murdered . . . after scrubbing his blood

232

off of my hands and getting into an elevator and getting down to the lobby of those buildings and crossing through the lobby. And somehow as I'm walking through that lobby. . . consumed by my own pain and hurt and rage, I somehow remembered as I'm walking through it, that that was the lobby Ms Jones's son came out [of]. And then I'm in the courtyard, and poof, Ms Jones is on the other side of the courtyard.

I'll never forget. Almost as if she heard me screaming on my inside one hundred feet under water, she turns around and does exactly the only thing I need. She just opened her arms. So how did she know that I needed a hug? And so, I run to her like a child and yet I'm a grown man, six-foot-three, and much bigger than she is. And she throws her arms around me and I just break. I start crying, angry tears, hurt tears, broken tears, hopeless tears. And she just says over and over again the two words that became a mantra to me and got me through tough days in Newark where I was broken again. Even weeks like this one where I feel like I'm banging my head against implacable walls of resistance, the one government of the G7 countries that wants to be stingy in terms of the relief that they give. The words she said over and over as she's rubbing my back, nothing to do with religion, everything to do with how we have endured, how we got over, as the song says. She says to me, 'Just stay faithful. Stay faithful, stay faithful.'

And so, I have tried to be in a position like this and not get stuck in a bubble of privilege, as a senator. I go to meet with an incarcerated, pregnant woman, immigrant, detained, who wasn't getting medical care; go across the border and meet with women who have been sexually assaulted, who were denied asylum; go to the lowlands of North Carolina and meet with people who have been so deeply affected by factory farm CAFOs [concentrated animal feeding operations] that have trapped them in their own homes. And I've tried to stay connected to this fight because I know that the best way to resurrect hope is to stay connected to those people that are not denying the wretchedness, and brokenness, and jagged shards; to those people who are living there and yet still are in the fight, and still believe, and still have faith.

LADIPO MANYIKA: There's a wonderful documentary entitled *Street Fight*, which is about your first mayoral campaign. Many moments in the documentary were poignant to me, but one in particular, when you were staying connected with people, you were talking to people in the community and they were asking you questions. And I think the youngest person, at least in the documentary, asked you a question. His question was, 'Is you lying?'

BOOKER: Yes.

LADIPO MANYIKA: I wonder how that question made you feel then, and how that question would make you feel now, given the environment in which we're living, where there's arguably even less trust of what politicians are saying.

BOOKER: First of all, a lot of praise for the filmmaker, the artist [Marshall Curry]. He has now won Academy Awards. This was his first documentary that got nominated for an Academy Award and lost to a film named *March of the Penguins*.

LADIPO MANYIKA: But you would approve! You're a great lover of animals.

BOOKER: If Morgan Freeman had narrated our documentary . . .

LADIPO MANYIKA: Yeah. Exactly!

BOOKER: He just did this brilliant job, but he caught me in so many real moments. In fact, I don't think that many people would let documentarians in like that. We gave this guy amazing access. So, here we are in a basement of a building, at a community meeting. I'm getting crushed by my opponent who is challenging my Blackness, who's challenging my authenticity, who's challenging my very living in the community where I lived and these things are gaining currency. I often have to deal with skeptical people who think that everything that I present is just too good to be true, and I still remember that moment. It wounded me. It just took the breath . . . like a gut punch.

Again, everything I know I learned in Newark. I learned then and through those early campaigns about the understandable cynicism we have about politics and politicians. I get where that comes from, especially when you're in communities like the one I live in, where you voted so often, and it just doesn't seem like much is changing. So, I deal with that sentiment all the time. On the presidential campaign trail, my staff would sometimes say things like, 'Oh, people think you're too good to be true, so they don't believe you.'

So I just know that's why we need artists in every profession. The elected leaders I look up to most are those who not only have the prose right but are masters of poetry – who can touch something real in themselves and connect it to something real in you. And that's sort of what I try to do in inspiring people to believe. Not in me, but to believe in us.

LADIPO MANYIKA: We've been talking with a particular focus on America. I want to talk about the world, the broader world. I know that you have visited the continent of Africa in recent years, when you went to a couple different countries, including Zimbabwe. Why that trip?

BOOKER: Well, I'll tell you, but I want to get there a little bit differently because, when I was mayor, Henry Louis Gates, Jr, calls me up and says, 'Hey, I really want to talk to you. I do this show called *Finding Your Roots*.' And I'm like, 'Of course, I know you do the show, *Finding Your Roots*.' And I thought he was going to ask me to come to a premier or something. He's like, 'No. I want to do a show on you.' And I was sort of blown away, like I hit the lottery. This was really exciting, until he tells me, 'I'm going to partner you with John Lewis.' Which was so sobering to me because, in the beginning of that episode, they give the bios of both people. It's like, 'John Lewis, hero of the civil rights movement. On the Edmund Pettus Bridge, he literally bled the Southern soil red for freedom.' And then it goes to me. 'Cory Booker, growing up in suburban New Jersey, falls off his big wheel, skins his knee.' It's like the mountain and the boy with John Lewis.

But the one thing I loved about it was that he broke through. For most African Americans, unless you are an immigrant African American, it's very hard to trace your history back beyond the first time a Black source showed up in the census with the 1870s. And [Gates] came back to me sort of wide-eyed and just said, 'You hit the lottery. I've never been able to get this far back with many Blacks.' He was able to identify a lot of the people who were enslaved in my family, beautiful portraits of these incredible folks, and also my European ancestry. My grandfather's grandmother was a woman named Henrietta Stamper who was fought for by her slave owner because he was her father. And knowing then about the Stamper family, he traced them all the way back to coming to this country in 1640. The gift he gave me was testing my DNA and telling me literally where in Africa I was from and that my DNA led me back to Sierra Leone and Cameroon.

Gates telling me all this ignited an even deeper feeling of connection. I've always known I'm descended from slaves, but now I somehow know the beginning of those trips, those horrific thefts of . . . and bondage of human beings and it was a powerful connective cord that was then strengthened for me and to Africa, that was a gift that he gave me that I can never repay. As a mayor, you really don't deal with that much international issues, except for maybe parking at the International House of Pancakes. So now I'm suddenly a senator, and I'm on the foreign relations committee, and I'm able to work it so that I'm the top Democrat on the Africa subcommittee. I get this big delegation to go to Zimbabwe, amongst other countries, but Zimbabwe was very important to me and Jeff Flake who co-led [the delegation], a Republican from Arizona. Mugabe had just been . . . I don't know what the right term is . . .

LADIPO MANYIKA: Well, there was a coup that was not a coup, but he moved on.

BOOKER: Yes. Exactly. Emmerson Mnangagwa ascended, and we wanted to go meet with him because we also were talking to a lot of the pro-democracy folks in the country who really wanted a free and fair election. His nickname was 'the Alligator', I guess, and he'd been a part of the Mugabe regime. So we were flying there to have a bipartisan conversation. We already had sanctions on Zimbabwe, and we were talking about the sort of turning point. 'Will we tighten sanctions or will you relax and open up to free and fair elections and allow us to relax our sanctions as well?' We went there on that mission. I will tell you this, that was when I first got it because, as we're landing, Emmerson Mnangagwa was landing, too. He's landing from China and the Chinese message to him, as I read in local newspapers, was, 'We don't care if you oppress minorities or your political opposition. We don't care if you hold free and fair elections. We just want a . . .' I could say an *exploitative* relationship with you. That's very mercenary in my opinion. And so that's when I began to realize the sort of vast influence on the continent that China is beginning to have.

LADIPO MANYIKA: I'm smiling to myself at the emphasis on free and fair elections. That is something every nation on this globe needs to pay very special attention to.

BOOKER: I'll tell you a funny story. I was in India during the 2000 elections. I was a city council person and I was traveling to India to spend time in an ashram and meditate, I think. And when our election problem started, I loved it. I took a delight in the Indian newspaper saying, 'We need to send election observers to the United States to help work through this.' There is often this sense that has really been unaddressed right now about the assumptions we make about our democracy. And we fail to look at it from an external eye, the Americans. I don't think we realize, first of all, how fragile even our democracy is. I think we're realizing it now, but that we don't also have a corner on controversy.

LADIPO MANYIKA: The time flies by too quickly. So, I'm going to ask one more question, relating to the African diaspora. And that is: if there's one thing you could change about the way that people think about the African diaspora, what would it be?

BOOKER: America as a whole often looks at Africa through humanitarian lenses and it's just such an awful lens not to see the grandeur and the greatness and the glory of Africa. And as a person who has had the privilege of being very connected to Ghanaians, and Nigerians, and so many people who I know from the diaspora and that are here in the United States, prideful Americans honoring the connections of their ancestors, it is a glorious tapestry that is Americans of African descent. It's so hard to unpack this, but so much of it is implicit racial bias. So much of it is a colonialist sort of bigotry and more, but to know the diaspora here in the United States is to know the promise we have as a country and for our future. I would hope that more people could have the experiences I've had and know what I know, even about the contributions of Africans in the United States. They are our hope for ourselves. They offer this country a tremendous pathway forward to success and prosperity.

LADIPO MANYIKA: I love the way that you use the word promise and you've brought up the word hope again. I just want to end by asking: Cory, what grounds you?

BOOKER: Well, gratitude is my gravity. It has to be. To know that ancestral story of my grandmother's grandmother having a husband murdered, moving to coal mines in Iowa with eleven children, I can't think of a woman . . . I can't even understand how she could have done that. I just think of every string of mine that it took to get me here – the massive conspiracies of grit, and guts, and grace – how could I not be grounded in a sense of just gratitude? And so, gratitude is my gravity. That, I think, keeps me on the ground. I have such ambition for humanity. I do have a vision or a dream of a world, not [just] in America, where poverty is a thing of the past and where war is a thing of the past, where human achievement and human flourishing is the norm on this planet. So, I just get grounded by my sense of feeling blessed and lifted every day and that, maybe one day, three generations from now, they won't remember my name, but something I did will have made it better for those who are to come.

THE WHITE CONTINENT

On Meeting

'Guess what? I just got invited to travel to the South Pole!'

'Get out of here! Get out of here!!'

'You think I should go? It feels like such a crazy thing to do!'

'You go, girl! Go! How often Black folks like us get a chance to do something like this? I wish I could go, but I might be too old, huh?'

After weeks of feeling torn over whether to accept a friend's generous invitation to join a South Pole expedition – weighing everything from excitement to worrying about the cold, from traveling during a pandemic to the extravagance of such a trip – it's the voice of my friend Willard, a one-hundred-and-two-year-old African American woman, that convinces me to go.

ANTARCTICA

January 13, 2022
Union Glacier – 79.36S 83.19° W

'Thirty. Twenty. Ten.' I can hear the countdown from the cockpit and then comes the bump as we hit the blue ice runway, speeding forward, rattling and lurching to the left, to the right. I hold my breath and hold it, hold it . . . until I feel the plane begin to slow. Then, with relief, I join in a burst of applause. We have landed in Antarctica. When it's my turn to disembark, I do so tentatively, weighed down by a heavy polar coat and boots.

The little of me that isn't at least triple-wrapped – namely my nose – feels the sharp prick of cold as I squint in the blinding light, taking in a blue ice rink that stretches as far as my eyes can see. We have landed on a long strip of glacial ice blown free of snow. Next to it are two storage containers, several large drums of jet fuel roped together, and two snow vehicles which add a bright pop of orange and blue to the pale-blue ice and white snow. Even with sunglasses, everything here is bright, too bright – the sun, the ice, the snow.

I glance back down at my massive black boots and the slick ice and brace myself. The air is filled with ice crystals within which my breath turns to white puffs. With each step my clothes make shuffling noises. Half astronaut, half Matryoshka nesting doll, my outer layer is a long, bright red polar jacket worn over heavily insulated black trousers. Beneath these, I wear three more layers. We have stepped outside for just a few minutes, so the additional recommended layers – another fleece top, a windproof jacket plus neck gaiter, balaclava and extra-heavyweight woolen socks – remain in my duffle bag for when we get to camp further inland. But now, despite my layers, my legs have started to shiver and won't stop. It feels like malaria, but this is no illness. Just cold, damn cold! So cold that here, some eighty miles into Antarctica's interior, there are no birds, insects or vegetation. With the exception of the three humans here to meet us, there is no life.

The snowcat, which will take us twenty-two miles further inland, looks like a small school bus with four giant triangular tracks for wheels. I climb in through the back stairs, glancing at our luggage which is stacked up amidst fine trails of snow and ice. There are fifteen of us including my husband, expedition guides and a glaciologist. Outside, the snow-covered peaks look like meringues and on the white-white snow our vehicle's shadow is the same royal-blue as the sky.

As we set off, our expedition guide explains how the route has been mapped out ahead of time with ground-penetrating sonar to detect any cracks in the ice. These crevasses which run as deep as sixty meters and as wide as nine meters are invisible to the naked eye when lightly filled with snow drift. As such, whenever we stop, we're advised not to wander beyond the demarcated route. Our glaciologist, who has lost colleagues to crevasses, once had a narrow escape himself. If you hit one, he advises wryly, hope to fall deep and hard as there's little chance of being rescued.

We journey for another two hours, passing the Ellsworth mountain range whose peaks are completely submerged beneath glacial ice and snow. Occasionally, bare granite peaks, called nunataks, protrude from the ice like a monument from another era. The absence of life makes it feel both extraterrestrial and prehistoric. It's hard to even imagine what this place would be like without the thick blanket of ice, yet ninety million years ago, dinosaurs roamed the continent in temperate rainforests. I begin to think in geological time.

Growing up, I didn't know that Antarctica was the world's largest polar desert and the size of India and China combined, but I did know something about deserts. I lived in the northern city of Jos, Nigeria, 1,500 miles from the Sahara desert, and during harmattan season the winds brought in the fine cinnamon Saharan dust. I was mesmerized by tales of the Sahara – its vastness, the extreme heat, the beauty and terror of it, but most of all by stories of its nomadic peoples. Antarctica's polar desert feels analogous in terms of its striking beauty and lurking terrors, but it's bigger, much bigger, cold and empty.

In the weeks leading up to the trip, I'd followed a spate of articles about Antarctica's melting sea ice and wondered what visible marks of climate change I might see. Friends had asked, only half jokingly, if I were taking the trip before all the ice melted. To my surprise, our glaciologist explains that

Antarctica's ice, at least its interior surface ice as opposed to the ice shelves on the coast, will not melt any time soon. The ice, I learn, is on average two kilometers deep. *Two kilometers deep!* Contrary to what I'd expected, the continent's interior is one of the few places on Earth that looks almost exactly the same as it did thousands of years earlier. The surface feels so pristine that I have nothing to compare it to beyond make-believe landscapes that I associate with toothpaste or chewing gum ads – all bright, clean and twinkly. Ironically, unlike other parts of the world, such as where I live in California, here it's the absence of visible change that makes me want to do more to preserve what we have. I find myself thinking of how much of the environmental crisis messaging is, of necessity, apocalyptic in tone – sea levels rising, ice shelves collapsing – and yet now I wonder if such messaging may be doomed without some hope or inspiration. Instead of presenting visible signs of warming, Antarctica is a picture of what unspoiled, pristine environments *can* look like. It's a stark reminder that while our human species might perish, Earth will continue to exist on its own terms. The planet doesn't need us to exist; we need it.

Three Glaciers – 79.34S 83.44° W

The sun couldn't have been any brighter if it tried and yet it's midnight when we arrive at our camp nestled at the base of the three glaciers after which it's named. This is January in the middle of Antarctica's summer when the sun never sets. There is no distinguishing between day and night. I'm disorientated by constant daylight and soon the days and nights meld into one continuous stream of time. I am even more confused when I see, in the middle of the snow, a wooden table around which are arranged five deck chairs. It reminds me of a Maasai Mara safari lodge except in the middle of a snow world. Who's going to sit outside in minus-fifteen degrees sipping a cocktail? I notice solar panels and, when I peek inside our plush, double-walled tent, I see that there are heaters and I'm relieved and grateful.

The three-kilometer camp perimeter is marked out with blue flags around which we can walk safely. Beyond these are a scattering of black flags indicating where crevasses lie hidden beneath the snow. As the winds pick up, I worry that the flags will be blown away or covered by snow drift. To me, each black flag demarcates the boundary between life and death. They are not marked with skull and crossbones, but they evoke the same sense of dread.

We stay at the Three Glaciers camp for twelve hours before the next leg of our journey and while there I'm brave enough to try on a pair of skis for the first time, not only on the continent, but in my life. Standing at the bottom of a glacier slope I marvel at the insane beauty that surrounds us – nothing but brilliant shades of white and blue. I pull off my outer gloves and, wearing only liner gloves, I very quickly take a panoramic video before my hands start burning with cold. Then I stick the ski poles in the snow and, lifting them out, I see bright pinpricks of aquamarine ice. I want to love this sweet sparkle of color but it's the same blue as the gashes in the glacier ice all around us and my stomach churns.

THE BODY

Safety and Senses

I've never before been in a place where, for thousands of miles around me, there is no life form to fear. There are no bears, no snakes, not even mosquitoes, and, because I know all the humans around me, I walk without fear of sexual assault by a stranger male of my own species. Such a feeling of freedom would ordinarily have been liberating, were it not for the ever-looming savage power of mother earth. When I walk around the camp and crunch through the snow, there are moments

244

when my boots sink deeper than a foot and I'm gripped by fear. What if there are hidden crevasses? 'Fall deep and hard,' I recall. My fear is made greater by the fact that my sense of sight is upended. With so few landmarks on the landscape, it's hard to discern distance. Objects are much further away than they appear. Have I strayed too far?

Not only is sight altered but other senses feel all out of kilter too. My sense of touch and general dexterity is limited by having to keep my hands covered under three layers. My sense of smell and hearing is also magnified. Outside, in the vastness of space with no pollution or vegetation, the rare waft of smell hits the nose powerfully. One of our expedition guides says that around the continent's coastline you can identify the origin of science research stations by the tantalizing aromas of their cuisine, especially those of the Indian and Chinese stations. As for sound, noise is minimal, but that which there is carries – the squelch of boot steps, the human voice, snow shoveling and the out-of-place mechanical roar from a snow mobile or a Twin Otter plane. My ears seem to go through a retuning process for more intermittent frequencies and when the wind picks up then sound suddenly becomes deafening and frightening. Wind speeds here can reach a terrifying 200 miles per hour. Lying in the tent and listening to ferocious winds beating against the canvas reminds me of tropical storms from childhood, of nights in Jos with the terrifying clack of lightning and thunder while rain pelted down on our zinc roof. Then, as now, I fear my shelter may collapse, but, unlike in Nigeria, if this happens I'll freeze to death. I'm desperate to use the toilet but don't dare step outside.

Pee and Poo

The toilets are porta potties of sorts with toilet seats installed over boxes – one box for liquids, the other for solids and toilet paper. There are no flushes. All wastes, including these biological ones, are shipped off the continent. One does one's business on top of everyone else's where it piles up, sharp-smelling, in a frozen or semi-frozen state. In the designated women's toilet there's a plastic mesh for catching menses. I'm glad my menstruating days are behind me. As instructed, I've also brought pee bottles and a pee funnel – otherwise known as a FUD (female urination device) to use when it's too cold to leave the tent for the toilet box. The funnel is a hard piece of plastic tubing with a small opening which looks like a urinary catheter – I never use it.

Skin and Flesh

One of the things about being bundled up in layers of polar clothing and gear is that when outside you rarely see a person's skin color. The body is so covered up it's hard to recognize who's who. All that is clear is that a figure is human – not Black, not white, just human. The contours of a person's body are also hidden, which for me means fewer occasions to fuss about body image. In the extreme cold I gain a newfound appreciation for body fat and practical dressing. Everyone wears the same kinds of clothes and changes only every few days. All that matters is staying safe and warm. As for skincare, the priority is avoiding frostbite and sunburn. With water scarce (melting snow requires energy), skin cleansing routines are basic. The default is hand sanitizer and, for occasional use, an ingenious bucket shower. I miss running water, especially for washing my hands and face, but it's a good reminder. I waste too much water in my everyday world.

Breath and Life

The 'Basler' is a 1940s DC3 airplane equipped with landing gear skis. On the outside it's a gleaming beauty painted red and white with a black stripe around its belly. Its engines are retrofitted and powerful but there are no frills to the inside of this non-pressurized plane. In the passenger seats it feels like a 1940s metal warbird. It's noisy and smells strongly of jet fuel. I sit near the front, close to where the duffle bags are piled high behind a string net. We take off for the South Pole and soon reach a flying altitude of 10,000 feet. 600 miles to go. I begin to feel sleepy.

My body aches a little bit. Head hurts too. Might be all the flying, plus it's so hard sleeping when it's always daylight. Feel a bit sick. Nauseous. Eyes feel weird. Must be my contact lenses. It's noisy. Cold. Even with all my layers. I drink some water. Must stay hydrated. I drink more water. Sleepy. Lean against husband's shoulder.

Here comes lovely Hannah. I like Hannah. What's wrong with my eyes? I blink. Blink-blink-blink. Still blurry. God, I'm tired. How much longer? Hannah's got a . . . pulse oximeter. She's checking everyone. Oxygen saturation . . . I remember. Normal range is ninety-four to one hundred. Anything below is an emergency. My turn. Seventy. *Seventy!*

There's a plastic tube in my nose. How? When? Oxygen? Cockpit door is open.

Hannah's talking to the pilots. Pilots on radios . . . She pulls off my boots. Feels my legs. Oximeter still on my finger. Blood clots? She's checking. Pressing my ankles. She's asking: Are you on birth control? Birth control? She stares at my finger, at the oximeter. She does a calm voice. I know she's acting. She can't fool me. I smile. She hands me a Coke. It's medicine, she says. Drink! I drink. Digits flashing . . . Seventy-eight, eighty, seventy-eight. She smiles. I feel sick. I keep drinking. She fiddles with valve . . .

Someone asks a question. Heads huddled. Hannah nods. Oxygen on highest level? She nods. She watches. She hovers. She checks. Hypoxia. Hypoxia? Others hover. I drink. I close my eyes. I focus. Breathe in. Breathe out. Breathe in. Breathe out. Stats creeping up . . . Eighty-five, eighty-six, eighty-seven, eighty-seven, eighty-seven . . . Breathe in. Breathe out. Deep, deep, deep, to the bottom of my lungs. Then out. Ninety, ninety-one, ninety-one, ninety-one . . . Up please! Come on, up, up, up!

We've landed. I come off oxygen. Thank God. But Hannah won't let me walk. I must be transported in a snow vehicle to the food tent. My heart continues to beat wildly, my blood saturation levels hover just below ninety. I don't want to go back on oxygen. I tell myself, *Come on, Sarah, you've got to handle this!*

'AT POLE'

South Pole – 90.00° S, 45.00° E

The itinerary for our expedition has been built with as much flexibility as possible to fly to the South Pole when it's most safe to do so. There are no airports here and, as one pilot later explained it to me, not only does one worry about snow storms and ferocious winds, but visibility is also a challenge – it's hard to distinguish between land ice and sky.

Guided by hourly meteorological reports, a relatively good weather window of twenty-four hours is found on the day after we arrive at the Three Glaciers camp. That's when we fly, on the DC3, from base camp to the South Pole – five hours of flight made slightly longer by the pilots flying lower to aid my breathing. When I eventually step off the plane, albeit still woozy, I feel the instant freezing of my nostril hairs as the wind howls around the fur ruff of my polar coat. At 10,000 feet it's much colder here than at Three Glaciers. I try, unsuccessfully, to hold my hood up with my double-gloved and mittened hands. I need sun goggles to protect my eyes from the blinding sun, but my breath keeps freezing into ice on the inside of the goggles, which means I'm squinting through frosted patches.

Here, unlike base camp, the surface is completely flat and the wind unrelenting. There are no smooth-looking meringue mountains, just a flat expanse of nothingness, except for a sprinkling of man-made structures – shipping-container buildings, telescopes and antennas. I feel like I'm in *Star Trek* having just arrived on a planet where previous space explorers have left behind a smattering of their technologies that could easily be whipped up and tossed aside by this manic wind. The landscape is so alien, it looks like the moon's surface, only blindingly bright, even behind fogged-up sun goggles.

I discover that the South Pole, which is roughly at the center of this continent, is in fact two poles. One is the ceremonial pole marked by a red-and-white striped pole on top of which sits a silver-mirrored globe that makes everyone look fat and squat. Behind this is a semicircle of twelve flag poles, one for each of the original signatory nations to the Antarctic Treaty. Not far from the ceremonial pole is the 'real pole' marked by a large white board that says: *Geographic South Pole*. And because the ice cap on Antarctica moves by about thirty feet each year, the location of the geographical pole is also moved each year. In front of the board, stuck in the ice, is a metal pole with a round metal top. We learn that this top is changed each year and designed by those who have 'overwintered' at the station. I can't get over the fact that, in every direction I look, the direction is North.

We overnight at the pole in more basic tents than those of the Three Glaciers camp. These have sleeping cots, double-layer sleeping bags and a small heater. I try using hand wipes to clean my face, but the packet is frozen solid, as is a bottle of water I'd carried in my backpack with which I'd hoped to brush my teeth. With no water, I decide instead to chew some gum, but that too is frozen solid and nearly cracks a tooth. The temperature with wind chill is minus-fifty degrees, which we are told is relatively 'warm' for the Pole's summer. I'm happy to have been 'to Pole' as explorers say, but the extreme cold and desolateness leave me with no desire to return.

EXPLORERS

On the signpost marking the geographic pole are quotes from two legendary polar explorers – Roald Amundsen and Robert Falcon Scott. Although I recognize the men's names, I know little about them at the time. The first explorers I meet are women.

Preet Chandi

En route to Antarctica, at the southernmost tip of Chile, I meet Preet, by chance, at Hotel Dreams in the port town of Punta Arenas. Preet is tall and lanky and wears black sweats and a cream-colored sweatshirt each sporting the Sandhurst Royal Military Academy emblem with its motto: 'Serve to lead'. She looks casually chic and speaks with a British Midlands accent as she keeps apologizing for what she considers to be sloppy dressing. The laces on her tennis shoes are untied – she explains that she'd only ventured out of her room to order a Coke Zero, a drink she'd been craving while on her trek. Preet has just made history!

We head to the rooftop bar where we're asked to show our Covid passes. I wait for Preet to be recognized and am surprised when she isn't. Can't they see from her ID who she is? Preet Chandi, as in 'Polar Preet'! Don't they know that she's the thirty-two-year-old British army physiotherapist who, just days earlier, became the first woman of color, and only the eighth woman ever, to trek 700 miles, unaccompanied and unassisted to the South Pole?

Preet's two Coke Zeros arrive and confuse the server. Two? You ordered two just for you? Preet speaks rapidly and continuously and I wonder if this is her normal speaking pace or the result of having trekked solo for forty days without encountering a single living being.

For the previous two months, I'd been following Preet's online expedition blog (for which she'd used a satellite phone to send updates) and am now eager to hear more directly from her. She begins by describing her preparation, the ultra-marathons, her two and a half years of training, including crevasse training in the Alps, and her ongoing fundraising to pay for all the expenses. The rapidity of her speech is matched by how quickly she jumps from topic to topic, as though there's too much to say and not enough time. Granola, for breakfast – yes, far cry from pemmican, biscuits and dog meat of earlier explorers. Sleeping? Not much. On average maybe five, five and a half hours. Long hours of trekking. Sometimes as many as twenty continuous hours. Battling winds of 60mph and temperatures of minus-fifty degrees Celsius. Quickly, she whips out her phone to share her schedule – hours tracked and slept, food consumed, even bathroom breaks. Then she shows pictures of her tent, the snow and sastrugi – the ice equivalent of sand dunes. I wonder, Why show pictures when you could simply describe it? Only later will I appreciate just how difficult it is to describe such otherworldly terrain.

She speaks animatedly about the audiobooks that inspired her en route and kept her company, including *The Good Immigrant* and Malala Yousafzai's memoir. Then we speak of how she's become an inspiration to others, especially young South Asian women. Oh, and she's also started a charity, yet to be named, to support other women explorers. Preet's upbeat, can-do attitude matches the tone in her blog posts. On January 4th, the day she reaches the South Pole, she writes: 'I don't want to just break the glass ceiling. I want to smash it into a million pieces.'

Preet is already planning her next trip, to do what no human has yet done – cross Antarctica, solo and unaccompanied. As an afterthought she mentions her graduation day. Today! She's graduating with a first-class Masters degree in Sports and Exercise Medicine.

Hannah McKeand

Hannah is a giant who towers over everyone. When I first meet her, she's wearing sturdy polar wear and a short skirt over her trousers. The padded miniskirt, I learn, provides extra insulation to protect the waist and thighs from frostbite and chilblains. Hannah is the camp leader at Three Glaciers and she and her colleague, Gordo, are the ones that meet us when we land at Union Glacier. She welcomes us with smiles and waits patiently for everyone to get over the initial excitement before loading us into the snowcat. With silver-blue eyes and long, loose blond tresses, she resembles a modern-day Viking.

Once we set off, Hannah opens the plastic flap that separates her and Gordo in the front seats from the rest of us in the back and jokes about how she technically shouldn't be doing this. The world is still mid-Covid with the Omicron variant running riot and there is fear of the variant being brought to the continent. As such, even though we've all been PCR'd to the hilt, we keep masks on when talking with Hannah and her staff. Throughout the trip, Hannah is jovial and playful. In addition to managing the Three Glaciers camp, she also runs a coastal camp close to an emperor penguin colony and treats us to stories – complete with theatrical imitations – of the way young penguins waddle and flop about.

While at the Three Glaciers camp I watch Hannah pitching in and doing everything with her fellow staff. She leads by example and with passion, and seems to know everything about everything. When not on Antarctica, Hannah also runs a Polar Expedition Training Course and, as it turns out, was Preet's first polar trainer.

Later, reading up about Hannah, I discover she has sailed solo around the world, twice. In 2018, she fended off polar bears when stranded at the North Pole. In 2006, she set the world speed record for skiing solo and unsupported to the South Pole in thirty-nine days, nine hours and thirty-three minutes. She subsequently completed six expeditions to the South Pole covering over 6,000 miles of Antarctic sled-hauling, more than anyone else in the world. I also discover her love of music and theater and our shared love of literature and the writer Toni Morrison.

One afternoon, I seek Hannah out in her tent office. I'm eager to ask her about her adventurous life, but she insists that I hear about her co-workers, pointing to the two sitting with her at the time. Maggie, a chef and guide at the camp, is, in her other life, a camerawoman on Norway's blockbuster TV series *The Chef and the Comedian*. She also once guided a group of children to the North Pole. Similarly, Darren, who sits quietly listening, is a world-renowned mountaineer who, in his other life, is a ski instructor in the French Alps. It seems that those working at the bottom of the world are extraordinarily multi-talented and expert at many things.

These are the last weeks for Hannah at the Three Glaciers camp. Soon she will start her new job as director of the South Pole Station. Fittingly, it's Hannah who gives us the historical and scientific debriefing of the station. She describes some of the daunting communication and logistical challenges of running such a station, including the annual, 1,000-mile journey of a convoy of caterpillar tractors (all on tracks) that pull bladders of fuel totaling 100,000 gallons for the station's needs. She also tells the story of an emergency medical evacuation for an 'overwinterer' that took two weeks to plan and execute during the winter dark. The station itself faces a looming infrastructure challenge – built on stilts, it's designed to be raised each decade – yet a new station may soon have to be built. Hannah describes the station's many science projects, from earthquake monitoring to the neutrino observatory. At the end of her briefing, as we stand at the geographic pole, Hannah asks us to reflect on what it means to have set foot in a place where so few have been. She challenges us to think of what we will do with this gift.

The 'Heroic Age of Antarctic Exploration'

Meeting two women explorers causes me to rethink my notions of explorers – namely white men from the colonial era out to grab land. Hannah's Viking-like appearance also prompts me to consider the possible Viking ancestry on my maternal side. In another life, at another time, might I have been an explorer? Having met these two badass women explorers, I'm disappointed to hear anecdotally that women explorers in Antarctica must still fight hard to be taken seriously. As late as the 1950s, women scientists and explorers were prevented from going on shore and although there are place names bearing women's names in Antarctica, almost all are honorific or sentimental. I learn that the first African American woman on record to make it to the pole was a woman named Barbara Hillary. She was a nurse, just like my friend Willard, and made it to the Pole in 2011 at the age of seventy-nine. Women's stories such as these are not easy to find, whereas tales of male explorers are everywhere – podcasts, films, books (including most of the books on display at base camp). Even the tents in which we stay are all named after men. At the South Pole our tent is named after Olav Bjaaland who, I discover, was a member of Amundsen's team – the first recorded team to have made it to the South Pole. Bjaaland was a carpenter – a practical man with good common sense. He had tucked away cigars with which he surprised his team when they reached the Pole. I like the sound of Bjaaland, but I want a tent named after Hannah McKeand.

254

Other Explorers

Only cursory mention is ever made of peoples – from the Polynesians, Maoris or even Chileans – who might have arrived in Antarctica earlier. And yet when I consider the map in terms of proximity, it seems ludicrous that the first arrivals would have come from the Northern hemisphere rather than the much closer Southern hemisphere. What bodies, I wonder, will the melted ice reveal one day? There must be others, those original-original explorers, deep within the ice. I'm reminded of how it was only a hundred years ago that people thought humans evolved from somewhere in Europe or Asia. It took unearthing a human ancestor in Africa for the real answers to show themselves. Would the same happen in Antarctica? In 1980, a 175-year-old human skull and femur found on Antarctica's Livingston Island were identified as the remains of a young indigenous Chilean woman. No one knows how she got there, and nobody seems to be spending much time wondering who she was or why she was there. Time will tell.

AFRICAN AT THE POLE

Fela Kuti! I've encountered his Afrobeat all around the world but wasn't expecting to hear it here. The staff at the Three Glaciers camp are in the kitchen chopping and dancing and it's Gordo from Argentina who smiles and says, 'We're missing the African continent, so we have Fela Kuti to represent, represent!' And, just like that, Antarctica becomes the warmest coldest place on Earth.

It's Gordo who, at the South Pole, takes my phone and snaps pictures of us when, at the ceremonial South Pole, I clutch my green and white Nigerian flag alongside my husband who proudly holds his stripy green, yellow and red Zimbabwean flag. When we had learned we would be amongst the first from our respective countries of origin to set foot on the South Pole, we'd hastily purchased flags online which we attempt to unfurl in the foul wind and wave in our triple layers of gloves and mittens.

Afterwards, scrunching my way across the ice and breathing heavily from the thin air, I walk to the shipping container that serves as the passport stamping area for the Amundsen-Scott South Pole Station. There, one of my traveling companions stamps my passport with the official stamp – not once, but twice, just to make sure the ink is clear. *South Pole Station. United States Antarctica Program January 14, 2022.* I marvel at how carefree and lackadaisical the stamping has been. For the first time in my life there are no immigration officials scrutinizing my passport or looking me up and down deciding whether to give me a hard time or not. It feels too good to be true. Maybe it is too good to be true. What will happen next time I pass through American immigration . . . will they look suspiciously at these stamps? Will they ask me why there are two stamps rather than one? Will they ask me who stamped my passport, will they ask me to step aside for further questioning? What if they seize my passport? Does anyone else feel the way I'm feeling now? I look to my husband, the other African.

And yet and yet and yet, being in Antarctica makes me feel the least Black or African I have felt in a very long time and this surprises me. I'm thrown against a sharp white background here, but I feel the least colored, the most human. References to Black and white – be it to people or lands – are usually such loaded terms due to the ugliness of history, but here they seem to lose their baggage. This 'white continent' is merely a topographical descriptor for land that belongs to all. I learn that under the Antarctica Treaty of 1959, the continent is maintained by a coalition of nations. According to the treaty, no one can claim ownership of any of it, and no military exercises or mining of any sort can be conducted on the continent – only scientific research is allowed. The governing of this continent is extraordinary and has worked for more than sixty years. Here, on land that belongs to no one in particular, but to all, humans work together to be good stewards of the larger land, Earth.

Back in San Francisco, I walk again with Willard. She tells me how she researched Antarctica and the South Pole while I was gone. 'Cold, cold, cold. Cold, huh?!' she asks as we chuckle together. Instinctively, I reach for my phone, the way Preet did, to show just *how* cold – but then tuck it away. There'll be time enough for photos at the end when we sit on her stoop to catch our breath. And as we walk and talk, I keep returning to Hannah's question. What will I do with this gift of having been to the South Pole? It's a question I haven't been able to shake since I've been back. Several blocks later, as though reading my thoughts, Willard stops and turns to me.

'Remember when we stood here and you asked, do you think I should go? And I said, go, girl! Now you've brought us back all these stories. For your son, for his kids, and his kids' kids.'

I smile, squeezing her hand as we cross the road.

ACKNOWLEDGEMENTS

This book has emerged from multiple interactions with its twelve main subjects. Some pieces are essays, others are conversations. 'On Meetings' grew from encounters with the person featured, and their works, over time. 'In Conversations', as captured here, represent a single conversation, lightly edited for flow – a snapshot, in most cases, of many more conversations we have had over the years. I am deeply grateful to each of you – Anna, Claudia, Cory, Evan, Margaret, Michael, Michelle, 'Prof' (Soyinka), Skip, Toni, Willard and Xoliswa. Thank you for giving your time so freely and generously. Thank you for allowing me to record our conversations and for entrusting me with your stories. It has been a privilege and a joy. Thank you!

I also want to thank the many other artists, curators and changemakers quoted or referenced within the essays in this volume. Your writings, films and music have been in my mind as this collection came together.

My deep thanks to the Museum of the African Diaspora in San Francisco (MoAD), under whose auspices my series *Conversations Across the Diaspora* took shape. Special thanks to Elizabeth Gessel, for many delightful hours of collaboration and brainstorming, and to all who followed and supported the series, especially to Peggy Woodford Forbes for her generosity. I was also fortunate enough to include an exceptional array of 'pop-up' surprise guests, all of whom further enriched the series by engaging in the dialogue and sharing their experiences. Thank you to my extraordinary guests and speakers: Tatyana Ali, Kojo Apeagyei, Natalie Baszile, Jess Cole, Dela Dabulamanzi, Edwidge Danticat, Osato Dixon, Kenyon Duncan, Harry Elam, Bernardine Evaristo, Danielle Geathers, Meron Hadero, Chris Howard, Charlayne Hunter-Gault, Eric Khumalo, Jacob Koree, Kendall Laidlaw, Renée Lubin-Holmes, Ibrahim Mahama, Lwam Mahari, Brian Marombedza, Lieke Marsman, Strive Masiyiwa, Farai Mpofu, Rémy Ngamije, Rutendo Ngara, Peter Orner, Ashley Sango, Marcus Shelby, Tiffany Shlain, Rommi Smith, Kyla Thomas and Ron Tricoche.

To all my readers and friends who took time out of your busy lives to give me invaluable feedback. Thank you Akin Adeṣọkan, Bibi Bakare-Yusuf, Diana Dempsey, Michele Elam, Elizabeth Lamont, Katie Morris, Marti Paschal, Rob McCallum, Lavanya Sankaran, Rowena Singer, Claude Steele, Danielle Teller and Anne Whiteside. Your questions, suggestions and edits helped strengthen my work. A special thank you to Mario Kaiser for generously inviting me to share that incredible meeting with Toni Morrison. And my heartfelt thanks to my intrepid South Pole expedition group.

This book wouldn't have come together without publishers and editors. Thank you, Candida Lacey, for seeing the potential of this collection and for so thoughtfully and patiently shepherding it from birth to launch. Thank you to all at Footnote Press, and to Vicki Heath Silk and to Sara Bruya for your ever thoughtful and meticulous editorial notes and edits. Many thanks to *Granta, Transition, Medium* and *Africa Is a Country* for first publishing some of the pieces included in this book. And to Hedgebrook for the precious gift of time, radical hospitality and sisterhood.

Lastly, but certainly not least, thank you to my family. Thank you, David, Julian and Mum, for reading drafts of chapters, giving helpful suggestions and encouraging words. To Dad, my unofficial marketing and publicity director (how many copies of my books have you now sold?!), and to Eva for the cappuccinos and text messages of support. And, finally, to James. Thank you for being my most brilliant reader, always ready to give of your time to discuss and brainstorm ideas. Ever-patient and always encouraging, you read through endless drafts, sharing insights and suggestions that have made my writing infinitely better. This book is because of you, my starshine.

INDEX

Index

ABOUT THE AUTHOR

Sarah Ladipo Manyika is a British-Nigerian-American writer of novels, short stories and essays translated into several languages.

She is author of the best-selling novel *In Dependence* and multiple shortlisted novel *Like a Mule Bringing Ice Cream to the Sun*. She writes for publications including *Granta*, the *Guardian*, the *Washington Post* and *Transfuge* among others.

Sarah Ladipo Manyika serves as Board Chair for the women's writing residency, Hedgebrook; she was previously Board Director for the Museum of the African Diaspora, San Francisco; and she has been a judge for the Goldsmiths Prize, California Book Awards, Aspen Words Literary Prize, and Chair of judges for the Pan-African Etisalat Prize. She is a fellow of the Royal Society of Arts.